THE POLITICS
OF CONSERVATION

THE
POLITICS
OF
CONSERVATION

by Frank E. Smith

«««««««««««»»»»»»»»»»»

PANTHEON BOOKS

A Division of Random House / NEW YORK

FOR *My Mother*

« « « » » »

Contents

« « « » » »

Introduction

Not quite forty years ago a gentleman who was to become a good friend of mine, and who was to tell me the story many times, stood on the bluffs above Vicksburg, not many miles from where I was born and raised. Turning full circle, he scanned the horizon. The year was 1927. The horizon encompassed Mississippi, Louisiana, and Arkansas. All he could see was water. The man was Clyde Mathews. He was a newspaperman, and he knew that what he was looking at was the bitter fruit of the nation's failure to shoulder responsibility for its waterways. He is gone now, but he lived to see flood control on the lower Mississippi become a reality.

Much of the ground for that work had been laid before I began the twelve years I spent in the Congress of the United States. Most of those twelve years were devoted to promoting the conservation and development of natural resources, of which flood control is but one aspect. There were more of us in Congress in the fifties working on natural resource programs than there had ever been before, and there will be even greater numbers in the future, because awareness of the significance of resource development grows. Each of us had his own motivations, part innate idealism, necessarily part self-serving. Mine was the driving need to improve the economy of the South. Few of us had a really coherent understanding of the growth of conservation doctrine and philosophy in the United States, but most of us rapidly learned that to achieve anything, we would have to master the multiple art that is pork barrel politics—the ever-shifting coalitions, the compromises, the trades, the inter-agency lobbies, the special interest alliances—the lesser evil from which has come the greater good.

"Pork barrel" has become a term of scathing disparagement, a convenient shaft in the hands of editorial warriors, but the truth is that in the haphazard handling of resource development programs in both the executive and the legislative branches of our government, pork barrel methods have been the only way to achieve results. The system, like Topsy, just grew, sporadically and unplanned, and as it grew, it became entrenched. Undesirable and inefficient as it may be, without it we would have little of the conservation and resource development we have today. Virtually every major conservation success in our country's history, from the National Park system to the Tennessee Valley Authority to the Soil Conservation Service, has deep roots in what is commonly referred to as pork barrel politics.

In twenty years of studying and working in this field as a journalist, legislator, and agency director, I have found no outline of the political history of conservation. This book is an attempt to fill that gap. The building that houses the Archives of the United States is adorned with two statues. Under one is engraved "What is past is prologue," and under the other the injunction "Study the past." I hope this volume will be a reminder of the first and a guide to the second. By being aware of our past, we may be able to profit from our mistakes and capitalize on our achievements.

Emphasis in conservation problems shifts with the changing economy and the changing environment, but though there may be fluctuations, the importance of these problems will be even greater in the future than it has been in the past. The total national investment to date in water resource facilities alone is approximately $100 billion. During the remaining one third of this century, the public sector of our economy will probably need to spend at least $500 billion in this field, in addition to costly programs to stop air pollution and generally to enhance the beauty of our natural environment. The $500 billion may turn out to be a smaller part of our gross national product than the $100 billion, but that is no reason to relax our effort to spend it with more efficiency than has been achieved under the pork barrel system by which we spent the first $100 billion.

In advocating better coordination and planning of our present and future conservation programs, let me emphasize that I am not pleading for procedure over effective action. Too much valuable time and money has already been wasted on purposeless fights over methodology. Organizational charts conserve no resources.

It will very quickly become clear—probably about the middle of page one, if not by now—that this book is written with a decided bias in favor of viewing conservation as an essential element of the democratic faith that created and sustains the development of the American system of government and the American economy. One of the great mainstays of the conservation movement has been the deep-rooted philosophy that our natural resources must be developed in the interest of our economic wellbeing; that governmental development or regulation ensures their use for the greatest interest of all the people; and that governmental action is needed not only for protection against monopolistic exploitation but, equally if not more important, for the wisest future use. The great conservationists of our history—both the technicians like Powell, McGee, and Pinchot, and the politicians like the two Roosevelts and Senators Newlands and Norris —have been more concerned with economic justice in the handling of resources than with the mere prevention of waste. Noble as their motives were, these great technicians of conservation were practical men who recognized the value of politics. It is not coincidence that most major conservation achievements have been associated with political movements labeled progressive or liberal.

Part of the conservationist philosophy grows out of the concept of harmony between man and nature. In our own country that concept of harmony must prevail if we are to learn how best to live and work with each other in achieving the potential our nation so plainly offers us. In the world at large that concept of harmony can and should be a base for the resource development which is essential if the bare human needs are to be met, and without which there can be no hope of political stability. The comprehensive development program for the Mekong River Basin is a foundation for a stable Southeast Asia. The full development of the Indus is one of the hopes for a bridge between India and Pakistan, just as the Jordan might yet be the link for the Near East.

In this field, as in all other national adventures, the challenge is great, the burden is likely to be heavy, the cost will undoubtedly be high. But the price of failure would be greater, heavier, and higher. The rewards of success can be limitless, if we are willing to remember that plenty is not prosaic, preservation is not easy, and grandeur has never been cheap.

THE POLITICS
OF CONSERVATION

CHAPTER I

The Way
West

1

The first session of Congress, in 1789, passed an act providing that "a lighthouse shall be erected near the entrance of Chesapeake Bay." That lone lighthouse put the United States government into the business of public works—the utilization, development, and conservation of the natural resources of the country. The lighthouse has grown into a multibillion dollar investment, but there is little more real agreement on comprehensive resources policy today than there was in 1789.

Thirty-five years were to succeed the birth of that lighthouse before Congress and the executive could agree upon any responsibility for waterway development, meager as that agreement was, and nearly a century and a half became United States history before we achieved any appreciable recognition of the federal responsibility for the development and conservation of the nation's basic resources, the land and the water. In the infancy of the Republic, transportation was the overriding problem of the developing national economy. Congress and the governmental agencies looked upon the ocean, lakes, and rivers almost solely as liquid highways. The vast public domain was another problem entirely, but its fate was dependent upon transportation, and the need to move people and goods to and from the ever-advancing frontier.

Faced with this demand for improved means of movement, it was inevitable that the first federal participation in waterway development should be directed solely to transportation expansion, and this singleness of purpose was to foster an almost hereditary limitation on the outlook for potential development of the Corps of Engineers, the first United States agency assigned responsibilities in the field. The single-purpose concept was not confined to the Army, however. For the first hundred years of the government's existence, many Presidents and powerful members of Congress believed in even sharper limitations on federal action.

In 1802 President Jefferson approved an appropriation of $34,-000 for public piers on the Delaware River, in spite of his doubts about the constitutionality of federal action. As he began to re-evaluate this position, Jefferson helped instigate the official Senate request for Secretary of the Treasury Albert Gallatin's "Report on Roads and Canals."

The Gallatin report was a model for general national planning which has never been duplicated by any government agency. It pointed out that private capital was not providing the internal roads and canals needed for the expanding country, and that they could best be built through some form of federal assistance. A national plan of improvements was outlined, which included canals along the Atlantic coast similar to the present intercoastal system and canal and road connections from the coast to the western rivers. Government surveys were recommended as the best means of determining the desirable routes, and for developing a national plan of needed improvements. Construction of the various projects was to be accomplished directly by the government, through loans or grants to private companies promoting the work, or through subscription to stock issues in the companies.

The Gallatin report was submitted to Congress in 1808, the last year of the Jefferson administration. It aroused hopes among canal and road promoters throughout the country but accomplished nothing else. The first stimulus for the report had come at a time when there was a relatively large federal surplus, but this melted away when the Jefferson embargo on imports drastically reduced tariff revenues. With finances limited, Madison, the new President, and most of his Congress were reluctant to put their doubts about the constitutionality of internal improvements to the test. The denial of federal assistance to construction of the Erie Canal demonstrated the prevailing opinion.

2

The War of 1812 put off any real consideration of the issue, but Madison had virtually eliminated debate with his determination that the Federal government could not enter the field without a constitutional amendment giving it specific power to do so. Under the next President, James Monroe, the issue rose again in Congress, and in 1818 the House of Representatives approached it on the basis of what could be done under the cloak of national defense needs, a device that has been used repeatedly, right down to our own time. The House instructed Secretary of War John C. Calhoun to report "a plan for the application of such means as are within the power of Congress, for the purpose of opening and constructing such roads and canals as may deserve and require the aid of Government, with a view to military operations in time of war; the transportation of munitions of war; and also a statement of the nature of the works above mentioned, which have been commenced, the progress which has been made, and the means and prospects of their completion. . . ."

The Calhoun report went far beyond the official request. Prepared by the man who was later to symbolize opposition to power in the national government, it stands as a major contribution toward national development. Calhoun proposed a broad scheme for building both roads and canals, supplemented with improvement of navigation upon the inland rivers. After specifying the military value of the various projects, he stressed their civil value: ". . . many of the roads and canals which have been suggested

are no doubt of first importance to the commerce, the manufac-
turers, the agriculture, and the political prosperity of the country,
but are not, for that reason, less useful or necessary for military
purposes. . . ."

It is regrettable that Calhoun's idea about financing the proposed work were not as carefully thought-out as the program itself. Had they been, they might well have influenced future congressional decisions. Unfortunately, the financing proposals were
nothing more than a hodgepodge of suggestions for possible federal, state, local, and private contributions. They added nothing
new to then current thinking and, consequently, accomplished little toward the solution of what was—and too often still is—the
prime problem, where to get the money for the needed work.
Financing may have been the Calhoun report's weakness, but his
recommendations as to the administration of the program established a significant precedent. Secretary Calhoun's entire concept
of surveying, planning, and supervising the construction of the
projects was premised on its being wholly in the hands of the
Army Engineers.

3

George Washington, the young surveyor turned soldier, could
very properly be called the American army's first engineer officer. General Washington recruited a "corps of engineers" for his
revolutionary army, but their officers lacked the professional
competence of European military engineers. The limited peace-
time army which existed at the time of Presidents Washington
and Adams included few officers technically qualified to build
fortifications or compute firing data for the guns to be placed in
coastal and river forts.

It was to remedy this deficiency that President Jefferson encouraged Congress to establish the Corps of Engineers, created by
an act which he signed on March 16, 1802. The Corps was to be
stationed at the old Hudson fortress of West Point, and it was

directed to establish a military academy there. The possibility of invasion by either Britain or France was a real concern, and the Corps of Engineers and its academy were supposed to bring some mathematical and engineering competence to the professional army.

Between 1802 and the War of 1812 there was not much improvement in the quality of either the officers or the fortifications, as demonstrated by the relative ease with which most coastal fortifications were captured or neutralized by the invading British. The first years after the war were spent, as armies have spent them since wars began, preparing to refight yesterday's battles. Not until 1818, when Sylvanus Thayer undertook to transform the military academy from a crude military technical training improvisation into a school with both military and academic standards was there new emphasis on building fortifications and preparing officers to man them.

The war had made painfully obvious the Army's lack of engineering ability. In 1816 President Madison secured authority from Congress to employ a "skillful assistant" for the chief of the Corps of Engineers. Albert Gallatin, then ambassador to France, conferred with General Lafayette in Paris, and from the available list of unemployed military engineers from Napoleon's army, they recommended General Simon Bernard. Madison made him a brigadier general, and for the next fifteen years the Frenchman dominated the development of the most active branch of the U.S. Army, even though officially designated an "assistant."

By the time the nation was riven in the Civil War, the military academy was the nation's first and best school of engineering, but in the intervening years the national shortage of engineers was not relieved, and with the lack of civilians in the field, it was natural for the President and Congress to turn to the Corps of Engineers for technical advice.

A half-dozen officers had been added to the Corps in 1816 as topographical engineers, but they were not limited to mapping.

They began the first surveys in the interior of the country. State officials occasionally made requests for assistance with surveys of navigation proposals, but before Calhoun's report they had to be turned down unless the project could be assumed to have important military value.

4

Calhoun's report broke a great deal of the ice, and in 1820 Congress authorized and appropriated five thousand dollars for the first Corps of Engineers "survey." The project was the Ohio and Mississippi Rivers between Louisville and New Orleans to "determine the most practicable means of improving their navigation." General Bernard and Colonel Joseph G. Totten made the survey. Obstructions to steamboat navigation were their chief concern, and most of the work they suggested involved what was to become the traditional "clearing and snagging"—clearing the channels of sandbars and removing trees embedded in the channel or on its edge. They proposed a canal instead of a lock around the falls at Louisville, because a dam for the Ohio was entirely too expensive.

The big breakthrough came in 1822, when Congress passed the first appropriation for the Corps' river and harbor work. The sum was only $22,700, and no appropriation was made in 1823, but $115,000 was voted in 1824 and regular appropriations were made annually thereafter. Eventually the appropriation item came to be known as the rivers and harbors appropriation.

The records are not clear, but it is very likely, from the close supervision young Secretary Calhoun maintained over the entire War Department, that he personally cleared the project surveys for which appropriations were made in 1822 and 1824. It was presidential campaign time and the South Carolinian was ambitious. He had not yet been isolated as the voice of states' rights and sectionalist southern leadership, and his report on internal improvements was a bright feather in the Calhoun nationalist political war bonnet, evidence that he would be a spokesman for the advancing frontier.

Farsighted as the Calhoun report was, it did not become definitive national policy on internal improvements, nor did anything else. There simply was no policy, in spite of the fact that increasingly serious problems of transport and commerce warranted action and many responsible people were aware of this. Jefferson had moved toward recommendation of a government role in internal improvements, and the Gallatin report was part of that shift. That report failed to arouse action and support, because it came at a time when monetary and foreign problems urged caution; Madison compounded the failure by favoring federal action but insisting upon a constitutional amendment spelling out specific authority. President Monroe undercut the strength of the proposals of Secretary of War Calhoun by making it clear that he approved only limited federal authority in the field.

As the sponsor of the most advanced plan for federal action, Calhoun discussed his views in a letter that was part of his campaign when states' righters questioned his reliability. He denied that his plan would compel any state to accept federal improvements, although he naturally did not attempt to explain how the proposed Washington-New Orleans roadway could be completed if one of the states en route refused to accept it. The government should appropriate funds, he said, "not as a sovereign . . . but as a mere proprietor. . . . I have never yet committed myself beyond the mere right of making appropriations." It was a fair paraphrase of Monroe's position.

As Secretary of War, candidate Calhoun had specifically approved requests for the use of Engineer officers in surveying and planning a number of state and private projects. The Army gave no assistance to the Erie Canal, but it helped to survey the Chesapeake and Delaware Canal, the Delaware and Raritan Canal in New Jersey, and various canal routes to connect Baltimore with the Susquehanna River. Assurance was given Andrew Jackson that a survey would be made for a canal route around the Muscle Shoals on the Tennessee.

The most important immediate result of the Calhoun report was the passage of the General Survey Act of 1824, "An act to procure the necessary surveys, plans, and estimates, upon the subject of roads and canals." To carry out the act, the President was authorized "to employ two or more skillful civil engineers, and such officers of the corps of engineers, or who may be detailed to do duty with the corps, as he may think proper." The most significant part of the bill, however, gave the President the authority to make surveys "as he may deem of national importance."

Despite Calhoun's high hopes in 1824, he had to settle for the Vice-Presidency. He was to turn up as the chief figure at an internal improvement convention at Memphis a few years later, but this was directly related to a South Carolina railroad promotion venture and state politics. Calhoun's contribution to resource development had been made with his report. His suggested concept of coordinated priority planning followed Gallatin's ideas but was even more clear-cut. One permanent result of the report, and one of great significance, was the establishment of the civil functions role of the Corps of Engineers.

5

The interest of Monroe and Calhoun and the rising demand for "internal improvements" were the decisive factors in the passage of the General Survey Act of 1824. The bill originated in the Congress under the sponsorship of Representative Joseph Hemphill of Philadelphia, who deliberately designed the legislation to avoid forcing a decision as to whether the improvements would be built by the Federal government, the states, or private enterprise. A man who had served one term in Congress as a Federalist in 1803, had come back in the Monroe era as a Republican, and was later to be elected as a Jackson Democrat, Hemphill had no trouble skirting the conflicting constitutional viewpoints. He declared:

> Nothing can be more useful than an accurate knowledge of the natural capacities of the country for improvements. . . . Such information, accompanied with plans and estimates of expense, would be of the highest importance; for, whether the improvements of the country are to be made by the individual States, or by the General Government . . . this information will be essentially necessary. All . . . that are in favor of improving the country by any of the means that have been suggested, can, with consistency, vote for the present bill.

Henry Clay thought that the bill itself should resolve the constitutional issue of whether the "General" government could build the projects, but Hemphill was able to block this approach. The Hemphill bill left to the discretion of the President what surveys would be made, and Senator Benton of Missouri, who entertained no doubts about the constitutionality of federal action, wanted to assert this prerogative for the Congress. His amendment spelling out six canal and five road routes was turned down, however. The bill passed the Senate by a vote of 24 to 18. Two of the votes in the majority came from Senators Jackson of Tennessee and Hayne of South Carolina. The issue of constitutionality was not settled, but obviously those who favored the bill also favored a constitutional interpretation that would allow the Federal government both to finance and to build the resulting projects.

To administer the General Survey Act, President Monroe appointed a Board of Engineers for Internal Improvements, consisting of Chief Engineer Macomb; his assistant, General Bernard; and a civilian engineer named John L. Sullivan. Topographical engineers from the Corps were attached to the board, and an ambitious campaign to survey projects was soon under way, financed by regular river and harbor appropriations. Despite the precedent of the defeated Benton amendment, specific items for survey were named by the Congress in the appropriation bills.

President John Quincy Adams interposed no reservations about the constitutionality of the survey work or the projects that would eventually result. Andrew Jackson made his reservations well known but took the position that river improvements related to foreign commerce were the federal responsibility. The limits of foreign commerce were defined as those cities designated as ports of entry by the Customs Bureau. The elasticity of those limits was demonstrated when cities as far removed from ocean ports as Atlanta, Georgia, were designated ports of entry.

A clear-cut decision about the supremacy of federal authority on all streams was not to come until the *New River* case in 1940, but the Supreme Court under Roger Taney went a long way toward establishing a clear-cut power in 1845 with this declaration:

> It is evident that a definition that would at this day limit public rivers in this country to tide-water rivers is utterly inadmissible. We have thousands of miles of public navigable water, including lakes and rivers in which there is no tide. And certainly there can be no reason for admiralty power over a public tide-water which does not apply with equal force to any other public water used for commercial purposes and foreign trade.

Despite the long series of learned questions about the constitutionality of federal expenditures for waterways, neither the Congress nor the executive ever forced a clear-cut court test; they simply accepted the responsibility gradually over the years.

Both the Congress and the executive department of the Jackson era had a more realistic view of transportation problems than any which has prevailed since that time. The General Survey Act authorized studies of both canals and roads, and not long after that the Corps of Engineers was furnishing a major part of the technical skill for the first American railroads. The early railed highway was regarded as a public road both in England and in the United States. Pennsylvania and Massachusetts, among the first states which chartered railroads, did so on the principle of turnpike or common road, giving no railroad company exclusive rights to operate on the tracks. If this principle had been preserved for rail, road, and water, along with the first steps toward coordinated federal planning for their development, a vast part of the growing nation's transportation headaches might have been avoided.

As an example of the potential that existed before special interests ruled out the development of more imaginative transportation systems, in 1826 President Adams and Secretary of War James Barbour were petitioned to survey the Roanoke, James, and Kanawha Rivers to determine "the practicability, and if practicable, the cost of uniting them by a navigable canal, or if that be found physically impossible, the route and estimate of the best rail way which can be constructed between the highest points of their improvable navigation."

In response to this request from Virginia, Major William G. McNeill submitted a report which said that canal navigation was practicable between the three rivers, but that railroads might provide satisfactory connections. From this assignment McNeill moved north to Maryland to become a chief participant, along with Major Stephen H. Long, in the building of the Baltimore and Ohio Railroad, the first important railway in the United States. Popular histories like to tell how Charles Carroll of Carrollton, the venerable elder statesman of Maryland, when he laid the first stone for the B & O on July 4, 1828, described the event as being as important as his signing of the Declaration of Independence fifty-two years earlier. These stories rarely add that the road itself was surveyed and laid out, and its first section constructed, by Corps of Engineers officers.

Most of the railroad building of the 1830's, the decade of the most frenzied railroad promotion in the United States, was accomplished with the help of Engineer officers. Sometimes the offi-

cers were paid directly by the railroads (McNeill was chief engineer for several railroads while still on active duty), but almost
always there was the equivalent of a direct governmental subsidy
involved where such engineering talent was used. After the first
few years of railroad building by the Corps, it soon became apparent that the railroad promotions and resulting surveys were
not the response to a national plan, but the commercial efforts of
local promoters. The railroads were not being operated on the toll
highway-waterway concept. The same congressmen who had in-
terceded to obtain help for railroad surveys in their areas began to
complain about the use of Army officers for the benefit of private
monopolies. When a new law reorganizing the Corps was passed
in 1838, it included a provision which barred the employment of
Engineer officers by private companies. There were to be great
transcontinental railroad surveys by the Corps during the 1850's,
but the period of partnership in railroad engineering and building
was abruptly halted in 1838.

The 1838 Act was in good part the result of the still conflicting
constitutional viewpoints about the role of the Federal government in public works or internal improvements. Despite the reservations of President Jackson, new surveys for projects of "national importance" went forward at a steadily increasing pace
during his administration. The tendency would have continued,
despite the strict constructionist views of Martin Van Buren, had
not this Presidential opposition been combined with the panic of
1837, public reaction against assistance to the railroads, and the
assumption by the Whig party of national identification as the
party of internal improvements.

Although Whig Presidents Harrison, Taylor, and Fillmore
were more favorable to civil works programs for the Corps in the
period prior to the Civil War, no major expansion of this activity
took place during the entire period. The most restrictive action
was probably that taken by Franklin Pierce, through Jefferson
Davis, his Secretary of War. Davis ordered the Corps to start no

navigation work which it could not complete under its annual appropriation—in other words, unless funds were appropriated sufficient for the entire work to be completed. This ruled out most of the important work in improving navigation for the steamboats on the major rivers, which had become the chief activity of the Corps in this field.

6

The 1838 law had actually established for the first time the opportunity for the Corps of Engineers to become the chief scientific agency of the Federal government. The Topographical Bureau had existed in the Corps since the time of John C. Calhoun, but the Army Reorganization Act of 1838 provided for expansion of the bureau, charged it with responsibility for all nonmilitary engineering work, and gave it equal status with the regular Corps, with its chief engineer, Colonel Albert, reporting directly to the Secretary of War. The Topographical Corps officers lost their line status as troop commanders, and though this caused some problems for them later on, their morale benefited greatly from the chance to make careers as engineers.

Extensive surveys, of varying qualities, of all the eastern rivers and the Great Lakes were begun, but the most spectacular achievements were the first systematic explorations in the western territories, bringing the first reliable knowledge of most of the country west of the Mississippi since the Lewis and Clark expedition.

John C. Frémont was a young lieutenant of the Topographical Corps when he first met Senator Thomas Hart Benton of Missouri, a giant of the Senate in the pre-Civil War period when the Senate was often more powerful than the Presidency. Benton's expansionist ideas of opening up the country to the west were contagious, but Frémont needed little encouragement. He had already explored the upper Mississippi, Red River, and Missouri country that was to become Minnesota and the two Dakotas. Frémont was imaginative to begin with, but he shared these two trips with Joseph Nicollet, an immigrant French scientist who made the first major contribution to geology and hydrography by the Corps.

In Washington, Frémont was attracted to the Benton family, principally to their daughter Jessie. Mrs. Benton had the senator arrange the lieutenant's assignment to resurvey the Des Moines River in order to get the young officer out of Washington in 1841, but in a few months he returned and married Jessie. The father and new son-in-law talked of the value to the nation of an exploration across the Rockies into the Oregon country. Senator Benton got the appropriation, and Colonel Albert assigned Frémont three spectacular journeys over most of the western country not covered by Lewis and Clark. The national attention his explorations received contributed substantially to the territorial decisions about California, Oregon, and the southwestern territory involved in the Gadsden Purchase.

New surveys and explorations by the Topographical Corps were necessary during the Mexican War and after it to map the new domain. Wagon roads were mapped out for settlers, and the Pacific Railroad surveys were made after the Gold Rush opened up California. Jefferson Davis's bias in favor of the 32nd parallel or southern transcontinental rail route, apparently shared by Captain A. A. Humphreys, the engineer in charge, is worth a moment of speculation. Did this delay the building of a route further north that might have so served the whole nation as a route for easy western migration and expansion that it would have been an outlet for national energy and could have delayed the Civil War long enough to prevent that catastrophe?

Captain Humphreys' record with the railroad surveys is lamentable, but with Lieutenant H. L. Abbot he produced the monumental "Report upon the Physics and Hydraulics of the Mississippi River," one of the classic works of hydraulic science. The Mississippi Delta Survey, as it was called while in progress, was authorized and first appropriated for in 1850. The Humphreys and Abbot report, filed in 1861, is still useful for a knowledge of the Mississippi and its tributaries. The mass of detail it accumulated set a pattern for thoroughness in other hydraulic surveys and all similar studies since that time. Humphreys optimistically concluded his letter of transmittal of the report (made August 5, 1861, when all the states to be protected from floods were fighting to establish their secession from the United States) with the observation that, "Thus every important fact connected with the various physical conditions of the river and the laws uniting them being ascertained, the great problem of protection against inundation was solved."

Humphreys' conclusion that the problem was solved was dead wrong, as painful and costly experience was to prove in the years ahead. The tragedy of the conclusion was magnified by Humphreys' using his report as an attack on another report submitted ten years earlier by Charles Ellet, Jr. Ellet's period of study had been far shorter, and his compilation of data far less impressive, but his conclusion as to the flood problem solution included the building of reservoirs on the tributary headwaters and cutoffs on the lower river, in addition to levees. This was the eventual solution, in contrast to the Humphreys-Abbot idea of levees only, but the Ellet ideas were to be largely ignored by the Corps for more than 75 years.

Some of the Topographical Corps officers found to their dismay that their lack of authority over regular troops made it difficult to work out arrangements with frontier outposts during the western surveys. Frémont first solved the problem for himself by adding a howitzer to his expedition without authority, and eventually only by transferring out of the Corps. When the Civil War came, however, most of the Corps' officers sought transfers to duty as troop commanders. Nine went to the Confederacy, and eighteen were given line duty in the Union army. Joe Johnston was the most prominent among the Confederates, and John Pope

and George Gordon Meade among the Federals. Humphreys was
a brigade commander at the Battle of Gettysburg and became
Meade's very competent chief of staff, but it was ex-Topograph-
ical Engineer G. K. Warren, Meade's chief engineer officer, who
deserved major credit for the Union success. He saw the need for
guarding the confluence of lines at Little Round Top, and the
men he placed there to deny it to Longstreet are generally regarded as the difference between victory and defeat.

Four months before Gettysburg, the Corps of Topographical
Engineers had been abolished by Congress as part of "an act to
promote the efficiency of the Corps of Engineers." The war was
in the process of establishing the supremacy of the Federal over
the state governments. The Humphreys and Abbot survey had
demonstrated the technical efficiency of the Corps, if not its saga-
cious judgment, and made it appear an appropriate agency for the
collection of scientific knowledge in government. There would
be an opportunity for new starts in the postwar period. Hopefully, they would be pursued in an atmosphere characterized by
opinions like those of Abraham Lincoln when he was a Representative of the 7th District of Illinois:

Now for the second position of the message, namely, that the
burdens of improvements would be general, while their benefits
would be local and partial, involving an obnoxious inequality.
That there is some degree of truth in this position I shall not deny.
No commercial object of Government patronage can be so ex-
clusively general, as not to be of some peculiar local advantage;
but, on the other hand, nothing is so local as not to be of some
general advantage. The navy, as I understand it, was established,
and is maintained, at a great annual expense, partly to be ready
for war, when war shall come, but partly also, and perhaps
chiefly, for the protection of our commerce on the high seas.
This latter object is, for all I can see, in principle, the same as
internal improvements. The driving a pirate from the track of

commerce on the broad ocean, and the removing a snag from its
more narrow path in the Mississippi River cannot, I think, be distinguished in principle. Each is done to save life and property,
and for nothing else. The navy, then, is the most general in its
benefits of all this class of objects; and yet even the navy is of
some peculiar advantage to Charleston, Baltimore, Philadelphia,
New York, and Boston, beyond what it is to the interior towns
of Illinois. The next most general object I can think of, would
be improvements on the Mississippi River and its tributaries.
They touch thirteen of our States—Pennsylvania, Virginia, Kentucky, Tennessee, Mississippi, Louisiana, Arkansas, Missouri, Illinois, Indiana, Ohio, Wisconsin, and Iowa. Now I suppose it will
not be denied, that these thirteen States are a little more interested in improvements on that great river than are the remaining
seventeen. These instances of the navy, and the Mississippi River,
show clearly that there is something of local advantage in the
most general objects. But the converse is also true. Nothing is so
local as not to be of some general benefit. Take, for instance, the
Illinois and Michigan Canal. Considered apart from its effects,
it is perfectly local. Every inch of it is within the State of Illinois.
That canal was first opened for business last April. In a very few
days we were all gratified to learn, among other things, that sugar
had been carried from New Orleans, through the Canal, to Buffalo
in New York. This sugar took this route, doubtless, because it
was cheaper than the old route. Supposing the benefit in the reduction of the cost of carriage to be shared between seller and
buyer, the result is, that the New Orleans merchant sold his sugar
a little dearer, and the people of Buffalo sweetened their coffee a
little cheaper than before; a benefit resulting from the canal, not
to Illinois where the Canal is, but to Louisiana and New York,
where it is not. In other transactions Illinois will, of course, have
her share, and perhaps the larger share too, in the benefits of the
Canal; but the instance of the sugar clearly shows that the benefits
of an improvement are by no means confined to the particular
locality of the improvement itself.

The just conclusion from all this is, that if the nation refuse to

make improvements of the more general kind, because their benefits may be somewhat local, a State may, for the same reason,
refuse to make an improvement of a local kind, because its benefits may be somewhat general. A State may well say to the nation, "If you will do nothing for me, I will do nothing for you."
Thus it is seen, that if this argument of "inequality" is sufficient
anywhere, it is sufficient everywhere, and puts an end to improvements altogether. I hope and believe, that if both the nation and
the States would, in good faith, in their respective spheres, do
what they could in the way of improvements, what of inequality
might be produced in one place might be compensated in another,
and that the sum of the whole might not be very unequal. But
suppose, after all, there should be some degree of inequality: inequality is certainly never to be embraced for its own sake; but is
every good thing to be discarded which may be inseparably connected with some degree of it? If so, we must discard all government. This Capitol is built at the public expense, for the public
benefit; but does anyone doubt that it is of some peculiar local
advantage to the property holders and business people of Washington? Shall we remove it for this reason? And if so, where shall
we set it down, and be free from the difficulty? To make sure of
our object, shall we locate it nowhere? And have Congress hereafter to hold its sessions, as the loafer lodged, "in spots about?" I
make no special allusion to the present President when I say, there
are few stronger cases in this world of "burden to the many, and
benefit to the few"—of "inequality"—than the Presidency itself
is by some thought to be. An honest laborer digs coal at about
70¢ a day, while the President digs abstractions at about $70 a
day. The coal is clearly worth more than the abstractions, and
yet what a monstrous inequality in the prices! Does the President,
for this reason, propose to abolish the Presidency? He does not,
and he ought not. The true rule, in determining to embrace or
reject anything, is not whether it have any evil in it, but whether
it have more of evil than of good. There are few things wholly
evil or wholly good. Almost everything, especially of governmental policy, is an inseparable compound of the two; so that our

best judgment of the preponderance between them is continually demanded. On this principle, the President, his friends, and the world generally, act on most subjects. Why not apply it, then, upon this question? Why, as to improvements, magnify the evil, and stoutly refuse to see any good in them?

CHAPTER II

Clinton's Ditch

1

Adventurous men with their eyes on the West, most of them not averse to speculation in western lands, were the leaders of those who spoke out for American independence, and then continuously pushed the frontier westward. Foremost among them was George Washington, who made a long exploration of the Mohawk Valley in 1783, and reported back:

> Prompted by these actual observations, I could not help taking a more extensive view of the vast inland navigation of these United States and could not but be struck by the immense extent and importance of it, and with the goodness of that Providence, which has dealt its favors to us with so profuse a hand. Would to God we had wisdom enough to improve them. I shall not rest contented until I have explored the western country, and traversed those lines, or great part of them, which have given bounds to a new empire.

Washington was probably the first person of prominence to encourage the idea of a waterway west from the Hudson, through the Mohawk Valley and to the Great Lakes, even though there is evidence that the idea had been talked about before the Revolution. The former Virginia surveyor went to the trouble of exploring the Mohawk himself, but his chief personal promotion efforts were in behalf of a canal link between the Potomac and the Ohio. From the Ohio he expected to make a connection by tributary river and canal to Lake Erie. Even though the general himself lent his name as president of the company formed to promote the route, it never achieved success.

The first American canal was the Santee, in South Carolina, built to connect the Santee River with the Cooper, which flowed southeast to meet the Ashley River at Charleston and there, in the phrase of and sometimes in the minds of the Charlestonians, form the Atlantic Ocean. The completion of this project in 1800, through 22 miles of forest and swamp, with the help of twelve locks and eight aqueducts, was primarily due to the engineering genius of a Swede named Christian Senf. He was one of the prizes of war, an engineer attached to General Burgoyne's Hessian troops and captured at Saratoga. Someone, possibly General Gates, brought Senf to South Carolina, where he acted as engineer on the American side for the rest of the war.

Other canals of the same relatively small size were started and some were completed in the early years of the century, but by far the longest, and the most spectacularly successful, was DeWitt Clinton's Ditch, "the Great Canal to the Western Lakes," the Erie Canal.

2

The Erie Canal, like any great construction enterprise, was the product of a combination of visionaries, adventurers, solid businessmen, and both normal and avaricious speculators. Both the New Yorkers of the time and the judgment of history give the bulk of the credit to DeWitt Clinton, who could not win the Presidency but who did win the governorship of New York on the canal issue, then built it over continuing opposition and set the policies for its successful operation. Clinton was the state's best-known political figure, with more than the usual share of political enemies, when he assumed the leadership of the canal fight. The canal opponents tried to beat it by making it a personal issue. One of the results was this jingle:

> Clinton, the federal son-of-a-bitch,
> Taxes our dollars to build him a ditch.

In the middle of the construction of the canal, when there were still few concrete results to point to, "Clinton's Ditch" was as much a liability as an asset, and Clinton lost the governorship. When his opponents meanly tried to exploit their victory by removing him from the canal board, the whole scheme exploded and the ditch digger rode back into office on the wave of popular resentment. It was fitting that he be governor when the canal was completed, and that history accept the verdict "Clinton's Ditch."

Washington, the surveyor, had readily seen the potential of a water link between the Hudson and the Great Lakes—the Mohawk came out of the West between the Adirondacks and the Catskills. The Appalachian mountain range disappeared as it crossed from Pennsylvania into the lower tier of New York's western counties, and with no mountain range to cross, there obviously must be some way to connect the Erie with the Hudson. Only a water path was needed—the march of western development would more than supply the freight to be hauled, and a good supply of human cargo.

One of Washington's generals, Philip Schuyler, tackled the promotion of a western water route during the first President's first term. Schuyler became head of the Western Inland Lock Navigation Company, chartered in 1792 for the purpose of establishing a water route between the Hudson and Lake Ontario by way of the Mohawk River, Lake Oneida, and the Oneida River. The company lasted on paper until it was purchased by the state as part of the process of establishing the Erie, but it achieved very little in the way of developing new traffic. Most of its customers were boatmen who were already moving along the route with the help of portage over the impassable portions. Returns to the stockholders apparently did not equal the several assessments made against the stocks during varied periods of crisis.

General Schuyler attempted to cut costs by acting as the company's engineer, which brought forth the first recorded comment from young DeWitt Clinton about canal operations. Clinton published a letter in a New York City newspaper denouncing Schuyler as a "mechanic empiric," whose operations were "wasting the property of the stockholders." Apparently, most of the financial support of the company came from wealthy residents of New York City whose main interest was in land speculation in the Mohawk Valley. When the stockholders refused to accept new assessments, the company turned to the state for more direct assistance. Various schemes to secure land grants kept it alive, but even its strongest supporters soon began to realize that only a real canal could attract the traffic needed for a link to the West.

3

Perhaps the turning point in the fight for the great western canal came when Jonas Platt, a Federalist politician from one of the western counties, joined with Thomas Eddy, a New York City financier and promoter who had been an active backer of the Inland Lock Navigation Company, in urging DeWitt Clinton to take the lead in developing a canal connection to Lake Erie. It was hard-headed political sense to look for more attractive and aggressive leadership, and they found the right man in Clinton.

Today, Clinton is best known to the public as the obscure figure who is pictured on the tobacco stamp, but the Clinton name was the best known in early New York State, even during the eminence of Alexander Hamilton and Aaron Burr. George Clinton was governor of New York during the Revolution, and when the Constitution was ratified, the first governor of the largest state. He joined the Jeffersonian faction when party lines began to develop, and was Vice-President for Jefferson's second term. The Virginia dynasty passed him over for the succession to the

Presidency, but he was elected to a second term as Vice-President under Madison.

The Clinton name did not hurt his nephew DeWitt, but the second Clinton obviously was well endowed with personal ability. At the age of fifteen he became the first student, and at seventeen the first graduate, of the newly established Columbia College (changed from King's to commemorate the discovery of a republican country by Christopher Columbus). Governor Clinton then took him on as his private secretary.

DeWitt's first public office was in the State Assembly, and he quickly cashed in on the family name and his own ability to build a political faction which presaged latter-day New York and national politics. With the help of his uncle, he was made a member of the Council of Appointments for the state, a four-man group responsible, together with the governor, for virtually all employment by the state government. Rightly or wrongly, young DeWitt was credited with dominating the council and the governor, and by this means controlling some six thousand officeholders. Many political scientists describe him as the boss of the first political machine in the country; his political opponents at the time called him "father of the spoils system."

Clinton moved in and out of factions in city and state politics. Both he and Aaron Burr were adherents of the Republican party during the days of Jefferson, but the Clinton faction threw Burr out of their party while he was still Vice-President, before the Hamilton duel. As a by-product of this, Clinton fought a duel with a Burr ally named John Swartwout two years before Burr killed Alexander Hamilton. Clinton came out unscathed in the exchange of fire; Swartwout was shot in the leg. He survived to become one of Clinton's close associates in the fight for the canal a few years later.

DeWitt used his personal machine to place himself in the United States Senate, but he served only briefly, giving it up for the opportunity to become mayor of New York City. Leaving Washington to accept the local office did not take Clinton out of the national political picture, partly because the New York vote was always important. Despite the fact that his Uncle George was Madison's Vice-President, DeWitt allied himself with the Federalists in 1812, and became Madison's opponent for re-election. Clinton ran as the candidate of a "peace party" coalition, but the war fervor of that day was too much for his effort, and he lost, 128 electoral votes to 89. His personal opposition to Madison was undoubtedly stimulated by the little Virginian's interpretation of the Constitution as prohibiting any federal program of assistance to internal improvements like the Erie Canal.

His role as the Federalist candidate in 1812 did not permanently identify Clinton with that party. The fact that the party of Hamilton and John Adams turned to a leader of a Republican faction in New York was indicative of its weakness as the country moved toward the "era of good feeling" in national political contests. Tammany Hall came into being during the Clinton period, but the Tammany warriors were usually an anti-Clinton faction. During most of DeWitt's political life, politics in New York was simply pro- or anti-Clinton.

The unsuccessful Presidential campaign was DeWitt Clinton's only significant appearance in national politics. Afterwards he returned to the state legislature and concentrated primarily on the fight for the canal that brought with it the governorship. As governor he brought his political machine into the fight for the election of Andrew Jackson to the Presidency, and Clintonians from New York played a large part in establishing the Jacksonian doctrine of political spoils for political victors. Clinton himself was considered a likely prospect for an important post in Jackson's cabinet, but he died suddenly in February 1828, before the actual Presidential campaign got under way.

4

When DeWitt Clinton moved into the fight for the western canal in 1810, he suggested that the logical line of procedure was to secure the assistance of the Federal government. Thomas Jefferson, in one of his messages to Congress toward the close of his Presidency, had raised the question: ". . . Shall the revenue be reduced? Or shall it not be appropriated to the improvement of roads, canals, rivers, education and other foundations of prosperity and union . . . ?" The Gallatin report specifically mentioned the proposed Erie and Champlain canals, and recommended that, as of national importance, they receive federal assistance.

Clinton's 1810 resolution provided for the appointment of a board of canal commissioners, who would draw up a plan for the canal if they found it advisable to construct a waterway from the Hudson to the Erie. The seven commissioners named by act of the legislature were Gouverneur Morris, the famous financier of the Revolution, now something of a senior statesman of the Federalist party and long an advocate of a route to Erie; Stephen Van Rensselaer, the fabled landlord whose family holdings dated back to the days of the Dutch colony; William North, a wealthy New Yorker; Peter B. Porter, congressman from the Niagara area and prominent in land speculation in the Erie country; Simeon De-Witt, the state surveyor general; Thomas Eddy, and Clinton. Clinton, Morris (who was named chairman of the commission), Porter, and Simeon DeWitt made a trip over a good part of the proposed route. It was more a trip to arouse interest in the project than an actual survey—DeWitt had made a very limited survey a few years before. After the commissioners reported to the legislature, they were authorized to submit a request to Congress for aid in construction of the canal.

Morris and Clinton were chosen to make the appeal in Washington in person. Their formal written report stressed the national advantages of the canal, but from the time of their arrival in

Washington it became apparent that the prospects were not as bright as the 1808 statements of Jefferson and Gallatin had made it appear. The treasury surplus had shrunk in the intervening three years, and Gallatin was now opposed to any direct appropriation. President Madison commended New York State for "its honorable spirit of enterprise," but would make no direct recommendation to Congress for assistance, even though he submitted the proposal for the attention of the members.

Talking to members, and reading between the lines of their comment, Clinton soon concluded that the chances for federal aid were slim unless there was a general plan for similar assistance to other projects in other states, or some suggestion of a general program that would eventually include other canal and transportation plans over the country. The concept of reciprocity was already developing. In later years it might be called "scratching each other's back" or "pork barrel," but it was based on a natural belief that each section and each state was entitled to its share. With no national commitment to development of other waterway programs, the prospects for action in other sections of the country were too remote to attract support.

Morris and Clinton decided to make their request for a grant of lands as the means of federal assistance, and the bill that they had introduced provided for a grant of 4,500,000 acres of land in the Indiana Territory to New York State upon the completion of the Erie and Champlain canals. The bill never got out of committee. Some members of the House openly opposed it, and others took Madison's position that only a constitutional amendment would make it permissible for the national government to aid in the building of roads or canals.

The defeat in Congress was resounding enough to make it clear to the commissioners that the State of New York would actually have to build the canal if it was to be constructed in the foreseeable future. They began to plan for state action, and then the War of 1812 stopped all activity. Upstate and western New York were

scenes of important action in the war, and changes in the area
would have to wait. Clinton's campaign for the Presidency came
at a period of stalemate in canal development activity, and consequently it cost the movement no ground.

The war ended on an indecisive note as far as Americans on the
Niagara and St. Lawrence frontier were concerned. Most of them
were convinced that war would come again with England, and
involve a fight to annex Canada to prevent its use as an invasion
base. No one envisioned peaceful relations with Canada, and the
idea of a route to Lake Erie entirely within United States territory seemed more and more compelling.

5

Late in 1814 Clinton met with the surviving commissioners and
other chief proponents of the canal in New York City and outlined a campaign to secure quick approval of a plan for construction backed by the state. Gouverneur Morris, disappointed because
they rejected his plan of an "inclined plane" linking rivers and
lakes and concentrated on channeling a canal through to the Erie,
stayed out of the final campaign, but most of the others, whether
Clintonians, Federalists, or Sons of St. Tammany, were ready to
fight down to the wire.

The canal company would be chartered by the state, entitled to
certain special taxes to pay part of the cost of construction, but
the main cost would be met by issuance of stock against the full
faith and credit of the State of New York. The debts, it was assumed, would all be repaid from the company's income from
traffic tolls and fees. The Erie Canal Company would also assume
all the assets and obligations of the old Inland Lock and Navigation Company.

Clinton combined all of the arguments for the canal into a masterful presentation which he called "A Memorial of the Citizens
of New-York, in Favour of a Canal Navigation Between the
Great Western Lakes and the Tidewaters of the Hudson." The

memorial was prepared in petition form and scattered throughout the western counties, but it was no haphazard hope of favorable reaction that DeWitt Clinton relied upon. He took to the hustings himself throughout 1815 and 1816, speaking at virtually every western hamlet that hoped to benefit from the project. He went into the Champlain valley, probably with the full knowledge that a logrolling arrangement had to be worked out with the citizens of that area to assure the building of their planned connection between the Champlain and the Hudson. The alliance between the Champlain and Erie factions was quickly cemented. The Champlain valley was an important contribution but still relatively small in comparison with the support needed over the entire state.

Opposition to the Erie became more intense as the Clinton campaign moved toward a climax. The western frontier was almost unanimous for the canal, joined enthusiastically by upstaters north of Albany, but in New York City the strong support was largely confined to wealthy land speculators who wanted quick development of the West. As with most plans for economic expansion, some of those who stood to benefit the most by the change, such as the city merchants and bankers, were the most obdurate in their opposition. Some of the sparkling names of the old Federalist party were supporters, but they were also speculators with an eye to the value of their holdings. Many ordinary businessmen were convinced that the project meant bankruptcy for the state, threatening their prosperity and status.

The really active opposition, however, was among the farmers and businessmen of the Hudson valley. The canal, they believed, would destroy the market for their crops in New York City, and reduce the relative value of their landholdings, which were already creating some of the great fortunes of the state. In addition, the Long Island area and other rural southern counties simply opposed expenditure that appeared to offer no advantage to them. By contrast with later opposition to navigation projects, there was no single powerful special interest like the railroads to lead the attack. Opposition to the Erie was largely opposition to change and a means of registering support for the status quo. As always, any new enterprise carried the threat of more taxes.

The opponents of the canal were in powerful places. Chief among them was Daniel Tompkins, governor of the state, and about to become the next Vice-President of the United States, in keeping with the tradition of New York State's furnishing the second in command to Virginia Presidents. The Tompkins opposition was based on two considerations: the chief base of his political strength was in the Hudson valley, among people who opposed the canal; but more than that, it had become obvious that successful construction of the canal would carry Clinton into the governorship, giving that master of the political spoils system the chance to destroy the Albany Regency faction developing behind Tompkins, Martin Van Buren, Silas Wright, and William L. Marcy.

Clinton believed he had the votes to pass the canal bill in 1816, but Van Buren managed to hold him by maneuvering the passage of a resolution for a further study. Governor Tompkins was open in his opposition to the bill, but Van Buren was farsighted enough to realize that his faction could not openly fight it. A year's delay might change the picture.

There was no change, however, and Van Buren had to actively support the bill that passed in 1817. In the interim, Clinton and his supporters had worked out several schemes to cut down opposition. A tax on salt, most of which was produced in the western countries and would be reduced in price by cheaper transportation costs on the canal, was not too controversial. Clinton's master stroke, however, was to obtain the authorization of a special provisional tax on lands that would directly benefit from the canal. The tax was never to be collected, but it nullified the opposition of those parts of the state which were against any contribution to a project that would not benefit them. The hope of federal aid was left open, with a clause which allowed contributions "by the Congress of the United States, by individual states, corporations and individuals." One last fillip was the authorization to conduct a lottery in behalf of the canal, a possibility ultimately barred by the state constitution of 1821.

The Canal Act passed in April 1817, by fair margins in both houses, but in the amending process some of the vital provisions were saved by very narrow votes. There was still one element of high drama before it became law. The bill could be vetoed by the Council of Revision, another one of the councils by which the then New York constitution limited the power of the governor. Tompkins had become Vice-President instead of governor, but his successor, John Taylor, was also against the canal. Another council member was opposed, and two were strongly committed in favor. The decisive vote was held by the venerable Chancellor James Kent, a convinced pacifist who had opposed the War of 1812, but who was perhaps best known for his ultra-conservatism and his opposition to any new expenditure of state funds.

Vice-President Tompkins tried one last appeal to block the canal, and barged into the meeting of the council, supposedly in executive session. According to a contemporary account, he told the council:

"The late peace with Great Britain was a mere truce, and we will undoubtedly soon have a renewed war with that country; and instead of wasting the credit and resources of the State in this chimerical project, we ought to employ all our revenue and credit in preparing for war."

"Do you think so, sir?" said Chancellor Kent.

"Yes sir," replied the Vice President. "England will never forgive us for our victories, and, my word for it, we shall have another war with her within two years."

The Chancellor, then rising from his seat, with great animation declared, "If we must have war . . . I am in favor of the canal, and I vote for the bill."

With that vote the bill became a law.

A new governor was elected in 1817, and there was only one possible choice in the minds of most New Yorkers. Congressman Peter B. Porter of the Erie district had been well known in the western area as a proponent of the canal, and some of Clinton's personal opposition persuaded him to enter the campaign. Clinton swamped him by a margin of more than ten to one.

6

The Canal Act had wisely provided that construction should start on the easiest and most immediately productive section of the canal, a portion at the summit level in the vicinity of the town of Rome. Construction was a constant series of problems and crises, and each new step became a landmark in American engineering. The first locks were entirely stone and timber, but in 1818 an engineer named Canvass White developed a waterproof hydraulic cement, which was a major advance for all hydraulic engineering. DuPont's new blasting powder achieved most of the massive rock-cutting at the mountain ridge at Lockport, mastered with a series of alternate locks to become another minor marvel of the construction. The Genesee River was crossed with a Roman-style aqueduct. The embankment over the Irondequoit valley provided the spectacle of boats gliding along a mountain ridge. Schohaire Creek was crossed with an aqueduct in the form of a dam that was to become one of the perils of Erie navigation during flood times of the future.

No new solutions were found for one ancient enemy of construction projects, disease and epidemic. Irish laborers came from the bogs of Killarney and died by the hundreds in the Montezuma marshes, infested with malarial mosquitoes. In 1819, work had to virtually stop in the Cayuga area when more than one thousand workmen were disabled. There is no accurate total available for the casualities of disease during the eight years of construction.

Most of the canal opponents did not give up their fight simply because construction was under way. The history of such projects shows that most were never completed. Navigation opened on the middle section in 1820, and some of the residents of this area immediately said, "This is enough, any more doesn't help us." The counties of the "southern tier," along the boundary with Pennsylvania, threatened to block the whole program by joining the opposition. They were kept in line by an agreement to make the Chenango canal to the south part of the project. The Chenango never paid out, but it was worth its cost to the Erie system.

The great ditch was 363 miles long, 40 feet wide, and 4 feet deep. Eighty-two locks were necessary for a fall (or rise) of 571 feet. Half of the cut was through forest and swamp, but disease made some of the swamp work almost as expensive as the stone cuts and aqueducts. In 1816 the canal commissioners had estimated the cost at five million dollars. The total actually came to slightly more than seven million. In view of the limited planning, and the construction system of on-the-job-training in engineering, the estimate was not too far off. Canal bonds were skillfully sold both at home and abroad, and there was never serious difficulty in awarding contracts. Those who proclaimed the Erie Canal the engineering wonder of the world were correct. A good part of early American hydraulic engineering was learned on this job.

The Erie Canal opened officially on October 25, 1825. Cannons placed along the length of the canal and down the Hudson to New York announced by successive firings that the waterway was open from Buffalo to Manhattan. A long procession of canal boats moved eastward toward New York, with Governor Clinton at the head of the procession aboard the "Seneca Chief." Besides other political notables and canal commissioners, the cargo included potash from Detroit, Sandusky, Erie, and Buffalo; whitefish from Lake Erie; flour and butter from Michigan and Ohio;

and dozens of other western products, plus a menagerie of wolves, foxes, and raccoons. Later that year, the canal fleet moved past New York harbor into the Atlantic off Sandy Hook, and performed the "wedding of the waters" with a keg from Lake Erie and bottles from the Nile, Ganges, Indus, Thames, Seine, Rhine, Mississippi, Columbia, Orinoco, and La Plata rivers.

Proud words were spoken by Clinton and the other notables, and the achievements made possible by the canal were to make most of them come true. It was the peak of DeWitt Clinton's career. An untimely death cut him short before he had another chance for national office, but few men in American history have achieved so much in a career in state politics. Clinton's major accomplishment other than the canal was the establishment of a system of public education for New York State that was generally superior to any other in the country. Most Americans who see his picture on the cigarette tax stamp today are unaware of his background, but few relatively minor recognitions are so well deserved of history.

7

Freight rates dropped on a scale unbelievable to even the chief canal promoters. Rates for some wagon cargo were reduced from $32 a ton per hundred miles to $1 per ton by canal boat. Traffic developed at the same rapid pace. At its peak, ten years after completion, three thousand boats were operating on the canal. In the first year 40,000 immigrants passed Utica en route to the West by canal boat, and the total immigration by this route ran into hundreds of thousands. Seven hundred new settlers reached Detroit in one day. The rush to the West included both New Yorkers and New Englanders, but it more and more became Europeans who delayed only momentarily in New York before transferring to another boat for ports throughout the Great Lakes area. Many thousands of the New Englanders and Europeans stopped permanently in New York State. Syracuse, Utica, Rochester, and Buffalo were transformed from villages into cities. Land values in western New York rose $100 million in five years.

New York City, of course, was the great direct beneficiary. The canal ended any possibility that Philadelphia would be the major eastern port, and gradually made it certain that New Orleans would not be the leading American port. The path to the West through the Erie Canal made New York America's top commercial center.

Low-cost transportation was not the canal's sole contribution to either the state or the city. The tolls on the Erie made the enterprise self-supporting from the start. By 1825, the year of the official opening, half a million dollars had been received from tolls, $100,000 in excess of the amount needed to pay the interest on canal bonds outstanding. Arrangements were attempted to retire bonds ahead of schedule, but there were always large sums of canal receipts awaiting disbursement. In 1826 the canal commissioners began negotiating arrangements with banks over the state to become revenue depositories. For the next dozen years the canal funds were to be the prime stimulus to the banking economy of the state, and the source, directly or indirectly, of a considerable part of the capital which enabled the rapid progress of New York during this period. In the panic of 1837, canal funds were used to bolster the state banks, and considerably shortened the effect in New York of the economic blight that halted the boom period of the frontier. Governors Marcy and Seward, with the help of the canal commissioners, used the financial structure of the state, and its creatures such as the canal, to assist in the economic development of their people to an extent that was not to be matched until another New York governor became President a century later.

The detailed story of how the Erie Canal contributed so substantially to the economic development of New York has been assembled by Nathan Miller in a fascinating study entitled *The Enterprise of a Free People*. In addition to being the first major resource development project for the country, the Erie was undoubtedly the best exploited during the nation's first century.

Folklore and literature naturally developed out of both the construction and operation of the canal, with the cry of "low bridge" and the legend of the canal driver boys becoming lasting contributions. "Low bridge, everybody down!" was probably called more often on the Erie than "mark twain" on a Mississippi steamer, for the bridges over the shallow canal were a serious threat. Despite the "low bridge" alerts, there were repeated instances of boatmen crushed to death between bridges and cargo or knocked off into the channel.

Even though the first steamboat was built for canal traffic long before its official opening, most Erie barges were powered by mules and horses driven along the canal towpath. Some of the driver boys followed the Horatio Alger path to successful careers as barge and steamboat captains, but most of them were examples of severely abused child labor, lucky to escape crippling injuries or early transformation into "canawler" alcoholism.

The success of the Erie spurred the completion of other long-planned canal projects throughout the country, or the beginnings of new ones. No others matched the spectacular success of the Erie, for a variety of reasons, chief of which was its natural geographic advantage. The development of the railroad reduced some of the demand. In 1850, at the peak of state and state-chartered construction, there were approximately 4,500 miles of canals in use in the country. More than half of these had been abandoned by 1900.

The great achievements of the Erie came largely in the first twenty years of its operation, when it obviously reshaped the history of the country, opening the Midwest with ties to New York instead of the South Atlantic or Gulf of Mexico. The pioneer hydraulic engineers who began work in 1817 built a waterway that actually provided service in some fashion until 1918, when the New York State Barge Canal was completed. Clinton's Ditch was changed from a towpath to virtually a manmade river, but the ditch had done the job in becoming the first great success in the development of an American waterway.

« « « » » »

CHAPTER III

The Wide
Country

1

The land was the first great natural resource of the United States, and in spite of its profligate handling at the hands of our forefathers, however noble or nefarious their individual motives, it remains so today. Now, the problems of land use are both qualitative and quantitative; the pioneers of the succeeding frontiers recognized no such dilemma. Most of the original colonies had great surpluses of land, and seven of them laid claim to vast acreage, some of it stretching all the way to the Mississippi. The small states with fixed boundaries took the position that the national government, of which they would be a part, would be better able to deal with the western lands than the original claimants. Maryland refused to sign the Articles of Confederation until there was evidence that the new government would have control of the unsettled land west of the mountains, and weak as it was, the Confederation government was strong enough to enforce its position.

In 1780 New York broke the ice by ceding her claims, and the precedent for control of the unsettled territory by the national government was established. The largest cession was made by Virginia in 1784, but the final claims were not relinquished until Georgia did so in 1802. The ceded lands became part of the public domain. With further acquisitions, beginning with the Louisiana

Purchase in 1803, most of the remainder of the present day United States passed through public domain status.

Slavery was the only domestic political issue more important than public land policy in the years prior to the Civil War, and eventually the two issues were intertwined in the "free soil" controversy that reshaped the national political structure. Public lands policy, in its long, often haphazard, and hazardous growth, also led to the beginnings of an American conservation policy. Most of the land policy struggle was, in fact, conflict between the poor and the rich, the squatter and the speculator, the farmer and the banker. Only very slowly, and in the face of widespread scandal, did there develop a compelling recognition of the national interest, immediate and future, in the disposal of public lands. And this led to national conservation policy.

The problems of agreement upon methods of controlling, and disposing to settlers, the ceded lands emphasized the need for a true national government rather than the post-Revolutionary Confederation. Desperate for money, the Confederation had made sales of land in violation of its own ordinances, and in at least two cases had done so in arrangements involving speculative schemes designed to directly benefit the members of Congress who promoted the plans.

The two ordinances relating to western land, however, were the foremost contribution of the Confederation to American government. The Ordinance of 1785 divided all of the territory north of the Ohio and west of the Appalachians into sections and townships, as the first step in offering the land for disposal to either the settler or the speculator. The ordinance provided for sales of lands to the highest bidder, but through a system that had the effect of encouraging speculation rather than individual settlement. With the resources of the national government so limited, it is doubtful that any other system could have been adopted at the time. Other provisions of the 1785 Ordinance were so farsighted, however, that the law deserves to rank in value with the better known Ordinance of 1787, usually called the Northwest Ordinance.

The land survey system prevented utter chaos for the future new territories. The reservation of the sixteenth section of each township for the support of common schools provided a local opportunity for education and eventually staked out a federal responsibility in education. Congress, in addition, reserved four sections to national ownership with reservation of one third of the mineral rights thereon. It was a limited but significant assertion of a national conservation responsibility.

The Ordinance of 1787 established the system for the admission of new states to the Union, making it clear that they would be equal sister states, and not unequal provinces. Settlement of land in the West would carry no penalty in the transfer of citizenship, and that privilege carried forward in the creation of all new territories and states. The ban on slavery in the new territories was important not only as an indication of national viewpoint but also as an indication of national power.

2

The two land ordinances were for the "Northwest." With the addition of the states immediately west of the Mississippi, this territory is now popularly called the Middle West, even though most of it is in the East. Prior to 1800, everything west of the Appalachians was "west." Western lands were first those as far east as Ohio, and eventually became the western area of the continent. Although plantation influences were present from the start, the new territories of the South were primarily western in their orientation in the terms of the day. Not until after the Mexican War was the Deep South more southern than western.

The new Federal government under President Washington did little to disturb the land policy established by the Confederation. When change did come, it was primarily in the hope of securing immediate revenue for the straitened new government. When the

Land Act of 1796 was passed, it provoked the first skirmish in the Congress between the representatives of the western farmers and the established eastern interests. Albert Gallatin, then a congressman from western Pennsylvania, spoke out in favor of sales in small tracts. The farmer, he declared, would buy small tracts to farm, not to resell. Gallatin's amendment failed, however, and the new law raised the land price from one to two dollars per acre. The minimum purchase was 640 acres, with no credit beyond one year.

The severity of the new law inevitably gave rise to squatter settlement throughout the new western lands. Few of the settlers streaming down the Ohio or through the Cumberland Gap had $1280 in cash—if they had had that much, they would not have been likely to migrate. In the years before 1800 most of the settlers along the Scioto and the Miami were squatters, and their delegate to the Congress from the Northwest Territory was a transplanted Virginian, William Henry Harrison. Harrison teamed with Gallatin to write the Land Act of 1800. The price of the land remained at two dollars per acre, but the minimum purchase was reduced to 320 acres. Most important, partial payments were allowed over a four-year period. A young congressman from Tennessee, W. C. C. Claiborne, sought to amend the bill to establish the principle of pre-emption—giving priority to and excusing the violation of squatters. His effort failed, but pre-emption was to become an accepted part of federal land policy by the time most of the land acquired through the Louisiana Purchase was being settled.

The 1800 land policy changes became law under President John Adams, but the changes in the system were symptomatic of the changing political tides in the country that carried Thomas Jefferson to the Presidency later in the year. The farmer and Westerner were beginning to assert power, and the primary use of the power was to make land acquisition easier. Under Jefferson the belief developed that plenty of western land was always avail-

able, and on credit, even though the price and the terms were
never easy on a frontier where there was little cash and limited
opportunity to cultivate crops directly negotiable into cash.
Under Jefferson also arose the idea that national policy should
make new land available. A free port at New Orleans was essential
to all of the existing West. When Jefferson and his emissaries,
Livingston and Monroe, acted without procrastination on the
chance to buy the whole colony of Louisiana, they were respond-
ing to the voice of the land-seeking frontiersman as well as to
their own vision of a continental United States.

3

The Jefferson policy of more public land and land available for
settlement was followed by the Jacksonian policy of pre-emption
for settlers and squatters and the wholesale removal of Indians
from areas east of the Mississippi, often in open disregard of earlier treaties or agreements with the various tribes. A Supreme
Court decision by Chief Justice John Marshall upholding the
Cherokee tribe's right to lands in Georgia not only was of no
value to the Indians, but it inspired, instead, Jackson's comment,
"John Marshall has made his decision; now let him enforce it!"

President Jackson's refusal to enforce the Court's decision did
not prevent his vigorous enforcement of his own Indian removal
policy. Most of the Indian cessions were made through treaties
between the tribal chiefs and representatives of the Federal government wherein formal exchanges of land were made for territory west of the Mississippi, but most of the Indians were persuaded to agree only at the point of a gun. In two areas there was
armed resistance by the Indians. The Black Hawk War is perhaps
best known today because a militiaman named Abraham Lincoln
was among the soldiers who pushed the Indians out of northwest
Illinois, but it presaged the creation of the Iowa and Wisconsin
territories and the opening to settlement of the territory between
Lake Michigan and the Mississippi. In the South the Seminoles

resisted removal, and finally were tracked down through the swamps of Florida in a costly campaign that was to be one of the embarrassments inherited from Jackson by the Van Buren administration. The Cherokee Indians in Jackson's home state of Tennessee repeatedly postponed moving long after the deadlines established by their treaty date, and eventually followed a "trail of tears" to Oklahoma.

The injustice and the inhumanity of the removal policy are obvious to hindsight. But no other course was possible for the government of the day. If the Federal government had not taken the lead in the removal, the individual states themselves could not have been restrained, and this would have resulted in a far bloodier policy toward the Indians, with even less effort to protect their future needs. Jackson symbolized frontier democracy, but among the vast majority of the citizens of the country, regardless of political allegiance, few if any questioned the morality of taking Indian lands with a mailed fist.

The great theft of the Indian lands was often followed by corrupt administration of the land offices that handled disposal of the new lands. Most of the removal treaties provided that individual Indian landowners should remain in possession, and that the Indians who elected not to go west with their tribes should have a chance to become owners of individual tracts. All too often, corrupt and fradulent schemes to deny even these small benefits to the Indians who wished to merge with the white community were arranged or connived at through the land agents in charge of the disposal of lands in the ceded territory. The rights of the Indians were simply not considered by the American frontiersman, and not very often by his government.

The compacts made with the Indian for removal to western lands usually carried the commitment that the new territories given him in the Great Plains would be forever his, free from any future encroachment by the white man. An act of Congress in 1834 established the High Plains of the west as permanent Indian territory. The same Jackson administration that carried out the ruthless removal program also created the Bureau of Indian Affairs in 1832. The abuse of the Indians during the years prior to the Civil War was no partisan political affair—no significant political group was in opposition, and no important political figure raised his voice in protest.

Henry Clay was the Whig nominee against Jackson in 1832, and the two fought out a public lands issue which was highly important to resource development potential for both that period and the future. The Clay public lands distribution proposal was linked with both the tariff issue and the purely personal political rivalry between Jackson and Clay, but it carried over into the area of internal improvements at a time when, with the early success of the Erie, national interest in canals was at its height.

Clay proposed to distribute to the states, in proportion to their representation in Congress, 90 per cent of all federal revenue from the sale of public lands. The states could use the money for education, internal improvements, redemption of debts, or colonization of free Negroes. The bait was tempting. A Steubenville, Ohio, editor calculated that Ohio's share would pay for the state's canal debt, "and if the net income of the canals should be equal only to the support of the state government, the people of Ohio would be relieved altogether from state tax."

Senator Thomas Hart Benton fought the proposal through his Committee on Public Lands, asserting that Congress should retain unrestricted control of the public domain: ". . . National legislation over the same should be guarded by a policy which shall regard it rather as a means to build up flourishing communities, than as a source of revenue to the general government or of wealth to the individual states."

The combination of states seeking revenue for internal improvements, or simply to abate local taxation, plus the protective tariff interests allied with Clay, pushed the bill through Congress over the opposition of Jackson, Benton, and John C. Calhoun, who was willing for South Carolina to nullify a tariff act but was strongly opposed to the denationalization of public funds. Jackson resorted to a pocket veto to kill the bill, claiming that it would have the effect of federal aid for internal improvements, which he considered unconstitutional, and that it might lead to similar demands for distribution of proceeds from the tariff.

Even though Jackson vetoed the Clay distribution program because of his fear that it might be a method of indirectly contributing federal funds for internal improvements, the long-range effect of the veto was to establish federal pre-eminence in the public lands field and to ensure federal sponsorship and financing of a wide range of "internal improvements"—specifically the natural resource developments now accepted as primary federal responsibilities. The viewpoint of Senator Benton that national legislation should be a means to "build up flourishing communities" has prevailed. Even if the Clay plan had been adopted, the present federal system would eventually have come into being, but probably only after compounded waste in state projects planned and built with no central coordination or relevancy.

4

Until the Mexican War added new acreage for disposal, the chief issue involved in public land policy from the Jackson administration on was the dispute between the small farmer and settler and the land speculator. Despite opposition in the Congress and from Jackson and other Presidents, speculators seemed to acquire the major share of any new tract or cession opened up for sale. The panic of 1837 punctured most of the speculators' hopes for vast overnight fortunes, but it also ruined many of the bona fide settlers who had purchased land either from the government or from private speculative syndicates.

One of the results of the panic was a permanent pre-emption law based on the principle that public domain sales should give priority to the small farmer who actually intended to settle on the land. Among other changes, the bill reduced the minimum land price to $1.25 per acre.

The pre-emption bills were labeled "locofoco" legislation by Daniel Webster, and "Log Cabin" bills by the supporters of President William Henry Harrison, who owed his election in 1840 in good part to his reputation as a friend of the frontiersman in the passage of the Land Act of 1800. The Westerners voted for Harrison, the log-cabin boy, and pushed pre-emption through Congress, locofoco or not.

Throughout most of the struggle over land policy the division was largely geographic: East against West. The occasional deviations came from fiscal conservatives who happened to get elected from the western territories. Despite the party line-ups, few members of the Congress from the eastern seaboard, or influential citizens outside of Congress, favored liberal land policies in the West. Among other reasons, there was no desire to encourage migration from the old established areas of the nation. A changed attitude began to show when the 1837 panic brought real hardship and suffering to the seaboard states for the first time since the Revolution. For the first time in the life of the country, large numbers of men and women were hungry and suffering, with no immediate prospect of jobs.

Horace Greeley, then in the beginning of his career and editing a paper called the *New Yorker*, had regularly followed the general Whig party policy on land grants and sales. He was one of the staunch supporters of the Clay distribution proposal, but when he found 50,000 unemployed in New York City, Greeley took up his historic cry of "Go West, young man, go forth into the country." He advised the workers, identified as mechanics and seamstresses, "Do not wait here to share and increase its horrors [the coming winter]. Fly—scatter through the country—go to the Great West—anything rather than remain here."

After the immediate panic had subsided and job opportunities began to return to the East, the vision of opportunity in the West remained. When the Mexican War brought even more public land for development, social reformers in the East began to join the Westerners in the Congress seeking reform of land policy. The idea of free land was not long in developing, and it was a basis for the formation of the Free Soil party. The philosophy of free land for free men was to bar the new political group from support in the South, but it evoked support over all the rest of the nation.

The first actual homestead bill was introduced in 1844 by Representative Robert Smith of Illinois, who proposed to grant eighty acres to any head of family unable to purchase such land from the federal domain. Smith's bill attracted no great attention, but by 1846 Felix G. McConnell of Alabama and Andrew Johnson of Tennessee were sponsoring similar proposals. From that time forward until the Homestead Act became law, the fight for free land dominated the struggle over land policy, and eventually so entangled it in the slavery issue that only the Civil War made a resolution possible. A homestead bill passed the House in 1852, bitterly opposed by those like Josiah Sutherland of New York, who said that it would "take labor from the manufacturing states to the land states—from the manufactories of the East to the farms of the West—and thereby increase the cost of labor and the cost of manufacturing." Most of the representatives from such still undeveloped southern states as Arkansas, Alabama, Mississippi, and Louisiana voted for the bill, but their senators were heedful of free land's threat to slavery and did not resist when the plan was quietly buried in the Senate Committee on Public Lands.

Another big push for a homestead bill did not come until 1859, after a period when most of the public land controversy was obscured by the fight over slavery in the new territories of the High Plains, where the demand for land was enough to cause the Congress to forget the old pledges of permanent Indian territory. The Graduation Act of 1854 made large blocks of land available for as low a price as 12½ cents per acre, but it was the only change in

land grant policy for individuals allowed by President Pierce. The
Pierce policies were carried on by James Buchanan, elected by
the same northern Democrat-southern planter coalition. Buchanan was put to his biggest test on the issue in 1860, when Andrew Johnson rewrote a homestead bill designed to meet southern
objections and tortuously nursed it through both houses despite
protests from both pro- and anti-slavery elements.

One of the side issues was the provision that allowed nonciti-
zens to claim homesteads, yet barred slaveholders from doing so.
Senator John B. Thompson of Kentucky gave vent to a remark-
ably candid complaint:

> We obtained the land by browbeating the Mexicans, by flog-
> ging the Indians, and then when you come to make a distribution
> of the spoils is one-half the nation to turn round and say to the
> other half, you smell of the nigger and you shall not have any
> land; we will give it to the foreigner and you shall not take a
> particle?

Despite all the compromises Johnson accepted to make his bill
palatable to the Senate, it was vetoed by President Buchanan. Perhaps the knowledge that Buchanan would kill the proposal was
one reason why southern senators let it pass by a heavy margin
after so long a delay. The veto, in June 1860, became a major campaign asset for the Republican candidate for President. As Horace
Greeley editorially inquired, "Does anyone suppose that Abraham Lincoln would ever veto such a bill?"

Abraham Lincoln signed such a bill, but a much better one, on
May 20, 1862. The right to homestead not exceeding 160 acres on
surveyed public domain was given to all heads of families. Title
would be acquired by continuous residence and improvement for
five years and the payment of $26 ($34 on the West Coast). The
applicant had to swear that he was entering the homestead for his
own residence, not as an agent for speculators. Free land was now

available to all prospective settlers, thanks to a Congress without representation from the Confederate states.

5

During the long struggle to establish the principle of free land for the settler, Congress had been extremely generous to other interests before it got around to concern for the individual pioneer. Great chunks of the public domain had been granted to railroads, or to states for the specific purpose of transfer to railroads being promoted within the state.

The first great railroad land grant by the Congress created the Illinois Central Railroad, and, as a by-product, the Mobile and Ohio. The legislation was in good part the product of the logrolling skill of Senator Stephen A. Douglas of Illinois, who drafted a land grant plan designed to attract the support of every region which might benefit directly or indirectly from the line that would parallel the Mississippi River, or which might secure grants in the future from the precedent set by the grants for a rail connection from Chicago to the Gulf. An example of the bargaining Douglas accomplished was the merger of the Illinois Central plan with the proposal for a rail line through Alabama and Mississippi into Tennessee and Kentucky, where it would be joined with the Illinois line at Cairo to form a route from Chicago to the Gulf. A branch was also designated to carry the Illinois line into Michigan, where it could connect with a line already being built as a direct link between New York City and Chicago. Despite general opposition from the Atlantic seaboard, most of New York's votes supported Douglas.

The Douglas bill provided that the land grants would be to the State of Illinois, and to the States of Alabama and Mississippi for the Mobile and Ohio. It passed the Senate without great difficulty in 1848 but provoked a much harder fight in the House. An agreement being negotiated by the Governor of Illinois and the

Massachusetts Western Railroad, whereby the Massachusetts firm would contract with the State of Illinois to construct the new line, may have been the decisive factor in swinging additional votes for the bill, which passed the House in 1850.

Since under the terms of the subsidy, grants to the state, made in turn to the Illinois Central Railroad Company, would be based on the mileage of the line constructed, the total land subsidy was not known until the line was completed in 1856. The actual grant was 2,572,800 acres. The total grant to Alabama and Mississippi for the Mobile and Ohio Railroad came to 1,156,659 acres.

Various states received grants for railroads during the next few years, but most of the land was granted direct to the railroads by Congress. Before these wholesale rail grants were finally halted, something like 180 million acres had been given away to states or private corporations. Eventually some of the less desirable lands were returned to the government, through failure to meet the terms of the grants or because of the failure of some of the promotion schemes. The total land donated wound up at 129,028,558 acres, of which 37,789,169 were in twelve states (Illinois, Mississippi, Alabama, Florida, Louisiana, Arkansas, Missouri, Iowa, Michigan, Wisconsin, Minnesota, and Kansas), and 91,239,389 acres were given directly to the dozen or so railroads who shared in the bonanzas. In addition to the land, more than one hundred million dollars in direct loans were made to the railroads in the same period.

Federal grants of land were the largest part, but not the whole story, of the grants to the railroads. Various states also made grants of hundreds of thousands of acres for railroad construction, as well as loans and direct money contributions. It was all part of the race to open the West to settlement and development. Even though the programs were often pushed by the same people, practices sharply contrasted with the theory of the Homestead Act. Most of the railroad grants were made before homesteaders had a chance to take their pick of the choice lands available for free settlement—75 million acres, for instance, were given the railroads during the Lincoln administration, when the war had reduced migration.

Speculators did not have to operate through the railroads to secure vast portions of the homestead lands. Through pre-emption frauds it was relatively easy for large tracts to be assembled by development companies in areas where there was a likely market for farmland. The Homestead Act made no proper distinction for timberlands, and lumber operators looking for a quick cutover and departure were among the chief offenders in pre-emption violations. The Timber Culture Act was passed for the worthy purpose of promoting the growth of timber on the prairie lands of the Great Plains, long before anyone foresaw the disastrous dust bowls. Together with the Desert Land Act, it was used, for the most part, to help acquire large tracts for grazing purposes. The storied conflicts between homesteaders and cattlemen naturally developed over conflicts in land use, and were quite often the by-products of concerted programs to keep the small farmer out of large tracts that the cattlemen wanted to keep entirely for grazing purposes, even though many cattle ranches were simply the combination of tracts originally homesteaded and pre-empted on the land office papers, if not in fact.

Through the first century of administration of the public domain, Congress set a pattern of profligate waste, with irreparable damage to the basic resource. The long struggle to achieve free land for settlers was a demonstration of the democratic process breaking down the seemingly endless resistance of the speculators and the vested representatives of the status quo. And even then, the homestead victory was diluted by the corruption in the administration of the program and the prior handouts to railroads of the choicest areas available in the public domain.

Land grants, perhaps more than any other government activity, were part and parcel of the stench of corruption which pervaded all the government during the Grant administration. More than one hundred companies maintained up to a dozen agents each in Washington for the purpose of pushing through land grant bills, or for influencing administrative regulations controlling the public domain. The corruption was enormous, but under cover of the conflict over reconstruction policy, it was possible to get by with a great deal. Congressional opponents of the raids on the national wealth, like George W. Julian of Indiana, spoke out and eventually began to be heard. A future President, James A. Garfield, had to apologize for his support of the Texas Pacific grant by saying: "I fully share in the general sentiment of the country, that we ought to put a speedy and effective end to the policy of granting lands to railway corporations, but justice to the South dictates this one."

The most brazen example of the corruption, at least among those promotions that became widely publicized, was the affair of the Crédit Mobilier, the firm which completed the building of the Union Pacific. The Crédit Mobilier took $23 million from Union Pacific's capital, most of which was derived from land grants. When a congressional investigation was requested, financier Oakes Ames distributed 160 shares of stock in his firm to some of the most influential members of Congress. He succeeded in blocking the first suggestion of investigation, but the Presidential election of 1872 broke the story and resulted in a partial exposé. A few careers were ruined, including that of a former Speaker of the House of Representatives, Schuyler Colfax, but the most important result was a reaction effectively stopping further wholesale railroad grants.

Whether the Congress of the United States or the President could break the pattern of corruption, lassitude, and spoliation was a test that had to be forced. For the first hundred years of the nation's existence, its land resource had been parceled out for mutilation and destruction. The time was urgent for some policy to reverse the tide and make some attempt at conservation.

CHAPTER IV

Federal Responsibility
for the Land

1

Robert J. Walker was a native of the western region of Pennsylvania, frontier country during his childhood in the early years of the nineteenth century. The intensely ambitious son of a local judge, Walker married into the talented and prominent Bache family of Philadelphia but decided that the southwestern frontier was the best place to make a name and fortune. He never quite achieved the fortune, but in 1832 he was elected United States Senator from Mississippi over George Poindexter, a bitter foe of President Jackson. His frontier background served Walker well in the Senate, where he was perhaps the chief advocate of preemption for public lands. President Polk made him Secretary of the Treasury, and he was probably the ablest man in the office since the departure of another Pennsylvania frontiersman, Albert Gallatin. Former Secretary Walker never returned permanently to Mississippi. As governor of strife-torn Kansas he became an active Unionist and during the war was a skillful Union propagandist in Europe.

Walker's major achievement in American resource development was a legislative afterthought in the last lame-duck days of the Polk administration. The General Land Office had for years been somewhat of a nuisance as part of the Treasury Department.

Walker suggested that it be combined with a few other house-keeping agencies as part of a Department of the Interior. Without great fanfare or lengthy debate, his idea was adopted by Congress in March 1849. Even though the new department was little more than a regrouping of such agencies as Pension and the Bureau of Indian Affairs, conservatives of the day expressed fears that it marked another milestone in the destruction of state powers.

"Mr. President, there is something ominous in the expression 'The Secretary of Interior,'" John C. Calhoun declaimed. "Everything upon the face of God's earth will go into the Home Department. . . . This is a monstrous bill. It is ominous. It will turn over the whole interior affairs of the country to this department; and it is one of the greatest steps that has ever been taken in my time to absorb all the remaining powers of the States."

Senator James Mason of Virginia was equally pessimistic about the dark intent of the new department but more accurate in his forecast of its effect. He predicted that the new cabinet agency would "absorb hereafter as much power as those who hold the reins of Government will see fit to place in its hands." For more than twenty years, very little was to be placed in its hands, and the century was nearly gone before the department began to assume real responsibility as a conservation agency.

2

The first Secretary of the Interior worthy of note was the famous German immigrant Carl Schurz in the cabinet of President Hayes after the cloudy election of 1876. He was the first active proponent of the idea of giving the Indians a chance to homestead some of the land which had been taken from them, and he introduced other ideas and actual reform into the administration of the Indian agency. Although he had settled in the German colony of St. Louis after fleeing from repression in Germany, Schurz, the liberal reformer, had a natural appeal to reform groups in the East, both native and foreign born. His awareness of Indian policy transgressions helped prepare the way for the emotional appeal of Helen Hunt Jackson's denunciation of government Indian policy in her book *A Century of Dishonor* and in her novels like *Ramona*. Negro slaves were now free from legal servitude, and the liberal groups in the East needed a new cause, ignoring the need of the freedmen for northern support as their rights as citizens were rigidly suppressed in the segregated South. Indian policy in itself is not part of this story, but it bears an inextricable relationship to the whole history of federal land policy.

Secretary Schurz's chief contribution to the development of the department's conservation role was to focus attention on the need for a general reform of the whole system of land grants and land management. The scandals of the Grant years had forced a halt, even under Grant, of the most corrupt abuses, but the penniless would-be small farmer was still not getting a fair chance at public lands. The timber resources on the lands were being ruthlessly depleted with little return to the government. For the first time, it was officially proposed that Congress "enact a law providing for the care and custody of such timber lands as are unfit for agriculture [potential agricultural lands were still to be homesteaded] and for the gradual sale of the timber thereon and for the perpetuation of the growth of timber on such lands by such needful rules and regulations as may be required to that end."

With the help of President Hayes, a halting legislative step was taken in the passage of the Timber Cutting Act and the Timber and Stone Act of 1878. For the first time in the history of the public domain, it was now possible for the government to sell timber from it. Hundreds of thousands of acres had been stripped and razed without return to the government. Now the new authority to sell offered the prospect of control, although meager appropriations brought little significant improvement during Schurz's years in office. Congress had been induced to take slow steps toward reform with the carrot of potential government revenue, but the lax and inept administration of the new laws turned them into mere tools in the hands of the land grabbers who evaded the homestead law.

Schurz, the scholar in the Interior Department, developed many of his ideas because he was not reluctant to expose his mind to some of the scholars and scientists of the day. The first great achievement of the American Association for the Advancement of Science was reformation of national forest policy. The association's 1873 convention became a rallying force for reform. A few newspapers took up the cause, and this attention in the intellectual community became the public opinion base for the Schurz-Hayes program. Timber reform had popular support in the still sparsely settled and represented Rocky Mountain and Pacific states (fast becoming the last "West") whenever the timber depredations could be identified as the work of absentee exploiters who left no opportunity for local development.

3

A figure even more important than Schurz in the development of national conservation policy was also beginning to make his presence felt in Washington during this time. John Wesley Powell, a self-educated product of an Illinois Methodist parsonage, left an arm at Shiloh but was a highly competent artillery officer in the Union army throughout the remainder of the war. He was "Major" Powell for the rest of his life, perhaps because the military title was useful in his explorations and surveys of the uncharted lands beyond the hundredth meridian but also most certainly because the rank of Union veteran was helpful in the uncharted course of building a bureaucratic toehold for science and conservation in the maze of Washington politics in the last quarter of the nineteenth century.

The country owes thanks to Major Powell for his courage and audacity in running the Colorado River, the first scientific exploration of the passes south through the Rockies, in 1869, and for his integrity and vision in the years that followed. To his shrewd talent as the builder of an expanding bureaucratic empire, without which his knowledge of the land and water would have been of little value to the nation, we also owe the legacy of government initiative to preserve and protect its resources.

Powell made his expedition through the Grand Canyon a springboard to government sponsorship of his western explora-ion and surveys. When his colleagues on the faculty of the Illi-nois State Normal College at Bloomington watched him promote a museum for the state Natural History Society and get himself appointed curator, some might have thought that the disabled army veteran was simply establishing his own sinecure, but this first Powell operation uniting politics and science was only a be-ginning. On the strength of his state position, and the intercession of Representative James A. Garfield, the Major managed an order from Washington allowing him to draw limited rations for his expedition from Army posts in the West. The promise of rations, together with a pittance from the Natural History Society and his own funds, was enough to finance the expedition through the Rockies, manned by family, friends, and volunteers.

The new transcontinental railroad made the start of the expedi-tion on the upper reaches of the Green River in Wyoming rela-tively simple, but the running of the Green and the Colorado ranks as a major feat of American exploration. Several of Powell's crew turned back along the way, and three out of the last nine left the misery and hunger of the trip just a few days before it ended, expecting a safer and more comfortable hike over a moun-tain plateau, only to be killed by Indians. Perhaps the major im-mediate achievement of the running of the river was to prove that there was no passage through the Rockies to the Pacific Coast, but its great value was that it enabled Major Powell to secure an appropriation from the Congress to begin a survey of the region he had traversed.

The ten thousand dollars appropriated for Powell's survey be-

yond the hundredth meridian was the start of another sporadic
uncoordinated survey of the western region. There were three
other major surveys going on at the same time, supervised by the
Interior Department, the War Department, or, in Powell's case,
by the Smithsonian Institution (probably as a result of a clerk's
error in transcribing the original appropriation for the survey).
Powell's appropriations were regularly increased, for he knew the
value of regular reports to Congress as well as articles for both the
popular and the learned journals published in the East. His most
valuable, as well as best known, government publication was *Report on the Lands of the Arid Regions.*

The report was the first step toward comprehending the necessity for scientific and realistic government management of the
public domain and toward the encouragement of those same factors in the private management of private lands in the West. After
its publication, there was no longer any excuse among learned
men for the popular myth of "rain following the plow," or the
widely accepted notion that the arid lands of the West were
adaptable for Midwest farming. The report specified that water
was the key to land use and that the sharply limited supply demanded classification of land for use and management. Almost all
the soil was fertile if water could be supplied, but even the most
careful irrigation plan could supply it for only a small part of the
arid region. Pasture lands without irrigation were economically
justifiable only in large acreages—with minimum units of four
sections, 2560 acres. Eighty irrigated acres were sufficient for a
family farm. Water rights would have to go with land, for they
determined its value. If private capital were given control of the
water, the farmers would be in peonage to the water owners. The
farmers themselves would have to be given authority to establish
irrigation districts and cooperatively develop and control the water supply for their land; otherwise, only the government would
be in a position to develop and distribute water supply.

Few government reports through the years have stood so well

the measure of hindsight. Although it is common for latter-day commentators to bewail the failure of the country to adopt the Powell recommendations for the western lands, a more realistic attitude might be one of thanks for the long-range guidelines which they laid down in a day when so little foresight was being shown. Tragically, much land and water resource was still to be destroyed, but the Powell recommendations were to become the basic philosophy of progressive federal conservation policy for the next two generations. Without the report, present reclamation and soil conservation policy would have come about far more slowly.

The American Association for the Advancement of Science's approval of the report was the tool Secretary Schurz used to bring about consolidation of the various western surveys in his department under a new bureau called the United States Geological Survey, established by a legislative rider on an appropriation bill on March 3, 1879. Schurz's choice for head of the new agency was not Major Powell but Clarence King, who had been in charge of the Geological Survey of the Fortieth Parallel, a War Department project. King was a product of eastern first families and schools, and a protégé and close friend of Henry Adams, who undoubtedly had a part in his appointment. But King was too erratic to be long interested in the administrative task, and he resigned after a year to be succeeded by Powell, now in a position of major influence and power. Powell was the logical successor to King, but the fact that his old legislative sponsor, James A. Garfield, was now President certainly was no handicap.

There was no Presidential budget in those days, and the fate of the Geological Survey was largely in the hands of its new director and the friends he could muster in the Congress. A proposal by Clarence King that the survey be broadened in scope to cover the entire United States, instead of the lands of the public domain, had lingered in committee and was obviously getting nowhere. In 1882, with the help of Representative Abram Hewitt, who was

later to be mayor of New York City, and John D. C. Atkins of
Tennessee, Powell circumvented the legislative committees by
adding a clause to a paragraph for the Geological Survey in the
Sundry Civil Appropriation Bill. Appropriations to the Survey
were made for its usual duties "and to continue the preparation of
a geological map of the United States."

With that clause Powell built one of the most successful personal empires in governmental history. His bureau owed its life to
an appropriations rider, and it became national in scope with another rider. By direct order of the Secretary of the Interior, he
became Special Disbursing Agent for the Survey. He was in direct control of all spending and hiring in the agency, and even the
Congress did not remember to seek an itemized accounting for his
expenditures and job allocations, thanks to the unorthodox way in
which the Survey had been established. If the civil service champions coming into prominence with the blessing of President Arthur had examined the situation, they might have described it
with a popular political phrase of later years—"a naked grab for
power." The flexibility thus created, however, allowed the survey
to produce the important breakthroughs in scientific knowledge
of the American land, water, and people that would have been
impossible under a more rigid system of operation.

4

Politically, the land scandals and the ferment in scientific circles
played a part in the electoral decision of 1884 which put Democrat Grover Cleveland in the White House. Cleveland's choice as
Secretary of the Interior was a somber-looking ex-Confederate
from Mississippi, Senator Lucius Quintus Cincinnatus Lamar. Lamar's knowledge and views of conservation issues did not enter
into the decision—Cleveland wanted him in the cabinet because
he was the chief national symbol of the mellowed former
Confederate, anxious to end postwar bitterness. That Lamar's integrity and intellectuality had made him another of the close

friends of both Henry Adams and Carl Schurz were extra dividends from the appointment. Lamar took the first serious look at some of the depredations of the western cattle barons, who ruled much of the public domain and Indian reservations with hired gunmen (some to be romanticized later into "cowboys"), and at the bribery of corrupt and inept Indian agents. Realizing that regulation and the elimination of corruption would not be a cure, however, Lamar recommended repeal of the Desert Land Acts, the Timber Culture laws, and the other legislation which was being used as a vehicle to consolidate huge corporate holdings.

These recommendations came in support of his Public Lands Commissioner, former Congressman William Andrew Jackson Sparks of Illinois, who was not afraid to speak out in favor of reforming the existing structure, which he called a nest of "fraud, favoritism and fees." With the support of Lamar and Cleveland, Sparks suspended all new entries into the public domain and even talked of requiring the railroad companies to meet the terms of their grants or return their lands to the United States.

Sparks estimated that his actions restored to the public domain more than forty million acres of lands fraudulently acquired, and at the end of his term President Cleveland claimed that in his administration the Interior Department had restored more than eighty million acres by halting illegal and "improvident" grants. Such progress was not to continue, however, for the embargo on land patents and the outlawing of fences on the public domain built up intense opposition to Sparks in the western states and territories. The powerful voices there were those of the established entrepreneurs, not the potential homesteaders or the occasional eccentric who was concerned about the future quality of the land. The early interest in reform died as the timber and mining interests gained effective control of western politics and public opinion.

To the average western congressman and newspaper editor, the aggressive Sparks was the chief villain of the lands policy, and he was offered up as a sacrifice in November 1887. A few weeks later, Lamar was kicked upstairs to the Supreme Court. The new Secretary of the Interior revoked most of the Lamar-Sparks reforms by an executive order in April 1888. It was the Presidential election year.

Another major development began in Cleveland's administration, the product of a meteorological disaster and the sure instincts of Major Powell. During the decade of drought that began in 1886, the average western settler began to realize the absurdity of "rain follows the plow." Even in the earlier years of normal rainfall, the successful homesteader had usually been forced to work out small-scale homemade irrigation systems. The drought now made it obvious that some planned program had to be established to provide a dependable source of irrigation water.

Western congressmen, including some who had previously ridiculed the idea that their area was deficient in rainfall, originated and pushed through, in February 1888, a resolution requiring a report from the Secretary of the Interior as to the feasibility of the Geological Survey's surveying and segregating irrigable lands and reservoir and canal sites in the western regions. William F. Vilas, the new Secretary, and S. M. Stockslager, his new Land Commissioner, were not anxious to take on new tasks in the face of the reaction against land law reform, but Powell was more than ready. Once again he suggested a rider on the Sundry Civil Appropriation Bill both to authorize and to provide funds for the irrigation survey. Senator William Stewart of Nevada and Senator Henry M. Teller of Colorado (the former Interior Secretary), both of whom had actively opposed the Lamar-Sparks reform program, were enthusiastic irrigationists and led the effort for the new authority for Powell.

In the House, however, Representative George Symes of Colorado was concerned about the possibility that the new program would be just one more boon to the land speculators. He managed to secure an amendment to the irrigation rider, ordering the withdrawal from settlement of "all lands made susceptible of irrigation" by the reservoirs and canals to be located by the survey. After considerable bickering about the effect of the amendment, the senators managed to get it modified to permit the President to restore for settlement any of the newly reserved lands. The appropriation act became law on October 2, 1888, establishing precedent for both the reservation from sale or homestead patent of the best remaining acreage in the public domain, and the historic Powell General Plan for irrigation, which eventually became the basis for the soundest aspects of the federal reclamation program.

Stewart, Teller, and their allies understood the importance of irrigation to the development of the West, but they could not fathom the attendant planning and control that would have to be part of a regional water use program, if land and water were not to be wasted and lost forever to the future. Powell's program involved planning, and few were ready for it.

"Do you conceive that there is any risk or doubt," Senator Eugene Hale of Maine asked, "in the government's assuming that relation [planning and control] and undertaking to deal with the flow of and use of water in the great streams? Do you think it is better than to leave it to nature and the common incidents of human life?"

"You ask me the question, and I will answer," Powell replied. "I think it would be almost a criminal act to go on as we are doing now, and allow thousands and hundreds of thousands of people to establish homes where they cannot maintain themselves."

The Congress chose to continue the "almost criminal" act. Funds for Powell's irrigation survey were virtually eliminated. The Symes restriction on new grants or sale of irrigable lands had been a warning to the exploiters and the pell-mell developers that the lands could actually be taken away from them, and they hastened to slap it down. It was not only repealed, but all entries made in "good faith" after its enactment were declared valid.

Powell had been relatively free to operate and expand his bu-

reaucracy of conservation science until he came into direct conflict with the powerful interests threatened by real conservation
policy. After sapping the irrigation survey, they turned on the
Geological Survey itself. When Representative Hilary Herbert of
Alabama discovered that the Survey had published a study on
Odontornithes, or toothed birds, the ultimate weapon had come to
hand. Why in the world was it necessary to spend taxpayer's dollars to find out whether birds had teeth?

In 1892 the Geological Survey appropriation was sharply reduced. What was worse, from Powell's viewpoint, its table of organization and salary schedule were spelled out to fit the ideas of
the congressmen instead of the director. Major Powell was no
longer in complete charge of his domain. After arranging for the
succession of Charles D. Walcott as the new head of the Survey,
Powell resigned in 1894. His mark is still strong on government
scientific and conservation programs. The national survey he
slipped through the side door in 1879 is still unfinished, like most
other conservation programs, but they and the country are better
for Powell's foresight and initiative.

5

Although the brakes had been tentatively applied following
Grant's second term, the first administration of Grover Cleveland
is entitled to credit for the first positive proposals for public lands
conservation policy. None of the Cleveland administration land-
law reforms became law, and the Department of the Interior had
given ground on most of its administrative reforms, but despite
the defeats, the ferment for change had taken hold in scientific
and intellectual circles, and the land reform ideas stayed alive in
the minds of some congressmen. In 1880 the basic proposals were
reintroduced by Representative Lewis Payson of Illinois. They
were not a specific part of President Benjamin Harrison's program, but at least they had his tacit approval. He signed them into

law on March 3, 1891. It was a sweeping reform bill which repealed the Timber Culture acts and the homestead pre-emption laws, barred the land auctions that had become the speculators' almost exclusive property, and then, almost as an afterthought, authorized the President to reserve areas of timber lands as national parks and to reserve other lands so future water supply could be protected.

The issues of public land disposal had probably absorbed more hours of congressional oratory than the tariff in the century-old life of the Congress. An ironic but perhaps fitting touch was that Benjamin Harrison, grandson of William Henry, the first congressional expert on public land, signed into law the bill virtually closing the public domain.

Although the Payson bill, which came to be identified as the General Revision Act of 1891, removed some of the worst defects of public land law, it was significant that it did not affect the Timber Cutting and Timber and Stone Acts, that had lately become the loopholes through which speculators and timber combines managed to ravage the land. As often happens, it was an afterthought provision of the law which became its most important part; the section allowing the President to set aside forest reserves for water supply and public parks was the bill's greatest achievement. Some of the credit for this section should go to the American Forestry Association and to the American Association for the Advancement of Science, both of which had recommended forest reserves. Neither proposal appeared to stir much interest in Congress at the time, which was probably helpful, for full debate might have aroused the curiosity of the western commercial interests who were later bitterly to oppose every new reservation.

During the first year under the law, Harrison created six forest reservations totaling more than three million acres. He added nine more reservations during his last year in office and evoked from a

Seattle newspaper what was to become a traditional complaint: "There is abundant room for pleasure without depriving the people of property of immense value in a commercial way."

When Cleveland came back to the Presidency in 1893, he supported fully the expansion of the forest reserves but thought the most important priority should be given to new legislation for management and protection of the forests along the lines of conservation practice being espoused by the American Forestry Association. The Interior Department's forestry bureau worked out improved regulations, but adequate appropriations and changes in the law continued to be a basic necessity.

Representative Thomas C. McRae of Arkansas supported Cleveland's program and introduced a bill that would give him the needed authority. McRae's bill provoked the full fury of the western states, now aroused over any attempt to stop the exploitation of the land. Populists like Sockless Jerry Simpson of Kansas lined up with open advocates of despoliation like Stewart of Nevada to oppose any step which would interfere with unregulated mining, grazing, or timber cutting. The McRae bill was introduced as a conservation measure, but it was eventually so amended as to become an effective instrument of anticonservation. Fortunately, the Westerners could not agree upon how strong to make it, and the original sponsors were able to block its passage after prolonged squabbles in conference.

The one positive legislative achievement in conservation policy during Cleveland's second term was securing appropriations for the expense of a special Forestry Commission to make recommendations about forest policy. It developed from the ideas of Walcott Gibbs, president of the National Academy of Science, and Secretary of the Interior Hoke Smith, and consisted of eminent scientists proposed by the National Academy. The only nominee without a national reputation in his field was a young man named Gifford Pinchot, an 1889 graduate of Yale, who had been working in the interim as forester for the fabled Vanderbilt Biltmore Estate in North Carolina.

The Forestry Commission was created just nine months before Cleveland left office, but its major recommendation, to establish thirteen more sizable reserves throughout the West, was unofficially agreed upon by February 1897. Pinchot, later to exhibit a mastery of Washington politics and bureaucratic infighting, had not yet developed this skill. He successfully delayed the commission's report until it included a statement of policy and a polished plan for the administration of the new reserves. Cleveland was more interested in simply getting the reserves, for a new President was about to be inaugurated, and William McKinley was unlikely to pick up Grover Cleveland's uncompleted chores.

On February 22, 1897, in celebration of the 165th anniversary of the birthday of George Washington, President Cleveland announced the thirteen new forest reserves of more than 21 million acres. A few eastern newspapers nodded in approval, but all hell broke loose in the West. Representative Frank Mondell of Wyoming spoke for most of the western congressmen when he called establishing the reservations "as outrageous an act of arbitrary power as a czar or sultan ever conceived." The Denver *Republican* seemed to speak for many newspapers when it said, "One trouble with Mr. Cleveland in regard to all matters concerning the West seems to be that he is imbued with an idea that the people of the West, especially those of the Far West, are ignorant, and, at the same time, hostile to the government." A mass meeting, reportedly of 30,000 people, at Deadwood, South Dakota, protested that the Black Hills reservation would "affect disastrously all the mining and dependent industries of this region and largely compel its depopulation." The general counsel of the Burlington and Missouri Railroad pronounced the end to further settlement of railroad lands.

The western congressmen answered immediately in the little

time remaining. They tacked an amendment onto the still pending Sundry Civil Bill rescinding all the reservations made by the President. Cleveland stood his ground by killing the bill with a pocket veto, which gave them no opportunity to attempt an override.

McKinley had hardly taken office before the attack on Cleveland's reservations was taken up again. The eastern supporters of the reservations, and conservation policy in general, fought back against outright recision of the grants, and gained ground daily, so much so that a Washington congressman cried out, "Why should we be everlastingly and eternally harassed and annoyed and bedevilled by these scientific gentlemen from Harvard College?"

McRae spoke out eloquently against blocking the Cleveland order, and he struck home to members from the Mississippi valley by pointing out that floods on the Mississippi might have been prevented if the forests had not been destroyed in the headwaters of its tributary system. Influenced by Major Powell's successor, Walcott, Senator Richard Pettigrew of South Dakota was unwilling to fight for a complete revocation of the Cleveland order. He proposed that it be set aside until March 1, 1898, with Presidential power in the future to modify any reservation already established. In addition, forest policy was changed by law, opening the reserves to mining and agriculture. The Secretary of the Interior was authorized to sell timber and to provide for the protection of the forests. This was a compromise of the old McRae proposals for improved forest administration, and it is still basic forest policy, no important changes being made in it before 1960.

CHAPTER V

The Water Barrel

1

In the generation between Lincoln and Roosevelt, the Federal government gradually moved toward a full-scale commitment to its responsibility for water programs, but the movement was haphazard, uncoordinated, and wasteful. The very wastefulness of the existing policies helped create the atmosphere that made possible the birth of a vibrant conservation movement under Theodore Roosevelt, but in the process so many ill-conceived, unplanned precedents were established by both the executive department and the Congress that the damage is still felt a century later.

Most of the policy decisions related to the civil functions of the Corps of Engineers. Although the Corps had virtually withdrawn from the business of improving rivers and harbors during the Civil War, Congress put it back to work at an accelerated pace as soon as the war was over. The two most important advances by the Corps prior to the turn of the century were an eventually full commitment to navigation development and a tentative start toward the assumption of responsibility for flood control work. The commitment of the Corps was largely uncoordinated, and the congressional control was even more haphazard.

An act of 1866 directed the Corps to resurvey all works of im-

provement for which appropriations had previously been made
and to give an estimate for each project of the cost of "its entire
and permanent completion." Estimates were also to be made of
"the amount of commerce and navigation which would be benefited by the completion of each particular work." It was the first
formal indication from the Congress that the costs of a project
should bear some relationship to the benefits to be derived from
it.

The same bill, however, required that these reports be submitted directly to Congress. There was no reference to national plans
for waterway or transportation systems. There is no indication
that either of the Presidents of the period, or the Corps of Engineers itself, had any interest in developing a coordinated national
waterway plan, but the law establishing almost direct control by
the Congress certainly discouraged any tendency in this direction.
It was a major breakaway from the system of public works envisioned by Gallatin, and it eliminated any possibility of the Corps'
fulfilling the role of planning engineers for the nation that might
have been derived from the Calhoun report.

The logrolling system came into its own as the control procedure. A President or a Secretary of War with firm convictions
against such a system could have held it in check, but there were
none in the first fifteen years after the war. A strong Chief of
Engineers might have brought about some semblance of national
planning, but the chief during most of this period was General A.
A. Humphreys, who not only accepted but strengthened the
Corps' tradition of never questioning a congressional determination. Thanks to his involvement in the original study of flood control on the Mississippi, however, the Corps was in no position to
resist efforts for a start toward flood control assistance on that
river.

The logrolling, pork-barrel system for approving water projects grew up in the same Congress which sharply cut back the
powers of the executive in every other field of government. Cries

of protest against the system rose right from the start, but most of them were directed not so much against the logrolling procedure in the Congress as against the mass of the projects themselves. Although the congressional procedure in handling water projects was criticized throughout the period, the chief criticism was aimed at the waste in voting federal money to assist obscure villages and remote sections of the country. Congressional supporters of navigation programs could answer back in righteous indignation that their projects were sound, and that the opponents were really objecting at the instigation of the railroads, or because they were unwilling for other parts of the country to share in the developing prosperity.

History supports both sides of the dispute but leaves no doubt that the waste grew out of the procedure, with its complete lack of planning and its uncoordinated haphazard development. The attitude of Representative J. Proctor Knott is a monument to those who shortsightedly ridiculed the value of federal public works to both a community and the country.

Knott had been attorney general of Missouri at the start of the Civil War. He returned to his native Kentucky during the war and was elected to Congress a few years later. Shortly after his "Duluth" speech, he was elected governor of Kentucky, and ended his long career as dean of law at Centre College.

On January 27, 1871, the House was debating a bill to extend the time on a grant of public land for a railroad proposed from the St. Croix River in Wisconsin to the west end of Lake Superior. The hopes for the railroad had been given new life with impending development of Great Lakes shipping through the locks at Sault St. Marie. Knott unloaded on the bill with one of the classic congressional examples of satirical oratorical flourish. A fair portion of the speech is worth reprinting from the *Congressional Record*, with the editorial notes (of laughter and roars of laughter), as an example both of congressional oratory of the day and of words destined for eating.

After paying his respects to a variety of subjects, including "those blushing damsels who are, day after day, beseeching us to let them vote, hold office, drink cock-tails, ride astraddle, and do everything the men do," Knott got to the heart of his subject:

Hence, as I have said, sir, I was utterly at a loss to determine where the terminus of this great and indispensable road should be, until I accidentally overheard some gentleman the other day mention the name of "Duluth." [Great laughter.] Duluth! The word fell upon my ear with peculiar and indescribable charm, like the gentle murmur of a low fountain stealing forth in the midst of roses, or the soft, sweet accents of an angel's whisper in the bright, joyous dream of sleeping innocence. Duluth! 'Twas the name for which my soul had panted for years, as the hart panteth for the water-brooks. [Renewed laughter.] But where was Duluth? Never, in all my limited reading, had my vision been gladdened by seeing the celestial word in print. [Laughter.] And I felt a profounder humiliation in my ignorance that its dulcet syllables had never before ravished my delighted ear. [Roars of laughter.] I was certain the draughtsman of this bill had never heard of it, or it would have been designated as one of the termini of this road. I asked my friends about it, but they knew nothing of it. I rushed to the Library and examined all the maps I could find. [Laughter.] I discovered in one of them a delicate, hairlike line, diverging from the Mississippi near a place marked Prescott, which I supposed was intended to represent the river St. Croix, but I could nowhere find Duluth.

Nevertheless, I was confident it existed somewhere, and that its discovery would constitute the crowning glory of the present century, if not of all modern times. [Laughter.] I knew it was bound to exist in the very nature of things; that the symmetry and perfection of our planetary system would be incomplete without it, [renewed laughter;] that the elements of material nature would long since have resolved themselves back into original chaos if there had been such a hiatus in creation as would have resulted from leaving out Duluth. [Roars of laughter.] In fact, sir, I was overwhelmed with the conviction that Duluth not only existed somewhere, but that wherever it was it was a great and glorious place. I was convinced that the greatest calamity that ever befell the benighted nations of the ancient world was in their having passed away without a knowledge of the actual existence of Duluth; that their fabled Atlantis, never seen save by the hallowed vision of inspired poesy, was, in fact, but another name for Duluth; that the golden orchard of the Hesperides was but a poetical synonym for the beer-gardens in the vicinity of Duluth. [Great laughter.] I was certain that Herodotus had died a miserable death because in all his travels and with all his geographical research he had never heard of Duluth. [Laughter.] I knew that if the immortal spirit of Homer could look down from another heaven than that created by his own celestial genius upon the long lines of pilgrims from every nation of the earth to the gushing fountain of poesy opened by the touch of his magic wand, if he could be permitted to behold the vast assemblange of grand and glorious productions of the lyric art called into being by his own inspired strains, he would weep tears of bitter anguish that instead of lavishing all the stores of his mighty genius upon the fall of Ilion it had not been his more blessed lot to crystallize in deathless song the rising glories of Duluth. [Great and continued laughter.] Yet, sir, had it not been for this map, kindly furnished me by the Legislature of Minnesota, I might have gone down to my obscure and humble grave in an agony of despair, because I could nowhere find Duluth. [Renewed laughter.] Had such been my melancholy fate, I have no doubt that with the last feeble pulsation of my breaking heart, with the last faint exhalation of my fleeting breath, I should have whispered, "Where is Duluth?" [Roars of laughter.]

But, thanks to the beneficence of that band of ministering angels who have their bright abodes in the far-off capital of Minnesota, just as the agony of my anxiety was about to culminate in the frenzy of despair, this blessed map was placed in my hands; and as I unfolded it a resplendent scene of ineffable glory opened before me, such as I imagine burst upon the enraptured vision of the wandering peri through the opening gates of paradise. [Renewed laughter.] There, there for the first time, my enchanted eye rested upon the ravishing word "Duluth."

This map, sir, is intended, as it appears from its title, to illustrate the position of Duluth in the United States; but if gentlemen will examine it, I think they will concur with me in the opinion that it is far too modest in its pretensions. It not only illustrates the position of Duluth in the United States, but exhibits its relations with all created things. It even goes further than this. It lifts the shadowy veil of futurity and affords us a view of the golden prospects of Duluth far along the dim vista of ages yet to come.

If gentlemen will examine it they will find Duluth not only in the center of the map, but represented in the center of a series of concentric circles one hundred miles apart, and some of them as much as four thousand miles in diameter, embracing alike in their tremendous sweep the fragrant savannas of the sunlit South and the eternal solitudes of snow that mantle the ice-bound North. [Laughter.] How these circles were produced is perhaps one of those primordial mysteries that the most skillful paleologist will never be able to explain. [Renewed laughter.] But the fact is, sir, Duluth is preëminently a central place, for I am told by gentlemen who have been so reckless of their own personal safety as to venture away into those awful regions where Duluth is supposed to be that it is so exactly in the center of the visible universe that the sky comes down at precisely the same distance all around it. [Roars of laughter.]

I find by reference to this map that Duluth is situated somewhere near the western end of Lake Superior, but as there is no dot or other mark indicating its exact location I am unable to say whether it is actually confined to any particular spot, or whether "it is just lying around there loose." [Renewed laughter.] I really cannot tell whether it is one of those ethereal creations of intellectual frostwork, more intangible than the rose-tinted clouds of a summer sunset; one of those airy exhalations of the speculator's brain, which I am told are ever flitting in the form of towns and cities along those lines of railroad, built with Government subsidies, luring the unwary settler as the mirage of the desert lures the famishing traveler on, and ever on, until it fades away in the darkening horizon, or whether it is a real, *bona fide*, substantial city, all "staked off," with the lots marked with their owners' names, like that proud commercial metropolis recently discovered on the desirable shores of San Domingo. [Laughter.] But, however that may be, I am satisfied Duluth is there, or thereabout, for I see it stated here on this map that it is exactly thirty-nine hundred and ninety miles from Liverpool, [laughter;] though I have no doubt, for the sake of convenience, it will be moved back ten miles, so as to make the distance an even four thousand. [Renewed laughter.]

Then, sir, there is the climate of Duluth, unquestionably the most salubrious and delightful to be found anywhere on the Lord's earth. Now, I have always been under the impression, as I presume other gentlemen have, that in the region around Lake Superior it was cold enough for at least nine months in the year to freeze the smokestack off a locomotive. [Great laughter.] But I see it represented on this map that Duluth is situated exactly half way between the latitudes of Paris and Venice, so that gentlemen who have inhaled the exhilarating airs of the one or basked in the golden sunlight of the other may see at a glance that Duluth must be a place of untold delights, [laughter,]. . . .

* * *

As to the commercial resources of Duluth, sir, they are simply illimitable and inexhaustible, as is shown by this map. I see it stated here that there is a vast scope of territory, embracing an area of over two million square miles, rich in every element of material wealth and commercial prosperity, all tributary to Duluth. Look at it, sir, [pointing to the map.] Here are inexhaustible mines of gold, immeasurable veins of silver, impenetrable depths of boundless forest, vast coal-measures, wide, extended plains of richest pasturage, all, all embraced in this vast territory, which must, in the very nature of things, empty the untold treasures of its commerce into the lap of Duluth. [Laughter.]

* * *

Sir, I might stand here for hours and hours, and expatiate with
rapture upon the gorgeous prospects of Duluth, as depicted upon
this map. But human life is too short and the time of this House
far too valuable to allow me to linger longer upon the delightful
theme. [Laughter.] I think every gentlemen on this floor is as
well satisfied as I am that Duluth is destined to become the commercial metropolis of the universe, and that this road should be
built at once. I am fully persuaded that no patriotic Representative
of the American people, who has a proper appreciation of the associated glories of Duluth and the St. Croix, will hesitate a moment to say that every able-bodied female in the land between
the ages of eighteen and forty-five who is in favor of "women's
rights" should be drafted and set to work upon this great work
without delay. [Roars of laughter.] Nevertheless, sir, it grieves
my very soul to be compelled to say that I cannot vote for the
grant of lands provided for in this bill.

Duluth prospered from Great Lakes shipping, which opened up
the Mesabi range. The growth of Duluth has been the stock answer since that time to accusations of logrolling and pork barrel.
Knott's speech was made during debate on a railroad grant bill,
but most of the ridicule was directed at Duluth's aspirations to be
linked with the ports of the world through the Great Lakes. The
linkage of the lakes by a lock system was a major contribution to
navigation development in the waterway programs of the Corps
following the Civil War.

2

Most of the nation accepted the unappealable outcome of the
Civil War for what it was—the pre-eminence of the Federal government, which settled as well the constitutionality of river and
harbor expenditures, but doubts on this point were still occasionally raised. When Congress passed a record appropriation of $18,-
743,000 in 1882, the doubts and reservations of President Chester
A. Arthur boiled over, and he vetoed the bill. Arthur said the

money appropriated provided for neither the common defense nor the general welfare, and the bill was therefore unconstitutional. Besides, he pointed out, it was an extravagant expenditure which debased public morals. A substantial segment of the press and some of the Congress were impressed, but not impressed enough to prevent passage of the bill over his veto.

President Cleveland vetoed a similar bill during his last year in office, 1896, with a stronger message:

> Many of the objects for which it appropriates public money are not related to the public welfare and many are palpably for the benefit of limited localities or in aid of individual interests.
>
> On the face of the bill it appears that not a few of these alleged improvements have been so improvidently planned and prosecuted that after an unwise expenditure of millions of dollars new experiments for this accomplishment have been entered upon.

The message was characteristic of many administrations of the era in that it criticized the lack of planning for the projects involved but failed to recognize that the "improvident" lack of planning was actually a lack of administrative control over the agency involved. Despite the angry congressional reaction which passed the bill over his veto in an election year, Cleveland's message did help to arouse public interest in better planning and coordination of the river and harbor programs. Even if there was little administrative planning for coordinated development, waterway promotion groups were being organized for the purpose of promoting specific navigation schemes. The net result of all this change was impetus to the conservation concept of planning, and eventually to the program of over-all coordination soon to be advocated for the first time.

The Corps of Engineers had used contractors working under Corps supervision for a good part of its construction work through the years. The practice became firmly entrenched during this period, in part due to specific instructions from the Congress in the rush of expanding work. In the years ahead, the contractors who handled the work were to become a bulwark of support in jurisdictional conflicts and campaigns for appropriations, but they would also sometimes be a crippling influence, encouraging rigidity and conformity when initiative and enterprise would have benefited both the Corps and the contractors in terms of expanded work opportunity.

3

The period of widening federal activity in river and harbor work was also the period of indirect assumption of full federal responsibility for navigation facilities on the inland waterways of the country. Prior to the Civil War, federal participation in the various canals over the country had been limited to indirect assistance —grants of public land or purchase of company stock—and even this had been done in only a very few projects. Now the government, usually by specific amendments to rivers-and-harbors bills, began to take over operation and maintenance of the canals. Some were purchased and others acquired through virtual abandonment by the original owners or promoters. The old Erie, however, was still enough of a going concern to warrant reconstruction and rehabilitation by the State of New York, which converted it into the New York State Barge Canal.

In 1881 the Secretary of War, in behalf of the Corps, was authorized to draw upon the treasury for the funds necessary to operate and keep in repair four specific canals. Three years later, general authorization was given to operate and maintain all canals owned by the United States. In 1894 specific authority was given the Corps to establish and enforce rules and regulations for the use of government-owned waterways, and from this has grown the Corps' responsibility for the entire inland waterway system, shared with the Coast Guard in some aspects of safety.

During this same period of broadening water responsibility, the collection of tolls was forbidden on any canal owned by the government. This 1882 law was in keeping with the tradition of free inland navigation first recognized under the Articles of Confederation. The major compelling force behind American acquisition of New Orleans, and consequently all the Louisiana Territory, was the midwestern pressure to end the Spanish collection of tolls and tariffs and other interference with goods brought down the Mississippi to New Orleans. Obscurely, and without a rational growth pattern, the concept of free rivers became one of free waterways without tolls. The free waterways concept has been a bastion of regional and local development promotion through the years, an economic leverage of vital, if incalculable, strength.

4

With the growth of congressional acceptance of the full federal role in development of inland navigation, it was inevitable that the demand also grow for federal action to control rivers for flood prevention. The Ellet and the Humphreys-Abbot reports of the 1850's were the results of congressional demand for Mississippi flood relief. The Ellet report was apparently lost in the archives, but the continued presence of both Humphreys and Abbot in high posts helped keep alive the idea that the Corps had a flood control mission on the Mississippi.

In the years immediately after the Civil War the strongest voice in the Congress for a Mississippi River flood control program was Senator James L. Alcorn of Mississippi, an ex-Confederate officer described as a scalawag by many of his former comrades because he had joined the Republicans and had been elected to the Senate with Negro votes. Alcorn was a planter in the Mississippi Delta, that area of ceded swampland that was being reclaimed as an agricultural Eden. He could describe from personal experience the absolute futility of local efforts to secure lands from Mississippi River floods. Mississippi, like the other valley states, had failed to meet its responsibility under the Swamplands Act, but the landowners in the area were taxing themselves to support local levee districts in a fruitless effort to halt the floods which descended from more than a third of the continental United States.

Alcorn offered regular amendments to the river and harbor bill for Mississippi flood control work, but all were rejected. After he left the Congress, however, the most impressive progress was achieved. An act was passed requiring the President to appoint a board of commissioners to study and recommend "steps for permanently relieving . . . Mississippi River overflow." Doubting congressmen reassured themselves about the constitutionality of this idea with a long preamble to the legislation: "Whereas the Mississippi River is national in character . . . and whereas all improvements looking to the reclamation of the delta of such a river must conduce to the general welfare of the whole union . . ."

The report of the special commission was largely a rewrite of the Humphreys and Abbot report, not surprising in view of the fact that Humphreys was now Chief of Engineers and Abbot a member of the commission. It repeated the Humphreys-Abbot doctrine that levees were the only solution to the Mississippi flood problem, and that there would be no significant benefits from reservoirs on tributaries, or cutoffs on the main river. Its important conclusion, however, was that little effective flood control could be accomplished on the river without the assistance of the Federal government.

Although history has proved the error of almost all of General Humphreys' major conclusions as an engineer, he should be credited with pushing the first admission by the Corps that river management and development was a single, if dual-purpose, responsibility. He was willing to push for flood control, even though it would have to be disguised as navigation improvement. This, together with the fact that President Hayes was committed to helping the South as a result of his electoral college bargain, was enough to secure passage of the Mississippi River Commission Act of June 22, 1879.

Although the act specifically gave authority to the commission to prepare plans to "prevent destructive floods," the whole tenor of the general language and the debate on the bill emphasized the points to "improve and give safety and ease the navigation thereof" and to "facilitate commerce, trade, and the postal service." The whole effort was to provide a limited coordination of the many local flood control efforts along the Mississippi. General Humphreys believed it would make the levee system work for flood control, even if the federal effort was called an aid to navigation.

The commission law required seven members appointed by the President, with three, including the chairman, from the Corps of Engineers, one from the Coast and Geodetic Survey, and three from civilian life, two of whom were to be civil engineers. The first of the civilian nonengineers named to the commission was Benjamin Harrison, the soon-to-be President. One of the civilian engineers was James B. Eads of St. Louis, one of the country's great civil engineers. Eads was a builder of both warships and bridges, most famous for the Mississippi River bridge at St. Louis. In the face of the determined opposition of General Humphreys and the Corps of Engineers establishment as a whole, Eads had risked a fortune in proving the value of jetties to hold open a navigation route where the mouth of the Mississippi poured into the Gulf. As a member of the Mississippi River Commission, however, for the most part he went along with the Humphreys doctrine of levees only as the solution to the Mississippi flood control problem.

The commission's first report in 1880 emphasized the value of levees as an aid to navigation. Another report in 1881 condemned both reservoirs and cutoffs as ineffective aids to the flood control system, after General Humphreys had had thirty years to digest the Ellet report. A severe flood struck the valley in 1882, and Congress appropriated more than four million dollars for Mississippi River "improvement," with the provision that no part of the funds be used for repair or construction of levees except where they were needed as aids to navigation. The commission parceled out most of the money to the various local levee boards for repairs of the levee breaks, and repeated that process through the years. After 1890 the restriction on levee building and repair was opened up to read "in such manner, to such extent, and in such proportions as in their opinion shall best promote the interest of commerce and navigation."

The system of flood control assistance on the Mississippi in the guise of aid to navigation was followed in a more limited program in California. In 1893 the Congress passed a law creating the California Debris Commission, consisting of three Corps of Engineers officers appointed by the President. The Debris Commission was given the duty of regulating hydraulic mining to prevent the debris from such operations interfering with navigation on the Feather and Sacramento Rivers, and for adopting plans for "improving the navigability, deepening channels, and protecting the banks of the rivers, and affording relief from flood damages."

5

The funds for flood control under the pretense of navigation were certainly limited in relation to the need, but in many years of heavy emergency levee repair work they made up the lion's share of river and harbor appropriations for the year. Each year they were attacked as unconstitutional by opposition members of Congress. In view of the pattern of other decisions of the day, it is highly possible that the Supreme Court might have held them unconstitutional, but no taxpayer ever took the trouble to carry a protest that far. Eminent authorities of the day were not hesitant to express their opinions, however. *The New York Times* in 1882 described spending money on levees as "ridiculous," in view of the undoubted unconstitutionality of the action. The *Chicago Tribune* outlined the case in the same year, when it rhetorically asked where Congress could find the authority for "confiscating the property" of the people of the nation for the benefit of the people on the banks of the lower Mississippi. An eminent historian, Albert Bushnell Hart, entered the ranks as a scholarly expert on pork barrel, logrolling, and general waste.

Senator Benjamin Harrison spoke up from his experience as a member of the Mississippi River Commission in 1882, and said that flood control was reclamation for the benefit of private property, and was not a proper or constitutional claim on the Federal treasury. Others pointed out that when the King of France originally granted lands in Louisiana, the grants contained the condition that the grantee would build levees at his own expense, and that whatever property loss he suffered from floods was a servitude incident to his grant. It was repeatedly pointed out that the land for which protection was demanded had originally been given away as worthless by the government.

Despite the cries of outrage from New York and Chicago over the expenditure of funds to protect private property in the Mississippi valley, relatively little money was being spent, and it accomplished very little in a system limited to providing flood control by levees only. The Mississippi River Commission became more wedded to the Humphreys doctrine each year, partly because of the continuing influence of the Humphreys-Abbot tradition, and, more realistically, because it was operating in a system where the major sources of funds were the local levee boards, each responsible for only a few miles of the entire river system. These local boards were unlikely to advance their funds for cutoffs far downstream, or for dams and reservoirs far upstream on the Ohio, Tennessee, Missouri, or Upper Mississippi. They could be the source of funds only for levee protection of their immediate frontage, and the River Commission did not tell them that this system would not and could not work.

The one hope for making the levee system successful was a vast supply of federal funds to underwrite its construction. The Interstate Mississippi Improvement and Levee Convention, an outgrowth of the original Memphis convention of 1845, met at Vicksburg in 1890, under the leadership of Charles Scott of Rosedale, Mississippi. Scott's program was based on the frank admission that only the Federal government could do the job, and no Mississippi valley organization has ever turned its back on that premise.

CHAPTER VI

T.R.

1

The end of the nineteenth century marked a changed America. The open frontier was gone. Most of the accessible and desirable areas of the West had already been opened up, homesteaded, or set aside in the reserves established by Cleveland and Harrison. For the first time in the nation's history, new principles of efficiency and scientific management were gaining acceptance among the better educated and economically favored elements of the population. The public was generally disgusted with the waste and exploitation so often evidenced in the government public lands policy. The railroad grants scandals were vivid memories, and they fitted into the reformist movement which was the eastern counterpart of the Populist revolt on the plains. The muckraker era of journalistic exposés was getting under way in the eastern press.

All of these factors coincided with the coming of Theodore Roosevelt to the White House, a man with some conservationist ideas of his own who was more than receptive to others. Other Presidents had made contributions, but Theodore Roosevelt is entitled to top Presidential credit for the American conservation movement. His actual achievements in the field were sharply limited in comparison with the accomplishments of Franklin Roosevelt, but the first Roosevelt laid all the important foundations. Gifford Pinchot, W J McGee, Francis J. Newlands, and a dozen others were major contributors to the conservation programs of the time, but without the impetus of Roosevelt's use of the Presidency they would have been far less successful. More than anyone else, Roosevelt dramatized the issues.

With a man in the White House who could be counted a friend, the champions of various conservation causes were ready to guide and advise him. All came with some background of special interest and special training in a single-purpose aspect of conservation or resource development, but most of them naturally supported adherence to a coordinated policy. Waste was something that they all instinctively reacted against, and waste was the major by-product of uncoordinated development. Most of them, knowingly or not, were touched by the reformist philosophy of the day typified by Henry George. They believed that the nation's resources had to be protected from waste, and preserved and developed for the best use of all the people. They joined in the popular reaction against monopoly, which meant to them monopolistic control of resources.

They conceived of the conservation movement as a fight for economic justice. Their foremost lawyer, Phillip Wells, later reflected that they conceived of economic justice as meaning, "so far as possible within the general limitations fixed by popular opinion as to fundamentals, and within the specific limitations fixed by constitutional provisions, the 'economic rent,' present and future, ['unearned increment'] in natural resources should be retained by the public which should also see that the resources are not wasted in order that the benefits of the new policy may be prolonged as far into the future as possible."

The heritage of Major Powell was an important factor among conservationists in the Roosevelt era. When the new President submitted his first message to Congress in 1901, Charles D. Walcott was still head of the Geological Survey, and this, as well as other scientific agencies, included men who had been influenced by both Powell and his pioneer sociologist friend Lester Ward, who found moral values in the use of scientific knowledge.

Foremost of the Powell heirs was W J McGee, an Iowa farm boy who taught himself to become one of the outstanding geologists and anthropologists of the day. He proved the worth of his homemade learning by making an extensive geologic and topographic survey of northeastern Iowa while he was still in his twenties, and then moved on to Washington to work for Powell. He was a principal organizer of both the National Geographical Society and the Geological Society of America, editor of the journals of both societies, president of the National Geographical Society and of the American Anthropological Society, and active in half a dozen other scientific groups. McGee was a scientist and a theorist from the start, and he became a skilled promoter and propagandist as well. He deserves to be called "the brains of the conservation movement." It was McGee who first conceived and promoted multipurpose development of water projects, which he pushed both as the scientific editor and as the chamber-of-commerce type organizer of business groups to promote navigation on the Mississippi River.

From the start, McGee linked his ideas of the use of new scientific discoveries with social purposes. Some of these ideas were presented in companion papers that he and his friend Lester Ward printed in the Smithsonian Annual Report for 1894. Meteorologist Samuel Langley, for one, was highly offended by their tone, which he termed "atheistic and radical," and he managed to get the report reprinted without the offending documents.

Langley had been a suitor of Anita Newcomb, daughter of the celebrated astronomer Simon Newcomb, but Anita had chosen McGee. Anita McGee was an intellectual from an intellectual family, but also a social one, and W J never did fit into the Washington social life. Anita studied and then practiced medicine, and there was apparently never a very happy family relationship.

Powell and McGee were self-educated Midwesterners, not too far removed from the soil and water that were the centers of the controversies they developed. The Eastern hero of the conservation movement, and by far the most influential figure in the field, was Gifford Pinchot. Born in Connecticut of an old Pennsylvania family and educated at Yale, Pinchot chose forestry as a career because of a youthful inclination, and his wealthy father encouraged him to get training in Europe, where the science was most advanced. His first job after Germany and France was the scientific management of Alfred G. Vanderbilt's forest estate near Asheville, North Carolina.

Few people in or associated with the timber business at the time believed that a sustained-yield forestry management system would be profitable in the American economy. Pinchot set out to show that it would, perhaps more than anything else to prove that the United States could support his chosen profession of forestry. His membership on President Cleveland's Forestry Commission catapulted him into the politics of conservation and he never left it, even as the Republican governor of Pennsylvania in the twilight of his career.

Especially in the years of conservation setbacks, complaints would be made about what some called the arbitrary and self-righteous nature of Pinchot's personality. However the contrariness in his nature might have offended some, the same personality inspired complete loyalty in others. Phillip Wells and George Woodruff, his Yale classmates, were outstanding among many attracted into government service through association with Pinchot. Others, outside government but important in national influence, first heard the doctrine of conservation from Pinchot, and accepted his leadership as gospel for some two decades.

Pinchot's most important friend, however, was Theodore Roosevelt. After his experience with the National Forest Commission in 1896, Pinchot had readily accepted the post of "Forester" in the Forest Division of the Department of Agriculture. In this role in 1899, he advised Governor Roosevelt on New York State forests. They were both Ivy Leaguers who had mastered the out-of-doors, both endowed with boundless energy and interested in translating ideas into action. Pinchot was ready with suggestions for Roosevelt's first message to Congress after he succeeded Mc-Kinley. From that time forward, the Forester became identified as T.R.'s conservation minister, even though his official position was subordinate to that of Secretary of Agriculture James Wilson. Part of the internal friction that hampered the Roosevelt program developed as a result of Pinchot's role as chief adviser, strategist, and spokesman, both public and private, for the President. It also was the official excuse for resistance and delay in both the Congress and the administrative agencies, but probably such foot-dragging would have existed even if Gifford Pinchot had not.

2

Roosevelt was no novice to conservation when he first encountered Pinchot. He was the most prominent among a number of eastern public figures of the late nineteenth century who took great personal satisfaction in proving themselves both physically and emotionally through some form of exposure to the rough life of the West. Before he became famous as the fabulous Rough Rider, he was friendly with Clarence King, the geologist; Bernard Fernow, the forester; Grant La Farge, the painter-naturalist; and John Muir and John Burroughs, the naturalists who popularized the conservation of natural beauty. In his autobiography, T.R. was to evaluate his efforts in behalf of conservation as the most important contribution of his years in the White House. More than fifty years after the autobiography, history supports his judgment.

Roosevelt's genuine interest, combined with the enthusiasm and promotional ability of men like McGee and Pinchot, reshaped the administrative structure and outlook of the Federal government on the whole conservation front. It was the misfortune of the over-all movement that the forces which had combined to give it such a favorable position in 1901 had not had a similar influence in shaping the Congress.

Unfortunately for Roosevelt, Congress could not match the executive agencies in producing champions of conservation. There was little political capital to be made in the issue outside the western states, and very little leadership in Congress from those states that showed any realization of the value of a coordinated approach to the varied needs of the region.

As one of the voices sporadically raised to seek flood control for the Mississippi valley, Representative Thomas C. McRae of Arkansas had directly related soil conservation and forest cover to an adequate flood control program. As a defender of the forest reservations, he would have been an invaluable ally among the southern Democrats, but he left the Congress in 1903 to become governor of his state.

The most influential figure in the House in water legislation was Representative Theodore E. Burton of Cleveland, Ohio, not only the chairman of the Rivers and Harbors Committee, but widely respected as a man who knew both the details of his committee's legislation and the full scope of the work of the Corps of Engineers, the agency that the committee virtually controlled. A graduate of Oberlin, Burton began his congressional career in the House in 1889. He served a term in the Senate from 1909 to 1915. After a period as a bank president in New York City, he came back to the House from Ohio in 1921, and died in 1929 after being elected to the Senate again in 1928.

Roosevelt's great legislative obstacle in the conservation field was his inability to gain Burton's support and cooperation, even though he recognized Burton's importance only belatedly. Burton's effective opposition to giveaways of power rights on navigable streams made it evident that he was aware of the national interest in water resources, and of their value in multiple use. Although a member of the commission, Burton was to give only half-hearted support to the National Waterways Commission report, and his opposition to the legislation to put it into effect was decisive. He was probably more responsible than even the Chief of

Engineers for the Corps' reluctance to take up flood control work, and he was usually the leader of the forces in the House that blocked the more imaginative programs of navigation development of the period.

The one congressman who wholeheartedly supported multipurpose resource development was Representative Francis G. Newlands of Nevada, who was introduced to the idea as one of many western supporters of federal aid for irrigation. After the passage of his reclamation act, he might have gracefully withdrawn from leadership in water development, for most of Nevada's interests could be taken care of under the reclamation program, but he continued to fight for multipurpose water development free from the traditional "pork barrel" approach.

Newlands was born at Natchez, Mississippi, in 1848, the son of a Scotch physician who had come to America with his bride only a few years before. Natchez was a center for the new-rich cotton South, but the young parents decided they would rather rear their child in the North, and moved to the outskirts of Chicago. Dr. Newlands died a few years later, and his widow remarried a local political leader, who was able to send his stepson to Yale and Columbia before his business failed and he had to take a job in Washington. The move brought young Newlands to the Georgetown Law School, which he left to practice law in San Francisco.

Success came soon in California, but it was assured when he married the daughter of Senator William Sharon of Nevada. After the death of his father-in-law, Newlands moved to Nevada to manage the family silver mining interests. It was a logical progression from this to the House of Representatives on a "silver" ticket in 1892, then firm allegiance as a silver Democrat, and promotion to the Senate in 1903.

His Nevada constituents knew of Newlands' role as the father of reclamation, but it did no harm to his political stability to be best known as a champion of silver. Today the Newlands Act is an impressive monument to his legislative record. The tragedy of his career was the failure of his long and often lonely fight to achieve a similar, but broader, program of water development for the entire nation.

Another young Federal official who met and impressed Governor Roosevelt in 1898 was Frederick H. Newell, chief hydrographer of the Geological Survey. As a proper protégé of Major Powell, Newell had worked for a program of federal irrigation that would make use of the water data his agency was developing. He found a ready ally in George H. Maxwell, a California lawyer whose specialization in water law had turned him into an irrigation enthusiast. Maxwell quickly realized that only a federal program could meet the need in the West, and in 1896 he persuaded the National Irrigation Congress to endorse a limited program of federal aid for irrigation.

Maxwell then moved from California to a base in Chicago, with a campaign to persuade business interests of the national economic value of irrigated lands, attempting to break through the Republican congressional opposition and the indifference of President McKinley. He worked with Congressman Newlands in hammering out an irrigation bill that met their goals and still had a chance of passing the Congress.

3

An outstanding psychological move was calling the program reclamation instead of irrigation. Newlands wanted to limit the water rights to eighty acres of land, to make sure that the benefits went to family farmers and not corporations. Eventually, the bill's sponsors had to increase the limitation to 180 acres, but they held fast for that limitation and established a principle of federal reclamation largely honored through the years, partly because community property laws usually made it 360 acres in actuality. To halt speculation, Newlands also wanted to give the Secretary of the Interior authority to withdraw from entry all potential irrigation lands. He settled for a provision that the areas of proposed projects would be barred from all private entry except those made under the homestead laws.

The first financing proposal was a Reclamation Fund established from the proceeds from sales of public lands. The struggle to provide a reasonable financial structure for the program eventually made it easier to establish the limited multipurpose concept for reclamation projects. Water power could carry part of the load for irrigation, and it was destined to become a standard benefit.

Newland's original bill provided that individual reclamation projects would be selected by the Secretary of the Interior on the basis of comparative national value, and that funds for their construction would be allocated from a general fund. There obviously had to be some relatively objective means of determining priorities, but Newlands also defended the plan on the more practical political ground that it was the one way to prevent regional fights over programs by western congressmen which could wreck the unified force the reclamation interests had to present in the Congress. Leaving the priorities to the executive department was Newlands' idea of the one way to prevent the logrolling system that controlled the river and harbor programs from getting the upper hand in the reclamation program.

From the beginning, "reclamation" has been identified with and sadly limited to the "western" states. The designation, of course, is a rough one which includes the "arid regions" of Major Powell's original report. Nothing but tradition, the existence of the original law, and the complexities of extending the Bureau of Reclamation's authority into new areas with differing experience in water rights law has prevented federal irrigation programs being made available to other states, but these have been potent forces, however illogical they may be. The reclamation program was limited to Arizona, California, Colorado, Idaho, Kansas, Montana,

Nebraska, Nevada, New Mexico, North Dakota, Oklahoma, Oregon, South Dakota, Utah, Washington, and Wyoming, with Texas added later.

Roosevelt did not hesitate to endorse Newlands' reclamation bill, thanks primarily to the influence of Frederick Newell. In protest against eastern opposition to irrigation, Senator Thomas Carter of Montana had meanwhile delivered major support for it by filibustering the 1901 rivers and harbors appropriation to death. Although Roosevelt could not persuade Speaker Cannon to support the bill, he did persuade him that with the new Republican President identified with the legislation, the Republican leadership could not block a vote, and this fortuitous combination of circumstance and event was enough to pass the bill.

The Newlands Act established the Reclamation Service as a branch of the Geological Survey, and Roosevelt placed Frederick Newell in charge of it. In 1903 the first four projects were approved by the Secretary of the Interior. One of them was the Salt River in Arizona, which was eventually to become a major success in both power and irrigation. (The massive Salt River project had a much easier start than the Arizona project, a similar major plan sixty years later, perhaps because the most prominent sponsor of the latter-day project was Senator Barry Goldwater, who opposed public power and water development projects in other states.)

In 1905 the first reclamation project was completed; it was the Truckee-Carson ditch in Nevada, where Representative Newlands now had been promoted to senator. In 1907, still under Newell's successful administration, the Reclamation Service was upgraded to the Bureau of Reclamation, becoming a separate major division of the Department of the Interior. In the years ahead, the bureau was to lose a great deal of its independence from congressional logrolling, but it was to make more progress in multipurpose development and a specific system of financial return from identifiable benefits. Establishing the Bureau of Reclamation and starting it on the road to success was probably Roosevelt's outstanding program achievement as President.

4

For many conservationists, the revolution in American forestry practices which Pinchot won during the Roosevelt years was as important as the bureau's establishment. The American timber industry, organized on a large and relatively efficient scale only after the Civil War, had moved with the frontier. Timberlands had been cut over and abandoned, with no thought of either their own future or the effect upon the land and the regional economy. The big timber interests had been confidently looking forward to cutting a similar path across the public domain, until the land grant scandals led to the first withdrawals from the public domain and the beginnings of national forests in the West.

Pinchot was the first American to train deliberately for a career in forestry management, as contrasted with the sons of lumber operators who followed their fathers into business. With the help of his European training, the young Pennsylvanian developed the theory of sustained-yield forest management. The system would not only preserve existing forests from wasteful cutting, but through selective cutting, it would enable the land to produce more timber for cutting over the long haul.

The American Forestry Association, formed in 1875, included few members who worked with trees for a living, but the combination of landscape architects and gardeners, estate owners, botanists, horticulturists, and scientists of varying other descriptions has had an important influence in favor of western forest reserves. After Pinchot became Chief Forester in the Department of Agriculture, he easily dominated the organization; most of its leaders developed his crusading spirit for reform in American forestry and for conservation in general.

One immediate problem facing the Forestry Division was the lack of professionally trained foresters to carry out the mission of

teaching timberland owners how to care for their trees. A program was set up to give college students on-the-job training, in the
hope that they would make government forestry a career. Yale
University established a school of forestry when Pinchot's parents
endowed it with $300,000, and the Chief Forester literally prom-
ised employment for all its graduates. (The senior Pinchots made
a career of nurturing their son's career. It was the elder Pinchot
who suggested forestry, and when their then bachelor son received his Washington assignment, his parents established a home
with him in the capital.)

The Forestry Division became the Bureau of Forestry in the
Department of Agriculture in 1900, but its enhanced status within
the department meant little to Pinchot as long as he had no control and little influence over the management of the vast acreages
of publicly owned forests that were still the responsibility of the
Department of the Interior, the heritage of the old Land Office.
Pinchot expended a lot of effort in the first four years of the
Roosevelt administration in an attempt to transfer the national
forest reserves from the Interior Department to his Forest Service
in the Department of Agriculture. It certainly made sense that the
nation's timber should be scientifically managed, and that the Forest Service would not be able to persuade private timber owners
to adopt sustained-yield practices if the government did not use
them itself.

Opposition to the change was well entrenched. The Department of the Interior did not care to lose a major part of its bureaucracy. Most of the jobs in the management and care of the
reserves had been parceled out as patronage prizes for important
members of the Congress. The Republican leaders did not want to
change this, and few of the western senators of either party favored the transfer. Through the various devices they used to
thwart the homestead law, many of the timber interests in the
West were able to obtain enough access to the public lands to
handle all the timber they could harvest and market. Those who

had found a niche in the existing system could see no advantage in change, and their influence counted heavily.

After failing to secure the transfer under McKinley, Pinchot found that even an outright recommendation from President Roosevelt could not bring it about; the timber industry itself would have to be at least partly converted. Lumbermen who saw the advantages of government protection and preparation of their future timber cuttings were encouraged to become active in the management of the American Forestry Association. Specific arrangements were made to protect existing interests. Secretary Hitchcock's policy had been to sharply restrict grazing in the reserves, and Pinchot made it clear that his sustained-yield theories envisioned a liberal grazing policy. His links to irrigation interests through Newell and Maxwell were cultivated.

Pinchot, the pioneer conservationist, was anything but a "preservationist." Teddy Roosevelt was the hero of the Boone and Crockett Clubs universal among prominent sportsmen of the East, but Pinchot persuaded him against their extensive plans to establish large hunting preserves in the publicly owned forests. The twin bugaboo of extensive hunting preserves and vast new national parks to limit lumbering operations gradually broke down the western opposition. Roosevelt choked off opposition within his administration, and the transfer plan passed the Congress in 1905. Pinchot was now in full control of national forest policy.

The forestry reserve states had in the main accepted the idea of the transfer of reserve control to the Forest Service, but they began to repent and rebel within a few months after Pinchot's young career men began to enforce his new regulations. For years, stockmen had been using the reserves for grazing, aided by inadequate regulations and lax enforcement. After 1905 they had stiffer regulations to contend with, and, for the first time, fees for the use of forest lands. Throughout the West, cries went up for state control of forests, along with strident attacks on federal bureaucracy and regimentation. Fighting back, Pinchot made annual

swings around the forest areas and built effective support among a
few farsighted newspaper editors, stockmen, and timber operators.

Except in California, few politicians spoke out in favor of his
policies. Although in some areas forest rangers were called
"Teddy's Pets," most of the personal reaction against the new
administration fell upon Pinchot instead of the President. In California, Nevada, and Utah most of the organized stockmen, lumbermen, and irrigation farmers saw the long-range economic advantage of the Pinchot policies and supported the new system of
administering the forests. Despite the clamor of such members of
Congress as Representative Frank Mondell of Wyoming and Senator William E. Borah of Idaho, opinion in the West was not
universally opposed to the new conservation program. Even
Borah, for example, talked much louder against the Forest Service
in Idaho than he did in Washington.

Presidential action to establish new forest reserves was the biggest scarecrow of those who talked the doctrine of western states'
rights. In 1907, this group managed to get a legislative rider added
to the Department of Agriculture appropriation bill permanently
barring the creation of any new reserves or expansion of existing
ones in Oregon, Washington, Idaho, Montana, Wyoming, and
Colorado. There was so little opposition in the Congress that Roosevelt accepted the political wisdom of signing the bill. Before he
signed it, however, he accepted Pinchot's recommendation for the
creation or enlargement of 32 national forests within the six states.

5

In 1907, Roosevelt named a new Secretary of the Interior. Pinchot had not been interested in the position, for the Interior Department was now largely removed from his direct interest in
forestry, and the new Secretary, James R. Garfield, son of the late
President, was fully acceptable to him. Despite the fact that Pinchot overshadowed him as Roosevelt's chief conservation officer,

Garfield became Pinchot's firm ally for the remainder of the Roosevelt administration and through most of the conservation controversies of the immediately succeeding years.

Garfield and Pinchot worked together for a leasing law for grazing rights on the public domain, even though it led to popular attacks on the administration's role as promoter of monopoly and the friend of cattle barons. Despite the active interest Roosevelt took in it, farmers and sheepmen joined with supporters of the old homestead doctrine and managed to beat the bill. Unregulated grazing continued, and new farming operations were started on land Major Powell had long ago identified as too arid for American farming. Garfield tried also to secure a leasing law for coal lands but was blocked by a combination in which the traditional western opposition was joined by Senator Robert LaFollette of Wisconsin, who feared that the proposal would lead to monopolistic combinations among coal producers.

Roosevelt's policies on water programs were chiefly influenced by W J McGee, both in direct advice to the President and in the widespread national sentiment for waterway development, a good part of which was due to McGee's promotional efforts. There were few legislative or program results in this field, but before Roosevelt had left office, a firm beginning had been made toward the philosophy of multipurpose waterway development. Senator Newlands was to be the chief congressional champion of this basic conservation doctrine for the rest of his life. Congressman Burton never fully accepted the multipurpose concept, but the firm opposition this conservative Republican waged against control of waterways by private monopoly was a real contribution to the conservation story and helped shape T.R.'s thinking.

Before "Fighting Joe" Wheeler, the ex-Confederate cavalry general, left the Congress in 1898 to accept a generalship in the United States Army (and serve as Theodore Roosevelt's superior in Cuba), he introduced a bill to give permanent authority for the newly formed Muscle Shoals Power Company to build a power dam on the Tennessee River at the Muscle Shoals in his district in north Alabama. Wheeler's bill declared that the Tennessee was "unused and unsuited for purposes of navigation" and gave the power company the rights to the river without any compensation to the United States government. Burton was chairman of the Rivers and Harbors Committee. Before he reported the bill, Burton amended it to strike out the navigation waiver and to direct the Secretary of the Army to collect reasonable fees for power.

The Muscle Shoals Power Company existed largely on paper, and the promotion failed without any construction activity. In 1902, Wheeler's successor in Congress, William Richardson, introduced a bill to allow a new promotional firm, N. F. Thomson and Associates, to build a power dam at Muscle Shoals. Richardson's bill was considered routinely and passed the Congress without great discussion. On March 3, 1903, Roosevelt vetoed the bill, saying that "The recent development of the application of water power to the production of electricity available for use at considerable distances has revealed an element of substantial value in streams. . . ." Burton vigorously defended the veto:

> . . . Such a bill as this fixes a precedent for the use of water power in every navigable stream in the United States . . . by which the Government after making expensive public works in rivers, constructing locks and dams or otherwise, absolutely barters away for nothing that which is of greater value than the cost of the works themselves [and throws] the door wide open for favoritism and monopoly.

After Roosevelt blocked the special bills for grants of power rights, pressure began to build up for a general authority for private power companies to build on streams. Congress passed the General Dam Act of 1906, giving this authority for dams to be built upon specific congressional resolution if the Chief of Engineers and the Secretary of the Army certified there would be no interference with navigation. The reservation of the right to charge for the water was dropped, and there was no time limit on the power rights. Roosevelt signed the bill but obviously had second thoughts a short time later.

By 1908, Roosevelt had decided that private companies should not be allowed to dam navigable streams unless there was a payment to the government, regulation of rates for the power produced, and provision for forfeiture in case of violation of the terms of the grant. He began to veto grants that lacked these conditions, even though they met the terms of the 1906 Dam Act.

When Roosevelt asked the Corps of Engineers to check plans for dams to see that his conditions were met before he acted on the various congressional resolutions, the Corps refused to comply with his request, apparently because no such power was spelled out in the General Dam Act. Secretary of War Taft thus had to report to President Roosevelt on the dams on the basis of information received from the Department of the Interior, instead of from the Army Engineers. Roosevelt sent a message to Congress proposing that the Interior Department be given authority over water power permits, but no action was taken, and Roosevelt left office with the policy still in confusion.

6

Beginning at the time of the Spanish-American War, railroad rates over the country started a steady climb upward. It was no coincidence that the rising rates came at a time when businessmen all over the country began to pick up the idea from scientists like McGee that the accessibility of water transportation would offset the rail rate structure and also become a major tool of economic development. Promotion groups organized to secure navigation on most of the major rivers, often just in time to block permanent navigation barriers in the form of single-purpose power dams to be constructed by private power companies. Various combinations of rivers and canals were proposed. Perhaps the most ambitious was the proposal to link Boston to the Rio Grande by way of an intracoastal waterway and a cross-Florida barge canal. (Completion of the dream is finally in sight in 1966.) Private capital sought authority from Congress to promote a canal connection through Pittsburgh between Lake Erie and the Ohio River. Atlanta, Georgia, interests proposed a combination of canal and river links to put Atlanta on a navigable path from the Atlantic coast to the Ohio River by way of the Tennessee.

In Canada, the idea of a St. Lawrence Seaway to bring ocean shipping up the river and into the Great Lakes was being talked about, but most of the discussion in Chicago was about the Lakes-to-the-Gulf waterway, to make it possible for ocean shipping to come up the Mississippi to Chicago by way of the Illinois River. The Lakes-to-the-Gulf Deep Waterway Association sought a 14-foot channel from Chicago to New Orleans. Chicago commercial interests wanted additional ties to the entire Mississippi valley, with more markets in the South made available by water freight rates. St. Louis businessmen had some of the same ideas, with more emphasis upon trade with Central America and the west coast of South America, which would become accessible upon the completion of the Panama Canal.

Hardware merchant James E. Smith had led in the promotion of the St. Louis Exposition of 1903 primarily as a spur to the economic development of St. Louis. One of the by-products of that fair came when W J McGee left his government post as head of the Bureau of Ethnology to come to St. Louis in charge of the anthropological section of the exposition. After the fair closed, McGee became head of the new St. Louis Museum, and a close associate of Smith in waterway promotion through the Latin-American Club of St. Louis. "Every consideration of geography and ethnology no less than that of immediate commerce commands our citizens to extend their enterprises beyond the Rio Grande and the thirtieth parallel, even beyond the Gulf and the Caribbean, to afar across the equators," McGee told the Missouri businessmen, ". . . St. Louis is the natural key city not only to our own Southwest but to all Latin America and much of the Pacific."

As chief spokesman for the Latin-American Club, McGee plunged into the work of the Lakes-to-the-Gulf Association, and sought to keep the organization from limiting its approach solely to navigational development. He was given considerable support by an influential young congressman from Louisiana, Joseph E. Ransdell, who was very much interested in flood control on the Mississippi. The city of Chicago wanted a deep channel for the Illinois, not only to carry ocean vessels, but to enable the river to carry a diversion of Lake Michigan waters sufficient to flush the city's sewage disposal system. Chicago interests believed that a good part of the cost of the Illinois River part of the project could be borne by a hydro-power project on the river. McGee emphasized the necessity of controlling the erosion that poured countless tons of silt into the Mississippi all up and down the big river.

In 1907, the Mississippi-Illinois waterway scheme came to a crucial test in the office of the Corps of Engineers and in the Congress. The Corps had approved a 14-foot project for the Illinois River portion of the waterway in 1905, but two years later it declared that a 14-foot project from Cairo, Illinois, south would not be feasible. It was not clear where the 14-foot traffic on the Illinois River was supposed to go, and the tonnage estimates for river traffic on the lower Mississippi have long been belied by the river's actual traffic. Under Chief of Engineers General Alexander MacKenzie, the Corps still viewed its function as limited to navigation work, and it was supercautious about even that.

In the Mississippi valley public sentiment was strongly against the Corps, and just as strong against Representative Burton. There was openly voiced suspicion that Burton's position as chairman of the committee influenced the Corps' decision, and newspapers pointed out that Burton secured $19 million for Great Lakes navigation work at the same time that he blocked any money for navigation on the Mississippi. Congressman Ransdell, president of the National Rivers and Harbors Congress, proposed that the civil functions of the Corps be abolished and the work put in the hands of a new Federal Department of Public Works.

Although he was from Illinois, Speaker Joe Cannon sided with Committee Chairman Burton in the fight over appropriations for the Mississippi. The recriminations that resulted from Cannon's stand played an often overlooked part in the historic revolt against him a few years later.

7

After the defeat at the hands of both the Corps and the Rivers and Harbors Committee, McGee came up with a plan to bypass these two bastions of conservative traditionalism. After consultations with Pinchot and Newell, he formally presented to Roosevelt on March 12, 1907, a request for the President to establish an Inland Waterways Commission. Two days later, Roosevelt announced the appointment of the commission. McGee had not only proposed it, but suggested its personnel, to be chosen from Federal agencies with responsibilities in the water development field: Pinchot, Newell, General MacKenzie, and Lawrence O. Murray, Assistant Secretary of the Department of Commerce and Labor. Instead of Murray, Roosevelt appointed Herbert K. Smith, Commissioner of Corporations and an old friend and publicist for Pinchot. He added four members of Congress: Senators Newlands and William Warner of Kansas, and Representatives Burton and John H. Bankhead of Alabama. To make McGee eligible to be the commission secretary, he was appointed to a job in the Bureau of Soils.

Roosevelt's charge to the commission was another suggestion from McGee:

> Works designed to control our waterways have thus far usually been undertaken for a single purpose, such as the improvement of

navigation, the development of power, the irrigation of arid lands, the protection of lowlands from floods, or to supply water for domestic and manufacturing purposes. . . . The time has come for merging local projects and uses of the inland waters in a comprehensive plan designed for the benefit of the entire country. Such a plan should consider and include all the uses to which streams may be put, and should bring together and coordinate the points of view of all users of water.

The commission toured a good part of the country and heard suggestions from all quarters. (Roosevelt joined it for a steamboat trip down the Mississippi.) Perhaps the most important developments of the period of study by the commission were some advanced ideas for multipurpose development from Marshall O. Leighton, Chief Hydrographer of the Geological Survey, who believed that power dams could also control floods, and drew up plans for a multipurpose Ohio River system.

The heart of the commission report was : "Hereafter plans for the improvement of navigation in inland waterways . . . should take account of the purification of the waters, the development of power, the control of floods, the reclamation of lands by irrigation and drainage, and all other uses of the waters or benefits to be derived from their control."

In endorsing and submitting the report, Roosevelt emphasized the recommendation for a single executive agency to coordinate water resource development and administration: "No single agency has been responsible under the Congress for making the best use of our rivers, or for exercising foresight in their development. . . . We shall not succeed until the responsibility for administering the policy and executing and extending the plan is definitely laid on one man or group of men who can be held accountable."

All of the members of the commission approved the report, except General MacKenzie.

In December 1907, Newlands introduced in the Senate a bill to carry out the commission's recommendations. It would have established a permanent Inland Waterways Commission, appointed by the President, with a responsibility for investigating water problems, authorizing projects, supervising construction, and coordinating the activities of all Federal water resource agencies. An Inland Waterway Fund would be established at $50 million, replenished whenever it fell below $20 million, without annual appropriations by the Congress.

The Corps of Engineers actively opposed the bill, although Roosevelt forced Secretary of War Taft to submit a favorable report for his department. More significant was the opposition of Congressman Burton. His committee did not want to give up its power of authorization, just as many individual congressmen were reluctant to give up the prestige and political value of sponsoring specific projects. Newlands agreed to compromise, to maintain a requirement for congressional authorization, but the sum of $50 million without "congressional controls" was raised as a new bugaboo. Then the Congress took up the idea that membership on the commission should be restricted to congressmen. Both the administration and Newlands stopped pushing the bill, and it died before coming to a vote in the Senate, after being so diluted in the House that it passed almost without opposition.

Roosevelt's administration ended on a depressing note brought about by the failure to enact into law the recommendations of the Inland Waterways Commission. The congressional leadership was angered by the end runs Roosevelt tried, to get around their failure to act or to prod them to act. A much publicized Governor's Conference on Conservation was held at the White House, guided and controlled by the Roosevelt forces, but it changed few votes in Congress. The governors proposed that Congress authorize a national conservation inventory. When Congress failed to act, Roosevelt appointed a National Conservation Commission to report on waters, forests, lands, and minerals, with Pinchot as general chairman. Congressmen were the heads of four subject commissions, but experts like McGee and George Woodruff were secretaries for the groups. The reports were the most comprehensive to that time, but produced without funds, they were of little permanent value because of the conditions under which they were compiled.

Congress refused to appropriate any sums whatever for Roosevelt's conservation meetings and committees, and sometimes even refused to print their reports to the Congress. Members of the Inland Waterways Commission had to pay for the printing of their report out of their own pockets. (Pinchot took care of General MacKenzie's share.) Finally, Congress adopted an amendment to a general appropriation bill prohibiting any federal administrative official from assisting in any way the work of any executive commission not authorized by Congress. They wanted no more advice on conservation from T.R.

CHAPTER VII

The First
Crusade

1

The successor Theodore Roosevelt officially designated, William Howard Taft, was on record as supporting the Roosevelt conservation program, but there was little in his record as an officeholder to suggest a commitment in keeping with Roosevelt's preoccupation with the subject. As Secretary of War he had gone along with Roosevelt in giving favorable reports on legislation in contradiction to the position of the Corps of Engineers, but, although the Corps had functioned under his authority, he had done nothing to really change their attitudes, or even to check their aggressive opposition to the President's programs.

From the hindsight of our present knowledge of Taft's views of government, it is likely that the new President was far more concerned about the propriety of Roosevelt's attempts to circumvent congressional defeats or stalemates than he was about pushing the uncompleted programs for conservation sponsored by his predecessor. Once in office, he sought to minimize any conflict with Congress, and he turned from those who had worked with Roosevelt in this field. He also, of course, sought to avoid any conflicts with the established business community, and vigorous conservation policy was now coming into active conflict with railroads and the developing private power interests.

The signs of changing policy became apparent as changes in personnel from the Roosevelt to the Taft administration were announced. The new Attorney General, George Wickersham, came straight from a post as legal counsel to a subsidiary of the Aluminum Company of America, which was seeking a perpetual, unlimited water power franchise on the Niagara River, over the objections of Roosevelt. Pinchot's friend George Woodruff, who had been Assistant Attorney General for the Department of the Interior, was moved upstairs to a judgeship in Hawaii. Not long after taking office, Wickersham announced that he regarded the idea of federal water rentals, so long cultivated by Roosevelt and Burton, as illegal. He readily admitted that his opinion was based on conclusions he had reached while acting as attorney for the Aluminum Company in its franchise bid.

Roosevelt believed that Taft had promised to retain James R. Garfield as Secretary of the Interior, but Taft told Garfield late in January that he would not be continued. Garfield's successor would be Richard A. Ballinger, who had resigned as Commissioner of Public Lands less than a year before. Ballinger's resignation had been made without fanfare, but conservationists were well aware that he had differed sharply with Garfield and Pinchot about lease policies within the department and had opposed creation of new forest reserves.

Born in Illinois and raised in Kansas, Ballinger had studied law at Williams College, where he first met James Garfield. Ballinger began the practice of law at Decatur, Alabama, a small cotton town on the Tennessee River, but set out for Port Townsend, Washington, not long after that state was admitted into the Union. In both Decatur and Port Townsend he was elected to office, but greater prospects for law practice continued to move him on. In 1897 he moved to Seattle to form a new law partnership in the town that was obviously going to be the largest in the Pacific Northwest. Seven years later, he was elected its mayor as the reform candidate of the local Republican leadership, but

turned down a re-election effort to concentrate on his law practice after one successful term in office.

The story of Ballinger's success in "cleaning up" Seattle was
not overlooked by his old college friend, Garfield. He seemed to
fit the image of Roosevelt progressivism, and the Interior Department was badly in need of more western representation in its
upper echelon. Garfield's Ohio origin was not western any more,
except to the most provincial of Easterners. Ballinger was also
high in the regard of his state's Republican leadership, and it was
through them that Roosevelt invited him to come to Washington
in 1907 to become Commissioner of Public Lands.

Quite a bit of cleaning up needed to be done in the Public
Lands Bureau, for the inefficiencies of the old days of congressional political control were still obvious in antiquated personnel
and methods. Ballinger's cleanups in this regard brought the normal protests but actually gained him far more favorable attention
than disfavor. His policy views were largely conditioned by his
legal experience back home, representing the local business interests in a new state where federal ownership of land was a major
irritant. In general, he opposed new federal ownership and believed that existing federal lands should be sold to the public
rather than leased; federal policy should assist the local business
interests wherever possible.

A man with these ideas could not be happy in a Washington
scene dominated by Roosevelt, Pinchot, Garfield, and McGee.
Nor was Ballinger happy about the financial opportunities slipping
away back in Seattle. He resigned and returned home after less
than a year in the office.

2

There was little public awareness of Ballinger's views when he
took office again. Most of the western papers and politicians who
commented praised the appointment of a Westerner to head the
Interior Department, and the appointment helped strengthen a

tradition that the office belonged to the West. Pinchot later revealed his reservations about Ballinger and his differences with
him, and obviously Garfield must have had questions about the
man he had helped bring into government, but in the first days of
the Taft administration the Pinchot group was hoping to guide
the new President without the pressures of an open break.

Ballinger was not long in making it clear that he wanted substantial changes in policy within his department. His first move
was toward a cutback in federal reclamation programs in favor of
private irrigation development. The easiest way to achieve this
would be to remove Newell as Commissioner of Reclamation, but
this proved virtually impossible to do. No prominent irrigation
engineer, or other public figure active in the reclamation movement in the West, could be found who was willing to replace the
original head of the bureau. Knowledgeable men in the field knew
that most of the better engineers in the bureau were loyal personal
supporters of Newell, who had often turned down attractive private jobs because of the high morale and sense of achievement in the agency. When Ballinger made open attacks on Newell's ability as an administrator and engineer, defense came from
both nonpartisan engineering journals and Republican newspapers
in the West. The new agency had built up a loyal constituency in
the few years of its existence.

Although Ballinger could not force personnel changes within
his department, he could force policy changes and concessions.
With the help of Wickersham, he established a ruling that no
projects could be started unless there was sufficient money in the
Reclamation Fund to pay for them entirely. He joined the Corps
of Engineers in advising President Taft to approve perpetual, unlimited franchises for the construction of dams on navigable
streams, including one on the James River in Missouri that Roosevelt had vetoed as late as January 1909.

Pinchot's unofficial role as chief conservation adviser and coor-
dinator for the administration was lost from its start. Before Bal-

linger's first year was out he revoked an agreement, begun under Roosevelt, whereby the Forest Service supervised timber cutting and fire protection on Indian reservation forest lands. Other cooperative arrangements between Interior and Agriculture were soon hauled over the coals, for revision or attempted cancellation.

Pinchot began to take his complaints about Ballinger to Taft. At first the President accepted some of his arguments, but yielded each time to Ballinger when the Secretary offered a rebuttal. Before long, the President was advising Secretary of Agriculture Wilson, Pinchot's long-time supporter and superior, to try to curb some of the publicity the Forest Service and its head were continually receiving.

Pinchot had begun to prepare for such restrictions long before the President tried to silence him. Working mainly with people outside government, like Emerson Hough and Charles W. Eliot of Harvard, he had organized the National Conservation Association. The purpose of the organization was to build popular support for Theodore Roosevelt's conservation policies, and Roosevelt-heir Taft could not take exception to that objective so soon after he succeeded to office. Just as important as the organization, financial arrangements were made for a national magazine that would be its official publication, with regular comment on conservation issues. When the reports of Pinchot's differences with Taft and Ballinger became more or less public, many of his friends urged him to resign in protest, but Pinchot told them he preferred to stay in office in the hope of modifying the President's attitude.

3

Most of the conservation leaders of the Roosevelt era, in and out of government, were men of deep conviction about the moral strength of their position. They believed that giving resources to private monopolists, or leaving them to waste, was just as immoral as stealing them for personal gain. Much of their popular support was in the metropolitan areas where the period of muckraking journalism then drawing to a close had built a popular tradition of a crusading press. In the face of national popular complacency, the general lack of public attention to the policy changes made by Taft and the apathy in Congress, the conservationists needed a *cause célèbre*, a moral issue that could be converted into a popular crusade. Without undue delay, Secretary Ballinger proceeded to give them their issue.

Myles C. Moore was an ex-governor of Washington and a long-time promoter of mining and timber enterprises in the Northwest. In 1902, he secured the backing of J. P. Morgan and Daniel Guggenheim in behalf of a mining and timber development in Alaska. Working for this syndicate, Clarence Cunningham, an Idaho mine operator, filed 33 claims for a total of 5,280 acres near the source of the Bering River. The claims were filed under the provisions of the Coal Lands Act, which allowed the sale of limited acreage in the public domain, but with restrictions on the amount that could be acquired for relatively nominal fees. After Roosevelt withdrew from public entry 100,000 acres that included virtually all of the remaining coal land in Alaska, the acreage Cunningham had filed for suddenly jumped in potential value from a few thousand dollars to several million.

Louis R. Glavis, a young career employee in the Public Lands Office, in the process of being promoted to head the regional office at Portland, Oregon, studied the Cunningham claims and decided that they were fraudulent because Cunningham represented a syndicate which intended to consolidate all the sites after they secured title, contrary to requirements under the Coal Lands Act. In June 1908, he reported to Assistant Secretary Frank Pierce that the claims were suspicious, and requested permission to make a detailed investigation for fraud. Pierce took no action, and shortly afterwards Secretary Ballinger ordered Glavis to suspend his investigation until an opinion could be obtained from the

Attorney General. Wickersham talked to Glavis about the case and left him with the impression that the claims would be approved.

Convinced that what he thought were fraudulent claims were about to be approved through the intercession or complicity of someone further up in the department, Glavis now took the story to his former chief, Garfield. The former Secretary remembered that after he had left the Land Office in 1908, Ballinger, in his capacity as a private attorney, had asked him to expedite action on the claims. In August, Garfield took Glavis to Pinchot to outline his story. Pinchot gave the information to Taft, including the details of Ballinger's interest in the claim shortly after having left his first Interior post. Garfield and Pinchot both expected Ballinger to be dismissed, and Garfield predicted that the President would pick Pinchot to succeed him.

Taft sent copies of the Pinchot charges to Ballinger with a request that they be answered in detail. The Secretary replied in a brief of more than 600 pages and presented it personally to the President at his summer home. A few days later, Taft gave his official reply to both men. In his opinion, Secretary Ballinger's actions were circumspect in all respects. Taft, the stickler for legality, pointed out that private attorney Ballinger had not violated the law in assisting in the preparation and prosecution of the claim, because the restriction against employment of former government personnel had applied only to money claims, and the Cunningham claims were for land, not money.

Glavis was fired from his job after the Taft decision supporting Ballinger. Pinchot put him in touch with his friend Powers Hapgood, editor of *Collier's* magazine. The result was a series of articles in the typical journalistic fashion of the era: "Are the Guggenheims in Charge of the Interior Department?" and "Ballinger—Shyster Lawyer" were two of the titles. Other newspapers and magazines picked up similar reports, and little appeared in defense of the administration's position, although a number of western politicians, well known for their opposition to Pinchot, did speak up for Ballinger. One of these was a Democrat, Franklin K. Lane, appointed to the Interstate Commerce Commission by Roosevelt and seeking reappointment from Taft (which he received).

Secretary Ballinger had been a good lawyer in Seattle, but he proved a poor attorney for himself. His chief defense was to denounce the magazine authors as "literary apostles of vomit" and to announce his allegiance to the conservation movement. Wickersham and other friends advised him against bringing suit against *Collier's*. His former law partner wrote a lengthy account of the firm's relationship with its various clients, but was so obscure about some of the most critical points that the brief was welcomed by Ballinger's opponents.

Not long after the President had considered the Glavis charges, he made it clear to Pinchot that he did not consider him indispensable to the administration. The showdown came in January after Ballinger invited the Senate to make an investigation of his department, and accused the Forest Service of being the source of the attacks on him. Without permission from his superior, Secretary Wilson, Pinchot answered with a letter to his friend Senator Jonathan P. Dolliver of Iowa, chairman of the Senate Committee on Agriculture and Forestry.

As chairman of the committee having jurisdiction over the forestry program, Dolliver had absorbed and supported the Pinchot ideas on forestry, and was turning toward a knowledgeable legislative role as champion of the entire conservation concept. His death at 52, later in the year, removed a skillful leader of the insurgent Republicans with a potential for greater heights. One of his legacies is a classic description of Taft: "that ponderous and pleasant person, entirely surrounded by men who know exactly what they want."

Dolliver read Pinchot's letter on the Senate floor. The next letter was from Taft to Pinchot, dismissing the Chief Forester from office for insubordination.

4

A congressional investigation was inevitable, and the regular Republican leaders had better control of the situation than Taft. A hand-picked committee might save the day for the administration, despite the beating it was taking in the press. A routine resolution authorizing appointment of the investigating committee by the Vice-President in the Senate and by the Speaker of the House— the regular party leadership—passed the Senate and came to the House. George Norris, a young progressive insurgent from Nebraska, took the occasion to make his first splash on the national scene. John Dalzell of Pennsylvania, a top lieutenant of Speaker Joe Cannon, was presiding. He would not have recognized an anti-Cannon man like Norris, but Dalzell vacated the chair every day at one o'clock for lunch. As soon as the chair was in the hands of another but friendlier regular, Norris got recognition and moved an amendment to the Senate bill to provide that the House members of the joint investigating committee would be named by the House as a whole, instead of by the Speaker. It was revolution, but it carried by a vote of 149 to 146, thanks to an alliance of insurgents, Pinchot conservationists, and Democrats. (With this precedent, and the impetus for the insurgent movement that the conservation issue had aroused, Norris was able to achieve his historic stripping of Speaker Cannon's powers a few months later.)

The investigation might have been routine, with little opportunity for the Pinchot side of the story to be presented, but for Norris's successful coup in the House. Thanks to that vote, an able insurgent Republican, E. H. Madison of Kansas, was named to the committee. More important, the Democrats as well as the insurgent Republicans recognized the value of a wide-ranging investigation that could discredit Republicans in general and the Taft administration in particular. Counsel for the interested parties, Ballinger, Glavis, and Pinchot, played the most prominent roles in the hearings. President Taft and friends suggested that

Ballinger retain as counsel John J. Vertrees of Tennessee, whose resulting performance was generally regarded as inept by most of the observers, including his client Ballinger.

Glavis was represented by Louis H. Brandeis, and Pinchot by George Wharton Pepper. It would have been difficult to find a more highly regarded pair of lawyers in the country, or two with such widely different backgrounds of legal experience. The intense national interest in the controversy, with the universal support among conservationists and political progressives in general, made it a highly prized assignment for even the nation's foremost attorneys. With Pinchot involved, there was no problem about fees for counsel on the conservationist side, but Ballinger was to find that he had one when it was all over. Presidential help in choosing a lawyer did not include assistance in paying Vertrees' fees, and Ballinger had to struggle with that personal debt after he was back in private life.

Ballinger offered no coherent defense or even summation of his resource ideas and policy during his long stay on the witness stand. Some of his denials may have been legally accurate, but they so obviously stretched points that even the committee chairman, Senator Knute Nelson of Minnesota, a Republican stalwart strongly opposed to the Roosevelt-Pinchot conservation ideas, could not defend them. The investigation was front-page news for months, but Ballinger and the other administration witnesses registered only negative impressions in the weeks that their testimony monopolized the coverage.

Glavis was the chief witness for the prosecution, a role that Brandeis managed to build as the hearings progressed, despite the best maneuverings of the majority members of the committee. The story of Glavis's long developing suspicions about the Cunningham claims, and the efforts to present his story to his superiors, would not be labeled an antiadministration or anti-Ballinger plot. Garfield and Newell, witnesses not involved as major protagonists, were able to identify Ballinger's disagreements with their policies as disagreements with Roosevelt policies. The biggest sensation of the hearings was the revelation from an Interior Department stenographer that the notes for Ballinger's brief to Taft had been ordered burned, and that Wickersham's opinion supporting Taft's decision had been pre-dated to make it appear to have been the basis for the President's decision.

Pinchot was a far better witness than Ballinger. He gave a spirited defense of the policies he had advocated and carried out, as well as those of Garfield and the Interior Department before Ballinger came to office. He accused Ballinger of taking office for the deliberate purpose of wrecking the programs established by Roosevelt and pledged to continuation by Taft. Ballinger's statements about his policies were false, because he was pursuing contrary policy, whether the President knew it or not. ". . . The interests of the people are not safe in Mr. Ballinger's hands, . . ." he concluded. "The Secretary of the Interior has been unfaithful both to the public, whose property has been endangered, and to the President, whom he has deceived."

The hearing had brought out the story of Ballinger's intervention in 1908 in behalf of the Cunningham claims at the request of Moore, but they also put on record his failure, despite repeated pressures from Moore and others, to order them approved after he became Secretary. There is no way of knowing what would have happened to the claims if Glavis had not brought the affair into the open, but it is not unreasonable, from this long distance, to guess that they probably would have been approved. Despite the ugly implications about Ballinger's connections with Moore and his backers made in the press at the time, there was no indication at all of bribery or corruption; the immorality was that in the judgment of the conservationists it was immoral and dishonest to give away a natural resource that was the property of the people of the country.

5

Taft's opinions on conservation must have been extremely hazy, but Ballinger far surpassed the President in trying to turn back some of the policies established by Roosevelt's administration, and they were Roosevelt's policies, regardless of whether they originated with Pinchot, Garfield, Newell, or McGee. Taft's Secretary could be properly accused of deceiving him in that he went far beyond Presidential directives in changing policy, but the accusation was a very long stretching of the point. Without doubt, Ballinger recognized and agreed with Taft's predilection for giving the highest priority to precise legalisms, especially when this resulted in checks on new federal power. Taft was probably unwittingly revealing his basic prejudice against the conservation philosophy when he wrote his brother Henry complaining about the "Jesuit guile" with which the "swelled head" Pinchot was pushing for the "socialist tendencies" of Roosevelt.

Taft's political ineptness allowed the Ballinger-Pinchot controversy to become a great moral issue of the conservationist crusade of the period. Ballinger's private character was made a central issue in the inevitable personalization of such controversies, in a day when sensation-mongering in the newspapers was at its height. When the committee majority gave Ballinger a clean bill of health, asserting that the charges originated in a "strong feeling of animosity created by a supposed difference in policy respecting the conservation of natural resources," the Democratic minority, joined by Representative Madison, came back with a strong attack on Ballinger, which was strangely cautious in its references to Taft, except in its conclusion that his Secretary "should be requested by the proper authority to resign his office."

The Ballinger scandal continued to dominate the conservation issue throughout the remainder of the off-year election. Hiram Johnson, who won the Republican nomination for governor in California as an out-and-out insurgent, used conservation issues

among the chief planks of his platform, and foremost among these
was opposition to Ballinger and his policies. Pinchot stumped the
state for him, and Johnson went on to win handily in November.

When the Ballinger-Pinchot controversy first began to develop,
Theodore Roosevelt was in Africa on his celebrated big-game sa-
fari. He waited out a year in public silence, but the fact that a
sharp break was developing became clear at the second National
Conservation Congress, which convened at St. Paul in September
1910, with Taft and Roosevelt as the featured speakers. When
President Taft spoke, he reviewed the conservation record of his
administration with self-satisfaction, and pointedly dodged taking
a position on whether the states or the Federal government should
have control of water power sites.

Roosevelt chose the occasion to draw a clear line between himself and his successor when he spoke the next day. Conservation
differences led to a public break with Taft policy, and, deliberately or not, the trail was broken for the Bull Moose party. The
National Conservation Congress had been one of the few remaining results of the White House Conservation Conference in 1908,
and T.R. was careful to make it clear that Taft had condoned the
disheartening failures in this field. He bore down on Taft's strad-
dling of the power issue, saying, "It is not a question of hair-split-
ting legal technicalities . . ." or "of state against nation. . . . It is
really a question of special corporate interests against the popular
interests of the people. . . . It's a comical fact that the most zeal-
ous upholders of states' rights are big businessmen who live in
other states, principally in the East. The most effective weapon is
federal laws and the federal executive. That is why I so strongly
oppose the demand to turn these matters over to the states."

The ominous signs of an open break with Roosevelt brought
some profound changes in Taft's public postures in conservation,
and a halt to the breakaway from the Roosevelt-Pinchot program.
After the conclusion of the congressional investigation, Taft had
again assured Ballinger of his full confidence in him, but the Sec-

retary spent the winter of 1910–11 constantly being rebuffed by the President. Newell and his assistant, Arthur P. Davis, had both testified in opposition to Ballinger's position at the congressional hearings. The Secretary tried to get permission to dismiss them because of this, but Taft pointedly refused. In March 1911, Ballinger resigned from office and returned to his law practice in Seattle.

In the years immediately ahead he might have made a fairly successful career spearheading western opposition to many aspects of public lands, forestry, and water power programs, but he continued to be an inept, obscure spokesman for his cause. The land business interests and western political leaders who had pressured and praised him for protecting their interest decided that the spokesman they required for the future needed a better image.

Thirty years later, Ballinger found a champion in the old Bull Mooser, Harold Ickes, Secretary of the Interior under another Roosevelt. Ickes published an article in the *Saturday Evening Post*, entitled "Not Guilty!" defending the Ballinger record and describing him as an "American Dreyfus." Ickes' defense, however, was nothing more than a demonstration that no evidence had ever been presented to show that Ballinger had been involved in any corrupt or illegal activity. He offered no evaluation of Ballinger's policy positions; it would have been embarrassing to do so, for most of them were directly contrary to Ickes' position on the same issues. The article was little more than an effort to strike a spiteful blow at the aging but still active Pinchot, who was openly opposing an Ickes proposal to return the Forest Service to the Department of the Interior.

6

As Ballinger's successor, Taft appointed Walter L. Fisher, a man whose conservation views were completely acceptable to Pinchot, and who had actually participated in the Pinchot-Garfield discussions about how to handle the Glavis exposure of Ballinger. In the next two years, Fisher was given a free hand by the President, and he turned regularly to Pinchot and Garfield for advice. Another Pinchot friend, Henry L. Stimson of New York, was appointed Secretary of War. If Stimson had been Secretary instead of Taft during the 1907–08 period, the Newlands bill might have passed. Stimson now announced his support of it and forced upon the Corps of Engineers a brief adherence to the Roosevelt policy on water power development.

Pinchot had been succeeded in the Forest Service by another disciple, Henry S. Graves. The post-Ballinger period of the Taft administration enabled him to help push through a major landmark in forest legislation, the Weeks Act of 1911. Representative John Wingate Weeks of Massachusetts was later to serve a term in the Senate and five years as Secretary of War to Presidents Harding and Coolidge, but the great achievement of his career was the sponsorship of the law which provided a breakthrough for federal forestry programs in the states outside the public lands area. The act provided federal financial aid to any state which would establish fire prevention programs for timberlands at the head of navigable streams. It also gave the Federal government authority to buy timberland and establish national forests where the timber was at the headwaters of a navigable stream.

The link of the timberlands to navigable streams in both these provisions of the bill was necessary to alleviate any doubt about the constitutionality of the act. The navigable stream basis could and would be used in the future for virtually any multipurpose conservation activity, although repeated court tests would be necessary before the last doubts were removed. The Weeks Act was not implemented on a broad scale until the New Deal days, but it enabled the Forest Service to accomplish much during the otherwise restrictive period of the 1920's.

Despite these many positive steps to prove his reliability as a Roosevelt conservationist, Taft had breached the dike for insurgency and the progressive movement when he appointed Ballinger and indicated his approval of the checks on the Roosevelt-Pinchot program. Other issues moved into the limelight as the insurgent revolt flared into a full-scale Progressive party, but Roosevelt would probably never have had so strong an inclination to break with his heir had not Taft betrayed his conservation program and conservation leaders like Pinchot and Garfield. Even without the progressive movement, Taft had so many weaknesses that he probably would have failed of re-election in a straight two-party fight. The conservation issue, however, insured the election of Woodrow Wilson, after having helped the over-all progressive movement that was one of the influences which brought about his nomination.

CHAPTER VIII

Democratic
Conservation

1

Although the conservation issue largely created the Republican schism that was to assure him the Presidency, Woodrow Wilson was never much interested in it. His whole political philosophy required that he support the dominance of federal over state policy, but his record in the field before 1912 was obscure enough to permit people on both sides of the question to support him. Little of the "New Freedom" was concerned with conservation or natural resource matters. No major achievements in the field were made in Wilson's eight years as President, and though comparatively little ground was lost, some great opportunities were missed.

Western Democrats included a large faction who by tradition had cooperated with Bourbon Democrats from the South, paying lip service to the doctrine of states' rights, and just as many in the Bryan tradition who had conquered the Populists of the nineties by taking over their doctrine of federal action to alleviate economic wrongs. Wilson, the political scientist, saw the danger of turning the Interior Department over to a Secretary who was identified with any western interests, and he briefly tried to persuade his friend Newton D. Baker to take the post. When Baker declined, Wilson turned the job of picking a man over to Colonel

Edward M. House. After consulting western Democrats of all factions and of all views on conservation policy, House recommended a Californian, Franklin K. Lane, a Democratic member of the Interstate Commerce Commission by appointment of both Roosevelt and Taft. Lane's performance was best described by A. N. Brown, an anticonservation lobbyist: "Any man who can get both the Ballinger and Pinchot forces to approve him is a smooth individual."

Lane's tightrope walking on policy matters did not satisfy the Democrats in the West who had talked loudly of ceding the national forests back to state control or ending further reservations of water power sites, because he sided with the federal interest on crucial issues, but he kept the anti-Pinchot people reasonably satisfied with his administration by consulting with them regularly, talking of "opening opportunities for the developer" and of "closer cooperation with the states." The significant conservation decisions of the Wilson administration were made in the Congress. With active administration support, better decisions could have been made in coordinated water control and development, and in federal water power policy.

2

Senator Newlands had continued to push actively for his federal water program throughout the Taft administration, bringing out his plan for discussion at every opportunity. Working with McGee and Maxwell, as well as friends in the several waterway organizations with whom he had worked through the years, and with various allies in Congress, he attempted to demonstrate the need for a plan to secure adequate flood protection in those river valleys being plagued with overflows year after year. The entire lower Mississippi valley, a regular victim of waters from throughout the interior of the country, was a natural ally, and Newlands cultivated flood control proponents from that area assiduously. Most of his early contacts were with Representative Randell of

Louisiana, impatient with the refusal of the Corps of Engineers to recognize a federal responsibility for flood control stronger than the limited assistance being provided under the Mississippi River Commission Act.

The cotton planters of the rich alluvial plain of the lower Mississippi valley were actively turning their entire attention to a federal solution of their problem. Largely through their own efforts, they had a levee system built, with taxes provided by a series of loosely coordinated levee districts. Every severe flood broke the levees, however, and the damage from levee breaks was not confined to areas that had financed the local levee system. There was no doctrine of states' rights in solving flood control problems in Mississippi, Arkansas, or Louisiana. Lawyers in New York or Washington might express doubts about the constitutionality of federal flood control, but none did in the Mississippi Delta. The planters and the commercial interests allied with them in river towns like Memphis organized to promote federal action. Most of them approved the ideas behind the Newlands bill, but they were coming to the conclusion that a plan for the lower Mississippi valley alone, a region they believed clearly entitled to national relief because so much of the water came from other parts of the nation, might not alarm the Congress so much as to either its cost or its constitutionality.

The chief congressional spokesman for this group was Representative Benjamin G. Humphreys, whose district encompassed the alluvial plain of the great river in the State of Mississippi, the area between the Mississippi and its tributary, the Yazoo. The major promoter of the idea was John A. Fox, secretary of the Mississippi Valley Levee Association of Memphis, who was to spend a lifetime as an effective promoter of flood control on the Mississippi. Ransdell moved to the Senate in 1912, to become the sponsor there of the Humphreys-Ransdell bill; he was to be an opponent of Newlands more often than a satisfactory ally.

The Mississippi valley was by no means lost to Newlands, despite the attractions of the single-purpose, single-shot Humphreys-Ransdell bill. Representative Robert F. Broussard spoke for a large segment of opinion in Louisiana, especially along the coastal swamps and in the city of New Orleans. Broussard claimed that levees alone would not protect Louisiana from floods, that there must be additional outlets to the sea to release flood waters before they spilled out near the mouth of the river in spite of the levees. In addition to more flood protection than levees provided, New Orleans needed the Gulf-to-the-Great Lakes Waterway, the greatest hope for which was wrapped up in the Newlands bill. The state accepted the Broussard philosophy sufficiently to elect him to the Senate in 1914.

Levees along the Mississippi were also no solution to the problem of interior flooding along the tributary streams of the river all up and down the valley. Organizations dedicated to federal assistance in "drainage" programs began to develop, and eventually these groups formed the National Drainage Association. Most of the drainage promoters favored the Newlands water commission idea, but they began to drift away after House Speaker Champ Clark of Missouri, whose district in northeast Missouri included drainage advocates, advised them to work for "a project," not a "policy." The Gulf-to-the-Great Lakes Association remained Newlands' stanch ally, and supported the multipurpose concept even after his death. Robert R. McCormick, the publisher of the *Chicago Tribune,* spoke for the association in 1912: "We have gone far enough where we will welcome any kind of a reasonably successful Federal law . . . to regulate to its best use all the water which falls upon the surface of our land, bearing in mind irrigation, navigation, drainage, and all the uses to which this water can be put; and the prevention of all the harm which it can do if misused."

In 1912, McGee died of cancer, and with him went Senator Newlands' best link to the intellectual leadership of the conservationist movement. He would still work actively with George H.

Maxwell, but Maxwell's long-recognized overriding concern with
irrigation earned him less than complete confidence among the
other interest groups in the conservation field. McGee had been
acknowledged as the servant of no special interest in the field,
simply a dedicated opponent of waste, which he believed was the
effect of the failure to take advantage of any potential water use.

After the Democrats won control of the House in 1910, in the
backwash of the Ballinger-Pinchot controversy, Newlands tried
to get action on his commission bill in the Congress, presenting
the idea to Speaker-designate Clark as a demonstration of the kind
of legislation the Democrats would enact if they were given control of both the Congress and the Presidency in 1912. Clark was
not greatly interested, and Newlands held up on a new push until
the beginning of the 62nd Congress in 1911. The bill had been
carefully prepared by Maxwell, with the help of McGee, Walcott, Pinchot, and others active in the field. It began to receive
committee consideration the next year, and Newlands had to
make modifications and concessions to overcome specific opposition or to gain new votes.

The basic Newlands proposal was that the commission established under the bill would draw up a coordinated program for
water development and regulation over the country. The work
was to be performed by the existing government agencies in the
field and financed by a continuing annual appropriation of fifty
million dollars. The very heart of the proposal was that the commission should have the power to approve the plans and allocate
the projects, to make sure that the objectives were reached without political considerations or concession to special interests un-
concerned with national water policy. In 1912, Newlands was
forced to modify this provision by allocating the funds to geographic areas, a change that he decided was essential to get the bill
out of the Senate committee. Within the year he had to accept
further changes: that members of Congress would serve on the
commission, that the fund authorization be reduced by a half mil-

lion dollars, and that the commission's work be limited to planning.

A major Mississippi River flood in 1912 gave Newlands further impetus for his effort. Candidate and then President-elect Wilson endorsed his general proposals. Then, early in 1913, Secretary of War Stimson, overruling the Corps of Engineers, presented a strong approval of the bill in behalf of the lame-duck Taft administration, along with favorable recommendations from the Departments of the Interior and Agriculture. But the same floods which spurred Newlands also stirred the Mississippi valley advocates of the "levees only" policy to come out in active opposition to his plan. They feared that under the Newlands program the needs of the valley would not receive adequate attention, and were convinced that a Democratic administration would reward their long-time Democratic loyalty by passage of the Ransdell-Humphreys bill.

At this late stage, Burton of Ohio now came around to general support of the Newlands bill, but he was now in the Senate, and no longer controlled his committee in the House. Newlands got his proposal approved by the Senate as an amendment to the rivers and harbors bill, but the House conferees solidly resisted it. The amendment was dropped by the conference, despite a threatened last-minute filibuster by Newlands.

The Ransdell-Humphreys bill was not law, either, and its sponsors began a period of cautious cooperation with Newlands and his chief Mississippi valley supporter, Broussard. President Wilson was an anxious third party in the discussions. He was committed to the Newlands position but never devoted much attention to the problem. His first Secretary of War, Lindley M. Garrison, accepted the Corps of Engineers position uncritically. Secretary Lane was not pushing the coordinated conservation concept in the cabinet, and there was no Pinchot at a sublevel.

Newlands worked out an agreement with Ransdell to incorporate a specific appropriation for levee construction on the Mis-

sissippi, under full control of the Corps of Engineers, as an amendment to his bill, which he now titled Waterways-River Regulation. In 1914 the simplest route to adoption appeared to be once
again adding the whole package to the rivers and harbors bill.
Unfortunately, Secretary Garrison and the Corps had gone along
with their traditional proponents in the House and agreed to a
rivers and harbors bill which came under withering attack for its
pork-barrel and logrolling ingredients. Its chief defect was that it
left out the upper Mississippi and most of the western states.
These areas, combined with Eastern votes traditionally opposed
to almost any programs, would have been enough to beat the bill
had it come to a vote. Eventually a blanket appropriation of
twenty million dollars, left entirely to the Corps to apportion, was
passed.

In the spring of 1916, President Wilson sent a special message to
Congress urging passage of the Waterways Commission-River
Regulation bill. A few months later, Newton D. Baker came into
the cabinet as Secretary of War and enthusiastically supported the
plan. This eliminated the threat of sabotage from the Corps, but
the critical test was still in the House. Humphreys had persuaded
the House leadership to establish a Flood Control Committee, of
which he became chairman. The first major legislation reported
by the new committee was the Humphreys bill, which promptly
passed the House itself. Newlands had left the Senate Committee
on Commerce, which received the bill, and Ransdell was a member. The committee also approved the Humphreys bill.

Newlands protested, publicly and privately, that the Mississippi
valley senators were violating the renewed agreement he had
reached with Ransdell and Broussard to incorporate the Ransdell-
Humphreys bill as part of his over-all water measure. Ransdell's
defense was that Humphreys was not a party to the agreement
since he had been absent because of illness from the 1916 meetings. Newlands made it clear to his supporters that the reported
bill alone would be the death knell of his plan. He blocked its

passage, and the Humphreys plan appeared headed for death with the end of the Congress on March 3.

Newlands' show of power was enough to force the final bargain with the Senate supporters of the Humphreys bill. They could not overcome the Nevadan in the Senate. Many of their constituents in the valley, and especially in Louisiana, were complaining about the failure of their strategy. Newlands had sent Maxwell down to Louisiana to bring the point home. Under the compromise agreement, the Humphreys bill was passed by the Senate on March 1, and the Newlands plan was adopted by an amendment to the 1917 Rivers and Harbors Bill. It became law on August 8.

The plan was law, but it was a long way from being put into effect. The war absorbed all the attention of both Wilson and Baker, who otherwise might have been ready to enter decisively into the matter from a viewpoint sympathetic to Newlands. Basically, Newlands and Maxwell thought that the commission should be dominated by cabinet members, in a position to insure a coordinated policy throughout the government. The Corps of Engineers favored a noncabinet group, one that would be more responsive to Congress and presumably more concerned for its viewpoint. Various tentative compromises were suggested. Newlands would not agree to plans that would reduce the commission to an arm of the Congress; his opponents operated on the theory that they were ahead as long as no commission was appointed.

They were still ahead on Christmas Eve, 1917. Newlands, too, was wrapped in the war effort and also in the compelling need to improve the national transportation system with a better planned railroad network. He spent a good part of the day talking over his ideas with the President. That night he died. No waterways commission was ever appointed.

The death of Newlands was not only the death of his waterways and river regulation plan. No other mind in the nearly two centuries of the American Congress has ever devoted as much study, unhampered and original thinking, and unending effort toward solutions of the nation's water problems. The Bureau of Reclamation is a good Newlands memorial, but some of his observations in defending and promoting his programs might be even better:

> I believe the Government can do work in a businesslike way in carrying out the granted powers, and I believe in giving its agents a pretty free hand to enable them to do business effectively. . . .
>
> . . . I insist upon it that Congress has attended too much to administrative matters, and the very reason of the inefficiency of our work upon our rivers and harbors has been that Congress has sought to do administrative work and has done it badly, as it always will do it badly. . . .
>
> . . . The National Government, has not, in my judgment, commenced to exercise its powers under the interstate-commerce clause of the Constitution. . . .
>
> . . . Would you today enter upon a process of decentralization? Would you attempt to divide these systems (of railways) up into the units of which they were once composed, each unit comprised within state lines? . . .

3

The last year of the Wilson administration brought to a climax, and what some hailed as a solution, another conservation issue first highlighted under Roosevelt and dramatized during the conflicts of the Taft administration. Hetch Hetchy and Muscle Shoals were the major struggles along the way.

Hetch Hetchy started as a plan to provide a better water supply for the city of San Francisco, and it eventually developed into the first major multipurpose water project authorized by Congress. It was also the first major fight between conservationists and preservationists, a side issue that often seemed the dominant one.

The idea of supplying San Francisco's water needs from the

mountains to the east was not new, and the Hetch Hetchy valley of the Toulumne River in the Yosemite National Park had been eyed as a source even before the park was created. As the plan to bring the mountain water to the city through a 175-mile aqueduct developed, the additional benefits to be derived from the necessary dam became obvious. A private water company was to be supplanted, and the dam could also generate electricity for the city. It would offer flood control benefits for the area below and a limited amount of irrigation for the San Joaquin valley. The proposal was thoroughly aired in California and introduced and discussed in the Congress for several years before decisive action came in 1913. Democratic Congressman John E. Raker introduced the bill, but its best-known sponsor, and the author of its most controversial amendment, was Representative William Kent, a progressive Republican of the Pinchot stripe, whose career is worth more than a footnote in the conservation story.

Kent was a Yale classmate of Pinchot. After graduation, he returned to his home in Chicago and became active in the local reform movement. He helped organize and served as president of the Municipal Voters' League there, and then moved to California. His election to Congress as a progressive Republican in 1910 was a direct product of the conservation issue and of the reaction developing from the Pinchot-Ballinger controversy. He left his mark in Section 6 of the Hetch Hetchy Act, with an amendment requiring the city of San Francisco to distribute the power generated by the project directly to the ultimate consumers, and expressly forbidding the city to dispose of it wholesale to any individual or private utility.

Kent's amendment assured the first full-scale, clear-cut fight between public and private power in the Congress. The Sierra Club and naturalist John Muir were the leaders of the preservationist groups opposed to the bill, but they were hard put to impugn the motives of Kent, who had been as active as any man in the fight to save California redwoods. He had personally purchased the tract to be known as Muir Woods, and presented it without benefit of tax write-offs to the state as a park. "Save the Yosemite National Park from destruction" was the cry sent out over the country, but most of the congressmen who had to decide the issue were able readily to comprehend that the Pacific Gas and Electric Company was the financial source of most of the sentiment about the park. The Hetch Hetchy bill passed.

The Sierra Club was founded in 1892 by a group of nature enthusiasts led by John Muir, the Scots-born, Wisconsin-educated Californian who had fallen in love with California's beauties when he migrated there in 1868. Muir traveled and lectured throughout the world, but his book, *The Mountains of California*, established him as the foremost champion of their untouched preservation. Although the club was organized, and is still based, in California, it has had a permanent national membership "devoted to the study and protection of national scenic resources, including mountain regions, wilderness areas, wildlife, forests and streams."

No one can question the purity of the club's motives; committed to an unwavering position against any infringement on nature, it has never hesitated to do battle with some of the chief vested interests of the economic exploitation of our natural resources. Unfortunately, the preservationists are determinedly uncompromising in their pursuit of absolutes. In their narrow definition of preservation, and their seeming inability to recognize that wilderness pristine is in fact wilderness lost, they have also at times, as in the Hetch Hetchy issue, found themselves on the side of the exploitation interests.

The Sierra Club and other groups like it have many times carried the first heavy burden of saving scenic beauty for the future. Their dedication is inspiring, and it would be impossible to fault them were it not that their unwillingness to recognize the inevitable claims of civilization usually leaves the accomplishment of constructive conservation to the "realists" whose ability to compromise they deplore but who eventually do thereby achieve both preservation and use of the lands they so highly, and so rightly, prize.

The San Francisco public power amendment was still to be fought over and circumvented in the years after the Hetch Hetchy Dam was completed, but Muscle Shoals was to be the continuing public power controversy of the Wilson administrations, and the impetus for an incomplete resolution of the broader issue. The dominant role of the power fight became fairly clear at the Fifth Conservation Congress, held at Washington in November 1913.

The power companies, alerted by the Hetch Hetchy fight, were moving to the offensive. M. O. Leighton, the former chief hydrographer of the Geological Survey, spoke to the congress on their behalf. Leighton had good credentials in his contribution on multipurpose dams to the 1908 Roosevelt Conservation Commission Report, but he had subsequently become a consulting engineer who did most of his consulting for power companies. The new influence was made plain when the resolutions committee of the congress came forward with a report favoring state control of power sites, and permits to private owners for indefinite periods. As the debate got under way, Harry Slattery, the secretary of the National Conservation Association, got the floor and read a long list of utility officials and attorneys representing utilities who were delegates to the convention by appointment of state governors. After this uproar, Pinchot offered a resolution from the floor affirming "the solemn judgment of the fifth conservation congress that hereafter no water power now owned or controlled by the public should be sold, granted or given away in perpetuity, or in any manner removed from public ownership, which alone can give sound basis of assured and permanent control in the interest of the people."

Senator John H. Bankhead of Alabama led the fight against the resolution as an extension of his fight to secure authority for a

dam at Muscle Shoals. Stimson and Garfield joined in support of Pinchot. His resolution passed, 317 to 96.

Attempts to get a bill through Congress authorizing private development of the Muscle Shoals had been an active enterprise for twenty years prior to 1916. During the first years, the power company case was handicapped because it was primarily a general promotion effort, seeking to sell stock to the public as well as to secure direct government assistance for part of the construction. In 1912, a major part of the money problem was eliminated when well-financed Canadian interests secured control of the Alabama Power Company, but the Congress which had passed the Hetch Hetchy power clause was reluctant to buy a scheme of government "partnership" with a power company. For a long time, Muscle Shoals seemed mired down in endless reports, with the Corps of Engineers after 1908 supporting the private company. The picture changed in 1916, when the National Defense Act became law.

As with many other proposals for governmental action, the threat of war was not so much the reason as it was merely the vehicle for passage of the act. From the days of the Populists, one of the unrequited pleas of southern farmers had been for cheap fertilizers. Various schemes for government work in the field had been proposed without success. Senator Ellison D. "Cotton Ed" Smith of South Carolina was the man who translated the old 'ream into positive legislative action. Smith brought before the ᵗe Agriculture Committee scientists and chemists who testi- ⁻ the huge munitions production of blockaded Germany ⁿ been impossible without the production of atmos- ⁿ. while the United States continued to rely on ni-

ᵗudy made it obvious that the extraction of ⁿuld be possible onlʸ with large amounts ⁿᵗ hydroe! ᶦc power. Senator ʰt r ⁿlants scattered

Senaᵗ thaᵗ
fied thaᵗ
would havᵉ
pheric nitrogeⁿ
trates from Chile.
The congressional s⁻
nitrogen from the air woᵗ
ᶜ low-cost power, and thaᵗ
had an original plan

over the country, obviously to better serve all the farmers. The practicality of national defense, and the interest of Senator Oscar W. Underwood in Muscle Shoals as a site, whether for government or private operation, eliminated the requirement of scattered nitrate plants. Two key provisions of the bill were sponsored by Senator Smith: "The plant or plants provided for under this Act shall be constructed and operated solely by the Government and not in conjunction with any other industry or enterprise carried on by private capital" and "the products of such plants shall be used by the President for military and naval purposes to the extent that he may deem necessary, and any surplus which he shall determine is not required shall be sold and disposed of by him under such regulations as he may prescribe."

4

The determination of the use of the facilities which President Wilson decided should be built at Muscle Shoals was to bring a decade of fruitful controversy, but, as far as the power issue was concerned, most of the war years were spent in an effort to pass legislation establishing definitive federal procedure in the field. Senator John K. Shields of Tennessee, who lived at Knoxville on the Tennessee River, took the lead in pushing bills favorable to the private power position. ". . . The United States has no proprietary interest," he said. "It has nothing to rent, nothing to lease, nothing to sell." The Shields bill was maneuvered into dying in conference with the end of Wilson's first administration, but the threat of its passage in 1917 moved the administration to come up with a bill of its own to provide some protection for the public interest and to make clear that there was federal jurisdiction over hydroelectric projects on navigable streams. A Federal Power Commission, consisting of the Secretaries of War, Interior, and Agriculture, was provided.

Representative Thetus W. Sims of Tennessee, chairman of the Interstate Commerce Committee, took up the Wilson bill in opposition to his senator, and got it through the House without major change. After long delays in conference, a compromise was reached which conceded federal jurisdiction in general, but made so many actual waivers of control that few good power sites were included. Even Muscle Shoals would have been lost, through a definition of navigability that had made the impassability of the Shoals reason for ruling the Tennessee nonnavigable. When the more liberal House accepted the conference report, passage of the legislation seemed assured.

Pinchot, Slattery, and Phillip Wells of the National Conservation Association made a desperation plea to the remaining progressive bloc in the Senate. With progressive help the conference report was delayed until the closing days of the session, but the Senate leadership believed there was no real threat of filibuster because four appropriation bills were scheduled behind it. This did not intimidate Senator Robert LaFollette of Wisconsin, however. With the help of Joseph France of Maryland and Lawrence Sherman of Illinois, he held the Senate floor from 2:00 A.M. on March 4, 1919, until midnight, blocking all legislation, including the appropriations and another bill which, it was believed, would open the path to raids on mineral rights in public lands. The March 4 filibuster is historic not only for its defeat of the power bill but for the disgusted sarcasm of Vice-President Thomas R. Marshall, who declared the Senate adjourned *"Sine Deo"* instead of *"Sine Die."* (The *Congressional Record* used the traditional spelling.)

The new Congress, elected in November 1918, was controlled by the Republicans. Senator Wesley Jones of Washington was not a former progressive, but he was more of a progressive than Shields had been on the power issue. He shaped a bill much improved over the old Commerce Committee version. Federal ownership and jurisdiction were established over all navigable rivers from source to mouth, without regard to shoals or falls. The Power Commission was given authority to make fifty-year leases for power development. One of the most important provisions for the future was a requirement for preference to public bodies in the case of conflicting applications and in the sale of the power generated.

To committed progressive conservationists like Senator Norris, the bill was a disappointment. Norris objected to the political composition of the commission, and to the fact that, despite the recognition of federal jurisdiction, there was still authority to grant private monopolies over public waters. Most of the 21 votes against the conference report were those who joined Norris in protesting its failure to fully protect the public interest. Pinchot and the Conservation Association, however, hailed the bill as a victory because it settled once and for all the long-fought question of state or federal jurisdiction.

There was one additional sad note about the power commission bill. With Senator Newlands gone, his old opponents had slipped in a provision repealing his waterways commission plan, which had been law for nearly three years but never activated by Presidential appointment. While the repeal clause was pending, George Maxwell made a last effort to get the President to act, but there was no response from the disabled White House.

5

Beyond flood control and water power, most of the conservation issues in the Wilson years did not develop into full-scale fights in Congress. Secretary of the Interior Lane was a disappointment to the Pinchot-Newell school of conservationists, but they could not develop useful opposition to the Reclamation Extension Act of 1914, which wrote many of Lane's policy changes into law. The bill extended the term of reclamation water payments from ten to twenty years, but the great loss was that it retracted from the Secretary the power to allocate the Reclamation Fund to specific projects, and assigned it instead to the Congress. The reclamation states as a whole supported the change, symbolic of the recognition of political influences that Newlands had hoped could be avoided. Roosevelt himself had taken pains to see that projects were allocated to all the reclamation states, recognizing practical political operations if the over-all program was to receive adequate funds.

The mineral lease bill which LaFollette had blocked in 1919 was revived and passed in modified form the next year. The bill represented acceptance of the idea that western lands would never be given to the states, but it was a victory for western interests in every other respect. The new law opened most public mineral lands to lease. The royalties received were to be divided 50 per cent to the federal Reclamation Fund, 37½ per cent to the state, and 12½ per cent to the general treasury. It was a major achievement for the "development" policy Lane had inaugurated.

CHAPTER IX

Pleasuring Grounds for the People

1

Our national park system is a natural by-product of the public domain; absent this largess, Congress would never have been so generous in the creation of the parks. The several reservations of public lands made by the Presidents, usually over congressional protests, made it possible to hold most of the park sites, but no President before Franklin Roosevelt made any real plans for a park system. Like most federal conservation policy, it first developed on a hit-or-miss basis.

Hot Springs National Reservation in Arkansas, for example, eventually was designated a national park but has never been really developed. The thermal waters of the springs were both curiosity and legend by the time Arkansas became a state, but the creation of the "reservation" by act of Congress in 1832 did set a precedent of lasting value.

The real concept of the responsibility of government in the preservation of natural beauty and scenic wonder first grew out of the successful effort to create Central Park in New York City. Before Central Park, the only park lands in American cities were the New England town commons and their equivalent in other town squares. The idea of Central Park originated with America's first landscape gardener and architect, Andrew Jackson

Downing, who adapted it from the parks of Europe—most of
which were remnants of royal holdings, preserved in earlier years
only because of their royal owners. Thanks to the fact that the
design and construction of Central Park were by another great
pioneer landscape architect, Frederick Law Olmsted, the country's first city park is still its masterpiece.

Andrew Jackson Downing was born in 1815, the son of a nurs-
eryman who lived and worked on the banks of the Hudson at
Newburgh, New York. With only the education available at the
local academy, he became the chief arbiter and designer of country living for that class of Americans who regarded themselves as
the proper counterparts of the English gentry. His first book, *A
Treatise on the Theory and Practice of Landscape Gardening,
Adapted to North America, with a View to the Improvement of
Country Residences*, was an instant success when it was published
in 1841; Downing was 26. A few years later, as editor and writer
for *The Horticulturist*, he was probably the most widely read,
and copied, columnist in the country. President Tyler chose him
to design and superintend the layout and planting of the "public
grounds" of the Capitol, from which developed the Capitol Mall.
A Hudson steamboat fire cut short his life in 1852, or undoubtedly he would be a better known figure of history today.

A visit to London in 1849 touched off Downing's first appeal
for a suitable park in New York, in the form of a letter published
back home calling attention to the lack of facilities. At the time,
the largest public park in the city was the Battery, 21 acres in all.
During the next year, Downing repeated his suggestions and further elaborated on his arguments in *The Horticulturist*; in 1851,
Mayor Ambrose Kingsland submitted a plan for a park which
would be perhaps as large as 160 acres, but Downing refused to
accept so modest a project. No less than 500 acres should be reserved, he declared, and he dwelled at length on such a park's
social values, which he pointed to as its most important aspect.
The mayor's site suggestion had been Jones's Wood, a stretch

along the East River between what is now 68th and 77th streets, but it was Downing who suggested the site of what was to become Central Park. Jones's Wood would be "only a child's playground," he said, and the larger Central Park site was one "with a real feeling of the beauty and breadth of green fields, the perfume and freshness of nature."

The first voice in favor of larger parks in New York City had been William Cullen Bryant's, in the *Evening Post*. Bryant took up the issue again when Downing began to promote a park, and it was probably the Bryant influence which accounted for the fact that both Mayor Kingsland and his 1850 opponent, Fernando Wood, supported the park idea in their campaigns. The state legislature gave the city authority to acquire the Jones's Wood site in 1851, but the *Evening Post* joined the clamor for the large Central Park site; in 1853, the legislature renewed the authority for the smaller park, but also authorized the creation of Central Park.

The idea of nearly a thousand acres of park land on Manhattan Island immediately evoked strong reactions ". . . A perpetual edict of desolation against two and one half square miles of this small island, might better come from the bitterest enemies of our city than from its friends," the *Journal of Commerce* complained. A new mayor, Jacob Westervelt, was opposed to both parks. He let the Jones's Wood site be sold for private development and backed a proposal in the legislature for authority to crisscross the Central Park site with residential streets. The *Evening Post* led the fight against the chop-up, and it was not won until a court decision in 1856 upheld the authority of the city to condemn and take the land to build the park.

But the park fight was still far from over. Fernando Wood was now mayor; the park plans and construction were in his hands, and he was an accomplished product of Tammany Hall, then in the process of becoming the instrument of Boss Tweed. Mayor Wood and his street commissioner became the Central Park Commissioners, but they had the foresight to get new public support for the park by appointing a consulting board, headed by Washington Irving, whose members included George Bancroft and C. A. Dana. The Irving board was little more than a front, however, and the lack of progress toward building the park gave the Republicans in the state legislature a chance to take it out of the hands of Mayor Wood in 1857. The new board in charge could use a Republican as superintendent, but one not so well known as to be obnoxious to the Democrats. Young Frederick Law Olmsted fit the bill and was hired, with little reference to his abilities as a landscape architect. Olmsted's books about his travels through the South, with their detailed accounts of slavery, had made him a local celebrity but had brought limited cash returns. He was 35 years old and wanted regular employment.

The same commission which hired Olmsted approved a competition for a design of the park. The entry which Olmsted prepared with his partner Calvert Vaux was the most imaginative and won the judges' approval almost automatically. Olmsted and Vaux called it the "Greensward" plan. One of its purposes was "to supply to the hundreds of thousands of tired workers, who have no opportunity to spend their summers in the country, a specimen of God's handiwork that shall be to them, inexpensively, what a month or two in the White Mountains or the Adirondacks is, at great cost, to those in easier circumstances." The park was to provide "conditions remedial of the influences of urban conditions." In their plan, they said, "The Park throughout is a single work of art, and as such subject to the primary law of every work of art, namely, that it shall be framed upon a single, noble motive, to which the design of all its parts, in some more or less subtle way, shall be confluent and helpful."

Olmsted was to be associated with the construction and operation of the park intermittently for the next 25 years, regularly resigning, being fired and rehired in various capacities. His original design was constantly threatened by efforts to cut corners, to utilize the park payroll as part of the political machinery, and otherwise interfere with orderly development. The park today is his monument. It has suffered from transient political influences, and the lack of city planning as broad in scope as Olmsted's social architecture. Central Park's great significance, apart from its actual existence, is the leverage it has given to local park development in every other American town and city. The blights have been bad enough, and it is difficult to conceive of American urban development in the past century without the example and incentive of Central Park.

When the Civil War came, Olmsted left the park for Washington, where he had been chosen as Secretary of the Sanitary Commission which furnished hospitalization for Federal troops and eventually evolved into the American Red Cross. In 1863 he was told to find different employment to protect his health, and the ideal job opportunity came along as superintendent of estates for the Mariposa Mining Company in California. Within a few months after taking the new job, he was involved in the promotion of a vastly different type of park.

Perhaps one reason Olmsted took the job with the Mariposa Company was because he might have read or heard of Horace Greeley's description of the Yosemite Valley as the "most unique and majestic of nature's marvels." At any rate, soon after he came to California, Olmsted was busy helping to prepare plans to make the Yosemite a public park. He helped Senator John Conness of California prepare a bill transferring the area from the public domain to the state of California, which passed the Congress with little notice or trouble in 1864. Although Olmsted was appointed chairman of the first state commission named to manage the new park, he soon left California to return to New York and more of the travail of Central Park. Yosemite Park was to remain a more or less indifferent state operation for 25 years and was not made a

national park until 1890. The first real national park was the won-
drous plateau area of the upper Missouri tributary, the Yellowstone.

2

Stories of the geysers, lakes, clear rivers, and waterfalls of this
patch of land along the Continental Divide first were circulated
by the trappers and fur traders who visited it or heard stories
from the Indians. Jim Bridger, one of the most famous of the
mountain men, told stories of some of the fantastic geysers, and
he was hired as a guide by the first exploration expedition sent
out by the Topographical Engineers. Captain (later General) W.
F. Raynolds of the Corps was in charge, with F. V. Hayden assigned as geologist to the expedition. Raynolds spent all the good
weather months of 1859 and 1860 exploring the area, but never
penetrated to the heartland of the present day park. A second
lieutenant of the Cavalry, G. C. Doane, was to make the major
Army contribution to the creation of Yellowstone Park.

During the 1860's, several groups of gold prospectors penetrated to the geysers and hot springs, but the first detailed reports
of the explorations were made by David E. Folsom in 1869. Folsom wrote an article about his trip which was rejected by several
eastern magazines as fiction, but was finally accepted and published by the *Western Monthly* of Chicago in 1870. Before the
publication, however, he had already talked with people at Helena, Montana, about preserving the Yellowstone headwaters as a
park, and added the final incentive in discussions with a Montana
territory group who were considering using the summer of 1870
to explore the fabled country primarily to satisfy their natural
curiosity.

Ten prominent men, most with imposing titles as officers or ex-
officials of the territory (and most no older than forty), made up
the party, and because of their prominence they were able to persuade Captain D. P. Hancock, the nearest military commander, to

assign them a military escort consisting of Lieutenant Doane and five men. Former Union General Henry D. Washburn, surveyor general of the territory, was the ranking official on the expedition; it also included Nathaniel P. Langford, who had been appointed territorial governor of Montana by President Johnson but denied confirmation by Johnson's opponents in the Senate. Another member was Walter Trumbull, whose father, Senator Lyman Trumbull of Illinois, was giving him a taste of frontier life through an appointment as assistant assessor of internal revenue for the territory. Trumbull persuaded the *Helena Daily Herald* to let him submit articles reporting on their exploration. The best writer in the party, however, was Doane. His detailed report, published as a congressional document, was to become a landmark of the Yellowstone story, and a good part of the reason the park idea was accepted by Congress. This is a paragraph of his description:

We kept the Yellowstone to our left, and finding the canyon impassable passed over several high spurs coming down from the mountains, over which the way was much obstructed by falling timber, and reached, at an elevation of 7,331 feet, an immense rolling plateau extending as far as the eye could reach. This elevated scope of country is about 30 miles in extent, with a general declivity to the northward. Its surface is an undulated prairie dotted with groves of pine and aspen. Numerous lakes are scattered throughout its whole extent, and great numbers of springs, which flow down the slopes and are lost in the volume of the Yellowstone. The river breaks through this plateau in a winding and impassable canyon and trachyte lava over 2,000 feet in depth; the middle canyon of the Yellowstone, rolling over volcanic bowlders in some places, and in others forming still pools of seemingly fathomless depth. At one point it dashes here and there, lashed to a white foam, upon its rocky bed; at another it subsides into a crystal mirror wherever a deep basin occurs in the channel. Numerous small cascades are seen tumbling from the lofty summits a mere ribbon of foam in the immeasurable distance below. This huge abyss, through walls of flinty lava, has not been worn away by the waters, for no trace of fluvial agency is left upon the rocks; it is a cleft in the strata brought about by volcanic action plainly shown by that irregular structure which gives such a ragged appearance to all such igneous formations. Standing on the brink of the chasm the heavy roaring of the imprisoned river comes to the ear only in a sort of hollow, hungry growl, scarcely audible from the depths, and strongly suggestive of demons in torment below. Lofty pines on the bank of the stream "dwindle to shrubs in dizziness of distance." Everything beneath has a weird and deceptive appearance. The water does not look like water, but like oil. Numerous fishhawks are seen busily plying their vocation, sailing high above the waters, and yet a thousand feet below the spectator. In the clefts of the rocks, hundreds of feet down, bald eagles have their eyries, from which we can see them swooping still further into the depths to rob the ospreys of their hard-earned trout. It is grand, gloomy, and terrible; a solitude peopled with fantastic ideas; an empire of shadows and of turmoil.

Thanks to Trumbull and the local connections of other members of the expedition, there were newspaper accounts which told of these same sites. They might have gone unnoticed in the East, however, without a dramatic scare story to go with them. Not long after the party entered the Yellowstone headwaters, Truman C. Everts, one of its civilian members, failed to return from a solitary scouting ride. After two days' searching, he was given up for lost, and the drama of his disappearance was the highlight of first reports from the exploration. More than a month after he had disappeared, two men from the Yellowstone Indian Agency found Everts wandering in the midst of a snowstorm. He had survived without so much as a pocketknife, having only some field glasses in his hand when his horse bolted with all his supplies attached. He had saved himself from freezing by sleeping near hot springs and fires he kindled from the sun with his field glasses, after overlooking this possibility during the first twelve days of being lost, when a fire might have attracted the other members of his party. Everts managed to keep from starving by eating thistle roots and an occasional minnow or snowbird, which he caught with bare hands. After the first fire he kindled, he always carried a burning brand, fearful that the erratic sun would not allow a new blaze.

Everts' miraculous rescue was a big national story for several months, but he was not the only member of the party who kept the Yellowstone in the public eye. Langford gave a series of lectures about the exploration and the wonders of the Yellowstone in several eastern cities, all under the sponsorship of Jay Cooke of the Northern Pacific Railroad (which was in the process of floating a new bond issue to be used for the extension of the line into new areas of the West like the Yellowstone).

Representative Henry L. Dawes of Massachusetts, chairman of the House Committee on Appropriations, included a provision to raise the pay of the United States geologist, F. V. Hayden, and complete the exploration of the sources of the Missouri and the Yellowstone, in the Sundry Civil Appropriation Bill of 1877. The boat which the Hayden party used was named for Anna, Congressman Dawes' daughter. Chester Dawes, his son, was assigned as one of the assistants on the expedition. This time, Hayden was able to locate all the Yellowstone wonders, by contrast with his trip with Captain Raynolds twelve years earlier. His report was a solid presentation in behalf of the park, and he was asked by Delegate William H. Clagett to help him draft the bill creating the park. We probably owe to Hayden the vital language establishing the park as a "pleasuring ground for the benefit and enjoyment of the people," and requiring "the preservation, from injury or spoliation, of all timber, mineral deposits, natural curiosities or wonders within said park and their retention in their natural condition."

Thanks to the bill's language, and the positive intervention through the years of such influential people as Senator George Vest of Missouri, the Yellowstone eventually established a fortunate pattern for American national parks. Active lobbying by Langford, Trumbull (back in Washington as clerk to his father's Senate Judiciary Committee), Hayden, and Dawes had enabled the authorization bill to pass. The Yellowstone was five hundred miles from the nearest railroad, but it was fortunate in its friends. Dawes was one of the top members of the Republican hierarchy in the House. He promised, and honored the promise, that he would seek no appropriations for several years, and could thus point out that the whole project involved no new costs to the government. Eventually, of course, the appropriations had to come; General Phil Sheridan had to help with soldiers to serve as the first park rangers; Senator Vest had to protect the area from various raids by congressmen and senators from the area which would have dismembered it, and other congressmen had to be kept friendly through relatives and friends on the park staff, but the Yellowstone survived, and set a unique pattern which was the foundation for the future success of national park policy.

3

The first real progress through local efforts to preserve scenic attractions came after the turn of the century. The American Scenic and Historic Preservation Society was a national organization active in this period. In an era before this type of public philanthropy was subsidized by the federal tax structure, the society helped make donations for state parks and scenic preservation a status symbol for wealthy Americans. The very important Palisades Interstate Park at the New Jersey-New York border on the Hudson is one product of this kind of effort.

All too often the success or failure of preservation efforts depended upon the luck of a few dedicated individuals in wheedling or cajoling local governing bodies and private financial interests into recognizing that the saving of sites and scenery had commercial as well as aesthetic and historical value. The successful effort to save the Great Stone Face in New Hampshire is an example of the tenuous thread by which some sites have been saved.

In 1805, a survey party was sent out by the State of New Hampshire to lay out a road through Franconia Notch in the White Mountains, and the first knowledge of the great granite profile came from the returning surveyors. Other white men had passed by, but apparently none of them had happened to look at the mountain at the right time and realize that the sharp outline of a man's face had been created where a cliff face fell away from its top. Ages of erosion had dropped rock away from the mountain in such a way as to etch a finely chiseled profile for those who saw it from precisely the favorable direction.

The mountain was given the name Profile, and some of the early accounts of the discovery gave the natural sculpture the name Old Man of the Mountains. Early in his career, Nathaniel Hawthorne wrote a story about it called "The Great Stone Face." The Hawthorne story, reprinted in millions of grammar school readers, with profile illustrations of varying authenticity, built an image in the mind of many a school boy that helped make Profile Mountain a major tourist attraction in the years following the Civil War. The mountain and surrounding territory were acquired early in this period by a firm known as the Profile and Flume Hotels Company, which built the traditional multistory frame resort hotel within walking distance of the profile view. Frame hotels burn eventually, and three successive Profile Hotel buildings, the last with 400 rooms, occupied the same site in succession before the company gave up after the last of them burned in 1923.

In 1872, a group of hikers from the Appalachian Mountain Club had climbed out on the head of the Great Stone Face and discovered that the two ledges which formed the forehead were hanging on in precarious balance. They contributed an article about the danger to a Boston newspaper. Charles H. Greenleaf, the managing partner of the hotel at the time, was aroused enough by the report to take a blacksmith and make a personal inspection. Greenleaf decided that any attempt to anchor the ledges would cost too much, and that they would last for a while, at any rate.

Thirty-four years later, frost and ice still had not dislodged the great forehead slabs, but the danger of their slipping was evident to the Reverend Guy Roberts of Whitefield, New Hampshire, when he climbed out on the ledge. The forehead which once retreated now jutted out, though the change had been imperceptible from year to year. Greenleaf was still operating the hotel and the company that owned the property, but Roberts could not persuade him to do anything about the cornerstone of his assets. For nine years Roberts bothered Greenleaf and anybody else who would listen with his story of the impending loss of the Old Man of the Mountain. In 1915 he met Edward H. Geddes, an experienced stonecutter and quarry superintendent, and persuaded him to take a look at the Old Man. Geddes decided he could stop the ledges from sliding further with a series of turnbuckles, which he could put into place with some hard and dangerous work.

Once again the Profile and Flume Hotels Company refused to underwrite the cost, but Greenleaf did endorse the idea of the repair work to Governor Rolland H. Spaulding. The Reverend Mr. Roberts managed to convince the governor that it was the duty of the state of New Hampshire to pay for Mr. Geddes' turnbuckles. The quarry man did a good job, with the help of Roberts, four laborers, and a blacksmith. The work was done in 1916, and each year after that until advancing age finally stopped him, Roberts made the trip to the Profile to paint the turnbuckles as protection against their rusting away. Today his devotion to the Profile is commemorated by a metal plaque beside the pathway from which tourists view the Old Man.

When the last Profile House was burned in 1923, the hotel company decided to list its 6,000-acre property for sale rather than to rebuild. Lumber companies were willing to offer $400,000 for the property, considerably more than the $200,000 appropriated by the state legislature. A bequest of $100,000 to the Society for the Preservation of New Hampshire Forests was the basis for a campaign for the additional money, promoted by women's clubs over the state, who secured contributions from all over the country to help make the Great Stone Face public property. The resulting Franconia Notch State Forest Reservation and Memorial Park was dedicated in 1928.

4

The outstanding contribution Franklin K. Lane made to the conservation movement, and to his Interior Department, was his active and successful support of the effort to establish the National Park Service. The idea of a national park system developed slowly, but moved with inevitable force after the passage of the Antiquities Act of 1906. The first dozen national parks had been established, or were in the process of legislative authorization, when Representative John F. Lacey of Oskaloosa, Iowa, chairman of the Public Lands Committee and the first great preservationist in the Congress, pushed through the National Antiquities Act. The new law gave specific authority to the government to protect "historic or prehistoric" ruins or monuments, but only those on the public domain or Indian reservations. The President was authorized to set aside these historic spots from any other use, and to accept gifts of such sites if they were outside the public domain. Before the end of his term, President Roosevelt had established a large number of national monuments under the act, and several of these were eventually to achieve full park status.

When the idea of a separate park service was first introduced, Pinchot scoffed that it "was no more needed than two tails to a cat." It was a natural reaction for him to propose that the parks be administered by the Forest Service. Most of them were either inside, or adjacent to, national forests, and it was the forest conservationists who had first fought for the reservations that made most of the parks possible. The Hetch Hetchy fight, however, which had broken the personal relationship between Pinchot and John Muir, made it impossible to achieve any agreement. J. Horace McFarland, another former Pinchot friend who had been estranged, took the lead as lobbyist and organizer for the park service fight, with an organization called the American Civic Association.

A significant new force, which eventually carried the day for the park service idea, was the railroad industry. In a day when railroads still made money hauling passengers, the lines that operated in the West recognized the value of well-developed national parks as tourist attractions. No group did more to advertise the early parks, to push for more funds for their administration, and to deliver the votes in nonwestern areas for the establishment of new parks and, eventually, the Park Service. The bill which created the National Park Service in 1916 was introduced by Representative William Kent of California, the man who donated Muir Woods. One of his consultants in drafting the bill was a second-generation park architect, Frederick Law Olmsted, Jr.

Secretary Lane made another contribution to the national park system when he persuaded another Californian, Steven T. Mather, to become the first director of the service. Mather had made a fortune in the borax business while still a relatively young man. Lane presented the Park Service to him as a challenge, and Mather's talents made it one of the vital, aggressive agencies during a period when much of government resource policy was simply marking time. The present National Park Service is largely the result of his efforts and those of his assistant and successor, Horace M. Albright, another one of Lane's Californians.

Three fundamentals encompassed their policy guide:

First, that the national parks must be maintained in absolutely unimpaired form for the use of future generations as well as those of our own time; second, that they are set apart for the use, observation, health, and pleasure of the people; and third, that the national interest must dictate all decisions affecting public or private enterprise in the parks.

Under Mather and Albright, the Park Service gained a status and employee morale equivalent to that of the Forest Service. By convincing railroads and local business interests that a free enterprise competitive system could not provide the most attractive facilities for tourists in the parks, Mather modernized and vastly improved the park food and lodging services. He convinced the leading eastern newspapers and magazines that the parks should be sacrosanct. He carefully cultivated the members of Congress from the park states, as well as those from other areas with committee assignments important to the service. The western congressmen were convinced that an expanding Park Service would be a great economic asset to their region, and after the first few years of Mather's administration, few of them ever joined in efforts to subvert park lands to irrigation or other local development purposes. Although installed under Wilson, both Mather and Albright survived under the following three Republican Presidents. Harding, Coolidge, and Hoover all gave lip service to the parks, but most of the legislative victories won by the service during this period were the results of the persistent lobby which Mather maintained with conservation groups, business interests, and influential congressmen.

As far as their accessibility to visitors was concerned, Mather found most of the parks in a primitive frontier condition. In 1923, virtually over the head of the Secretary of the Interior, he launched a full-scale campaign for roadbuilding appropriations, and began to get results in the form of rising numbers of visits to the parks: 750,000 people visited the parks in 1919; 1,750,000 in 1925, and 3,150,000 in 1931, in the full bloom of the depression. The first big roadbuilding programs brought objections from preservationists in the Sierra Club, despite a well-publicized effort to build the roads with the least damage to the natural state of the parks. The nature purists conveniently overlooked the fact that the noise and fumes of Model-T Fords brought considerably less pollution into the parks than the large stables of mules and horses that had been built to supply the tourists with stagecoaches, wagons, and packs and saddles.

In addition to the road program, the Mather-Albright administration of the Park Service was the spark which ignited the first real effort to develop recreational facilities in the national forests. Part of the rivalry between the Park and Forest Services was a hangover from those in the older agency who had never seen the need for a new one. Some normal jurisdictional conflicts were inevitable in work in adjacent areas, but Mather provoked others by approving a proposal for the Park Service to take over recreational development of the forests. The idea never made headway, but it did inspire the Forest Service to actively encourage camping, hiking, and fishing within the federal forests. The rivalry was often acrimonious, but it produced the healthy effect of better recreational work by both agencies. Eventually, the two services were to benefit equally from congressional appropriations for roads and trails to make their facilities more readily available to the public.

Mather did not take the full leadership, but he cooperated with congressional efforts to establish national parks in the eastern states, and the first breakthroughs came with his assistance.

The first national park was established in the East after a group of the summer residents at Bar Harbor, to protect their resort from commercialism, began to acquire nearby land under a charter from the state. When the state legislature threatened the charter, they persuaded President Wilson to accept it as a national monument in 1916. It was first called Sieur de Monts, then was named Lafayette when it was changed from a monument to a park in 1919, and finally became Acadia in 1929.

Local campaigns for parks had been talked about all up and down the Appalachian Mountain chain from the time of the Yellowstone, but the idea of national parks did not attract much support in New England, where there were few large scenic tracts in individual ownership. In the Southern Appalachians, timber operators had bought large tracts. Many of these reverted to the states for taxes after the initial cutover, and other areas were held after cutting with little hope for future development. There were a few splendid hardwood tracts still in virgin state, primarily because of their inaccessibility. As a consequence, the best organized campaigns for eastern national parks centered on the Great Smokies in western North Carolina and eastern Tennessee, and on the Shenandoah, along the crest of the Blue Ridge in western Virginia.

After the ground had been broken with a number of earlier bills, Senators Kenneth McKellar of Tennessee and Claude Swanson of Virginia got a law passed authorizing the establishment of the two national parks, along with one for Mammoth Cave in Kentucky.

Congress approved adding the new parks in the East, but it did not authorize the use of any federal funds to acquire the necessary lands. There was brave talk at the time of private contributions taking care of the costs, but land acquisition proceeded at a slow pace. The states voted contributions, and a gift of more than a million dollars from the Laura Spellman Rockefeller Foundation was a major impetus for the Great Smoky Park. Both proposed parks benefited materially from the first federal park land acquisition programs under Franklin Roosevelt. The Shenandoah National Park, centered on the hundred miles of Skyline Drive, was dedicated by President Roosevelt in 1936. The Great Smoky Park was not accepted for federal jurisdiction until 1942, although the Park Service had assumed its administrative control in 1934.

The relatively limited number of possible sites, and the much greater problem of nearby land already under development, have kept new federal parks in the eastern states at a minimum. The same enthusiasm which has fought to preserve inaccessible wilderness areas in the West has failed to respond to campaigns for coastline parks on the Atlantic, designed to preserve public access to the ocean shore. Small local sites have occasionally been won, but the only two important victories have been the Cape Cod and Cape Hatteras shoreline recreational areas. They are important, but they are not adequate to serve the need for preservation of a historic shoreline.

tion had begun. Harding still had faith enough in his friend to offer him a Supreme Court post as consolation, but the New Mexican had the courtesy to decline it. The inquiry brought the admission from Doheny that he had "loaned" Fall $100,000 while his lease was under consideration, and other evidence that Sinclair had given Fall $300,000. Fall became the only cabinet member in the country's history to go to jail for misdeeds in office, and Teapot Dome has become synonymous with corrupt misuse of natural resources. The leases were eventually declared invalid in the courts, but not before the oilmen had received a good return on their investment.

The sensational revelations of the bribery of a cabinet officer obscured the larger betrayal of conservation responsibility. As in the Pinchot-Ballinger controversy, personal corruption was more vivid to the public mind. Despite the fact that Teapot Dome became a byword for corruption, the Democrats did not succeed in transferring the guilt for it to Republicans in general. Perhaps this was because Doheny and Sinclair, the corrupters of the public servant, escaped without punishment, while Fall, broken in health, went to jail. Another reason was the revelation that the services of Franklin K. Lane and W. G. McAdoo, two prominent Democrats, had been retained by the oilmen.

Despite all this, Teapot Dome brought home the crusading element in the conservationists' position. It gave moral force to organizations like the National Popular Government League, soon to take the leadership in the fight for protection of public resources and public development of hydroelectric power. Through the years, conservationists have found it easy to become self-righteous, but in the great issues of direct public immorality where the geese have been stolen from the common, they have been on the moral side, just as they have been on the moral side in the broader and usually undramatized cases where the common has been stolen from the geese.

3

Thanks to the early denouement of Teapot Dome, few other important resource scandals developed in the twelve years of Republican administration that followed. With the encouragement of Secretary Wallace, the Forest Service moved cautiously ahead in promoting the management-for-use concept in the lands owned by the Federal government. The theory of developing better management of privately owned lands proved much easier to preach than to get practiced, although the various states did begin to develop limited cooperative programs, primarily in the field of fire control.

Several important programs were approved because Charles McNary of Oregon occupied a position of influence in the United States Senate and in the Republican party. McNary was a regular Republican who came to the Congress after the end of the progressive era, but he was a relative liberal on many conservation issues. His championship of resource development and programs to improve forest utilization (in a state with one of the largest percentages of U.S. forest lands) helped to re-elect him throughout the New Deal years and to give him the nomination for Vice-President on the ticket with Wendell Willkie. The Clarke-McNary Act authorized the cooperative fire control program, without the old limitation to activity in the watersheds of navigable streams, and also provided for another cooperative program with the states in the planting of seedlings. The McSweeney-McNary Act of 1928 authorized major expansion of forest research; the Woodruff-McNary Act of the same year authorized far greater forest land acquisition than under the old Weeks Act, and prepared the way for significant new holdings when vast acreages were forfeited to the states for unpaid taxes and needed federal ownership to prevent rapid deterioration.

Pinchot's influence on the early Forest Service personnel carried forward, even though the directors in the 1920's sometimes sharply disagreed with him over policy. The relatively high morale of the service and the opportunity to plan new programs authorized by the McNary bills helped make the federal foresters better prepared to meet the challenge of the depression and the New Deal than most of the existing agencies.

4

One of the by-products of the Roosevelt conservation movement had been the first national awakening to the necessity of federal programs to preserve wildlife. The U.S. Biological Survey was virtually the personal product of C. Hart Merriam, a veteran of the Powell era, when there were only a handful of scientists in government. Merriam headed the survey when it was created in 1885 to study the relationship between birds and agriculture. He soon managed to add a responsibility for the study of mammals, and saw his handmaiden elevated to the status of a separate bureau of the Department of Agriculture in 1906. The Lacey Act of 1900 put the importation of birds and mammals under federal control but had little regulatory effect on game birds and animals. The McLean Act of 1913 placed all migratory and insectivorous birds under federal protection, but neither the Wilson administration nor the Congress took it seriously because of the claim that it was unconstitutional. After a Migratory Bird Treaty was negotiated with Canada, a regulatory act based on its authority was passed in 1918.

Despite the power of the 1918 law, the Biological Survey spent the entire decade of the 1920's refusing to utilize its powers to regulate bag limits or otherwise provide any meaningful protection for migratory birds. Without prodding from the survey, Congress did nothing. Various states undertook some enforcement, but their uncoordinated action was of little value.

William T. Hornaday, director of the New York Zoological Society, carried on a continuous crusade to force the survey to establish and enforce migratory bird hunting regulations. Hornaday contended that there was a steady decline in migratory game birds and maintained that only federal action could halt their destruction. Even after Biological Survey scientists came to agree with him, they were reluctant to oppose organized groups of hunters, backed by the sporting arms and ammunition industry. Hornaday was a veteran of the Pinchot period, and his rhetoric fitted the conservation crusade of that day when he described the survey and its advisory board as "the organized defenders of big killing privileges, who take the field clad in the uniform of conservation and carrying the banners of false pretenses."

By 1930, it was clear that Hornaday had been right about the declining bird population, and the survey began to use some of its neglected authority. The survey had been trapped into supporting a bill for federal game refuges which also included public shooting areas, and the legislation had been effectively blocked by friends of Hornaday, including Representative Fiorello LaGuardia. When Senator Peter Norbeck of South Dakota brought up the proposal again in 1928, Hornaday persuaded him to take out the shooting grounds provision. With the help of Representative August Andresen of Minnesota, the first refuge act was passed in 1929.

5

Despite the reaction to the disastrous experience of Secretary Fall in the Interior Department, his resignation was followed by a procession of mediocre successors who continued in full retreat from the Roosevelt-Pinchot conservation concepts. Scientific contributions from the Bureau of Mines to conservation practices were lost when the agency was transferred to the Department of Commerce under Secretary Herbert Hoover, but the bureau's reputation had already been destroyed in the repercussions from Teapot Dome. An oil conservation program was needed in the 1920's, not only as protection from uncontrolled leasing of government reserves but to prevent waste in drilling, pumping, storing, and refining in both private and public fields. The Bureau of Mines was unable to supply assistance. Presidents Coolidge and Hoover acknowledged the problem, but both were reluctant to seek legislative authority for aggressive action.

Dr. Hubert Work, a physician better known as a politician, was Fall's immediate successor as Secretary of the Interior, shifting over from Postmaster General. Politically, the big problem in the department at the time was the dissatisfaction of the water users with the reclamation program. The farmers who were having to pay for the water were generally behind in their repayment schedules, despite the longer schedule of payments which had been written into the law. They contended that A. P. Davis, Newell's successor as head of the service, was only interested in fast returns so that his Reclamation Fund could enable him to build larger projects. Work's political solution was to change the name of the agency from Reclamation Service to Bureau of Reclamation, and to appoint David W. Davis, ex-governor of Idaho, as the new commissioner, with loud cheers from the Republican congressmen.

Davis's inadequacies were not long in becoming clear, however, and after a year Work brought in an experienced engineer, Elwood Mead, a University of California professor who was chairman of the state's Land Settlement Board. Mead had some understanding of the task necessary to get the various irrigation districts operating on a paying basis, and he remained at the job until his death in 1936. In a decade of declining farm prices, it was impossible to achieve any simple resolution of the financing problem. Constant agitation for change in the reclamation funding policy, from both the bureau and the Congress, encouraged many users to resist attempts at collection, hoping for better terms or eventual writeoff.

The financial problems of paying for irrigation water finally pushed the reluctant bureau into recognizing the value of hydroelectric power as a product of reclamation dams. The Boulder Canyon project was primarily the product of A. P. Davis; and when Davis left the bureau, it might have died from private power company opposition if Secretary of Commerce Herbert Hoover had not been assigned by President Harding to referee an arrangement between the states for disposition of Colorado River irrigation water that would be made available by damming the river. The Boulder project would provide a major water source for the growing city of Los Angeles, control the annual spring floods damaging the Imperial Valley, and irrigate approximately a million acres of agricultural land. In addition, the sale of 1,344,800 kilowatts of electricity generated at the dam would reduce the cost of the water. President Coolidge managed to avoid putting his administration into the power generation business, but Hoover was a committed advocate of the project, both as a Californian and a cabinet officer. When the plan was modified to make sure that most of the power was resold to private power companies for distribution, Coolidge relented. The Swing-Johnson bill was passed and signed in December 1928, after pending in the Congress for six years. The project benefited from most of the pump-priming appropriations of the Hoover administration, and became the first major multipurpose federal project to include power generation. The change of name from Boulder to Hoover Dam was a fitting recognition.

6

The 1920's were memorable for a continuing series of bitter fights in the Congress, as the private power companies mobilized to try to prevent federal construction of hydroelectric projects. It is a significant commentary on the changes in political posture in a forty-year period to note that such Republicans as Hiram Johnson and George Norris were usually the chief advocates of public power in the Congress. The position of Republican Presidents varied from reluctant support to hesitant opposition. The supporters of public power were the heirs of the Roosevelt-Pinchot conservation movement, making alliances with remnants of the reform element in the cities, who generally favored public power primarily because the old streetcar and traction companies had usually owned both the local power companies and the local political bosses. The boosters and promoters who wanted to use water development as a tool in economic improvement began to see that power generation would pay part of the cost of water programs, and they began to get behind it with more alacrity.

The power companies fought public power with all the traditional methods of national political lobbies: swaying local newspapers and paying retainers to local political leaders and influential lawyers. The system that has made power company contributions a leading source of congressional campaign funds for half a century was well under way. A more indirect campaign got under way on the general educational or propaganda front. Various "experts" set out to convince the American public that public power was poor economics, based on false or forged justifications, designed to serve the interests of pork-barrel politics.

The career of Samuel S. Wyer, a former consulting engineer, illustrates one of the power company weapons. Among other accomplishments, Wyer managed to leave a blot on the career of Charles D. Walcott, the chosen heir and pupil of Major Powell. While serving briefly as a dollar-a-year man in World War I, Wyer managed to be listed as an expert in his field of petroleum geology by the Smithsonian Institution. In 1925 he persuaded Walcott, secretary of the institution proud of its reputation for the scholarly integrity of government science, to let him privately print, but as a publication of the Smithsonian, a paper he had prepared entitled "Niagara Falls, its Power Possibilities and Preservation." The allegedly scholarly paper was a badly concealed attack on every positive view of the Ontario Power Authority, the agency by which the Canadian province was generating and distributing power from the Niagara River. The Canadian "sources" quoted by Wyer were either spurious, used out of context, or misquoted. The Federal Trade Commission investigated and presented evidence that power companies had paid for the paper's writing and printing. In Walcott's defense, it should be said that the veteran geologist was then in his dotage. When confronted with the fraud that had been worked on the Smithsonian, he repudiated the document, but echoes of "the Smithsonian report" were to turn up in Niagara power fights for years to come. Posing as a disinterested retired engineer, Wyer himself stayed into the 1930's on power company payrolls, ever ready to lecture or write on the engineering fallacies of the Boulder Dam plan, the Muscle Shoals project, St. Lawrence River hydro, Niagara power, or Governor Pinchot's proposed power grid for Pennsylvania.

Until the first public power projects went into operation and demonstrated their practical feasibility, the main line of power company attack was that government bureaucrats were incompetent to build power projects, and that they would not work or would not pay for themselves except through vast unjustified appropriations. From World War II forward, the attack has been primarily one of ideology: that public power is socialism and that it is consequently only one step removed from communism. The new approach of ideological attack has proven to be as generally effective, and is undoubtedly far cheaper, but the insurance derived from congressional campaign contributions has never been allowed to lapse.

Boulder Dam was the only public power fight that the private power companies lost in the 1920's, and even that loss was not complete. The victories, however, were by no means complete either. Senator Norris's fight for a Muscle Shoals hydro program was stopped only with the help of two Presidential vetoes. Power development on the St. Lawrence never reached the full planning stage, but the over-all St. Lawrence Seaway project was delayed not only by public power but by a combination of factors that included railroad and eastern seaport opposition as well. Franklin Roosevelt was stymied in his efforts as governor of New York to bring about state development of Niagara power, a program first sponsored by Governor Charles Evans Hughes, but the fight was good preliminary training in behalf of public power for the President who was destined to do the most for it.

Throughout the 1920's the federal interest in hydroelectric power development was supposedly under the protection of the Federal Power Commision, the cabinet agency created in 1920. Most of the Cabinet members who served on the commission during this period of its existence were frankly sympathetic to private power interests whenever they opposed public power development. The commission exercised no powers of regulation, and probably would have been an outright service agency of the power companies but for the integrity of its secretary, O. C. Merrill, and the reputation he had built as an engineer in the Forest Service, which made it impossible for his critics to have him fired without repercussions none of the Cabinet officers dared to arouse.

When Merrill gave up the struggle and resigned in 1929, the power companies could not resist the temptation to virtually take over full control, and chortle in public about it. A Senate investigation in 1930 made it clear that the commission staff was now being dominated by Washington representatives of the power companies, of whom Marshall O. Leighton was the most prominent. Senator James R. Couzens of Michigan led the fight for a bill reorganizing the commission, with five full-time commissioners appointed on a bipartisan basis. The first change in the commission staff voted by the new members was the firing of the two staff members who had testified before the Senate committee about the power company control. The Senate fired back by voting to recall the confirmation of the new chairman, George Otis Smith. Hoover refused to recognize any Senate right to recall a confirmation, and the net result of the investigation and reorganization was actually to strengthen the private power control of the commission, as most of the decisions it made within the next two years revealed.

7

During the 1920's the Army Engineers as a whole gradually adopted policies which indicated a steadily developing awareness of the need for multipurpose waterway control and development programs. However, the Mississippi River Commission, the Engineer division engaged in by far the largest operation in terms of appropriations, refused to budge from its 1861 "levees only" doctrine for the Mississippi. The passage of the Humphreys-Ransdell Bill in 1917, and the subsequent death of the Newlands' waterways commission plan, gave the commission a free hand. Serious levee breaks occurred above New Orleans in 1922, and many voices in the valley raised questions about the adequacy of levee protection. The congressional answer was to increase the authorization for the levee program, with no attention to any other program.

The Mississippi River handed down its own judgment in April 1927. The levee system proved completely inadequate. There were seventeen breaks in the main levee, most of them in portions which had been reported as up to the grade and standard of the project by the River Commission. The flood was a national disaster: more than 250 people were reported drowned, and at least 700,000 had to leave their homes. One official estimate of the total property damage was $364 million, and it is probable that a less limited calculation of damage would have come to half a billion. President Coolidge appointed Herbert Hoover chairman of a special Mississippi Flood Committee, with the task of coordinating relief for the disaster area. The favorable national press which this mission brought the Secretary of Commerce eliminated any doubt that he would be the Republican candidate for President the next year.

There was to be heated conflict over how to provide a remedy, but the immediate result was nationwide acknowledgment of federal responsibility for flood control on the Mississippi. It was not surprising for the liberal magazine *Survey* to suggest that

"Congress might provide that no little fellow should lose his place because the flood had made it impossible for him to meet the payments . . . ," but in the light of present attitudes it is interesting to note that the U.S. Chamber of Commerce voted in a 1927 referendum in favor of complete flood control on the Mississippi at federal expense by a margin of 2,629 to 156. Mayor William Hale Thompson of Chicago called a Chicago Flood Control Conference in June, with so much attendant publicity that congressmen, governors, and mayors seemed to make up more than half the two thousand delegates in attendance.

Before the smelly mud and scum of the flood could be shoveled and washed away, the voices which had been heard before, questioning the infallibility of the Mississippi River Commission's opposition to cutoffs and reservoirs as supplements to the levee system, were loudly raised again. New Orleans had been a center of support for the Newlands plan, and the city was now the largest sufferer from the failure of the straight levee system. Representative James O'Connor of New Orleans resubmitted his bill for a waterways and river regulatory commission based on the Newlands plan. The bill attracted wide support over the country in much the same circles that had supported Newlands, but received no attention from the Corps of Engineers or from the Coolidge administration. Despite the fanfare of the Hoover relief committee, the White House ignored any proposals which Engineer Hoover made, and left decisions as to legislative action to prevent new floods entirely up to the Corps and the Republican leadership in the Congress.

The disaster had been of the magnitude to invite drastic and imaginative remedies, and many were offered from throughout the country. Some of the more capable engineers for the levee districts in the lower Mississippi valley offered proposals that meant more assurance of protection than levees alone, and even the Mississippi River Commission modified its traditional plan to add a scheme of diversion channels which would be used at the time of flood peaks. The ultimate decision as to the plans, however, still was to be made by the congressional leadership and the Chief of Engineers.

Representative Frank R. Reid of Illinois, chairman of the House Flood Control Committee, was disgruntled with the Engineers' record, and encouraged widespread public testimony. One of the witnesses happy to oblige was Governor Gifford Pinchot of Pennsylvania, who termed the "levees only" theory the "most colossal blunder in engineering history." He added:

> At the end of a half century of control work by the army engineers comes the worst and most costly flood that we know anything about. And more than that, the Corps of Engineers, after a half a century of acting and responsible dealing with this, does not know what to do next, is without a plan for its control.

Despite the denunciation of the Corps' program from old-time opponents like Pinchot, and skepticism from former supporters like the local levee boards, the "levees only" solution prevailed. One reason for its persistence was the stubborn refusal of General Edgar Jadwin, Chief of Engineers, to accept any other viewpoint. The relative cheapness of the levee plan by comparison with other alternatives was all-important with the Coolidge administration, and probably helped establish the Jadwin position before any studies were compared in the Congress. A Jadwin-appointed engineer study group reported that a dependable reduction of six feet in flood heights on the lower Mississippi would cost $1,292,000,-000, if supplied by tributary reservoirs, but that the same protection could be given through higher levees for only $250,000,000. No evaluation was made of any reservoir purpose other than flood control. Congressmen from the lower valley area managed to get the Mississippi River Commission plan considered by the House committee, but the commission's heretical adoption of diversion plans helped make its cost more than twice as much as the Jadwin plan. Jadwin himself presented a report from another engineer board reviewing the commission plan and favoring the Jadwin plan.

Despite the Jadwin position, the House committee reported a bill authorizing most of the features of the Mississippi River Commission plan, thanks largely to the presence on the committee of Will M. Whittington, successor to B. G. Humphreys in the Congress. The Senate committee, headed by Wesley Jones of Washington, reported out the Jadwin plan.

President Coolidge let it be known that he was only reluctantly favorable to the Jones bill and was planning to veto anything more costly. The flood of enthusiasm for federal flood control legislation of only the year before had dried to a trickle in the areas of traditional opposition to government expenditures. The *Cleveland Plain Dealer* attacked both the bills as raids on the treasury, and the *New York Sun* agreed, predicting that passage of the Jones bill would bring on an "orgy of profiteering." Members of Congress began to speak in the same tone. The congressmen from the lower valley reluctantly read the changing mood the year after the flood. They managed to get the precedent established for federal purchase of levee rights-of-way, but the bill left very obscure the question of who would pay for the cost of floodways across open country, a cheap safety value added to the Jadwin plan. Led by Senator Ransdell, congressional opponents to the Jones bill gave up and joined in support. The final bill, called the Jones-Reid Flood Control Act of 1928, was essentially the Jadwin plan.

The passage of the bill was a significant victory for the long-time advocates of full federal responsibility for flood control, but it evoked no universal bell-ringing in the valley so recently inundated. There were too many memories of the failure of too many levees. Senator Ransdell had spent a quarter-century in the Congress fighting for federal flood control responsibility, but the "levees only" system had made the 1927 flood his chief monument. In 1930, Huey Long defeated him for renomination.

Fortunately for the Mississippi valley, the Jadwin plan was modified before it had to meet the test of a full-scale flood. A new
Chief of Engineers, General Lytle Brown, gave some attention to
the old but neglected concept of cutoffs to speed the waters to the
Gulf, after it was presented by W. E. Elam, engineer for the
Mississippi Levee Board at Greenville, Mississippi. The levees are
still an essential part of the Mississippi flood control program, but
they have been supplemented by cutoffs and a vast system of
tributary reservoirs, which now provide adequate protection for
the entire valley against the "project" flood.

8

At the same time the Corps of Engineers was demonstrating its
most glaring defects in the Mississippi River flood and the subsequent fight for the Jadwin plan, junior officers and civilian engineers of the Corps were beginning some of the most valuable and
comprehensive planning in the history of the service. As a result
of a provision pushed through Congress in 1925 by Representative
John McDuffie of Alabama, the Engineers had submitted a report
printed in House Document 308, 68th Congress, of a plan to evaluate the navigation, water power, flood control, and irrigation
potential of more than two hundred streams. The Rivers and
Harbors Act of 1927 directed the work to be done.

The "308 Reports" resulting from this act have been the solid
basis for planning most of the major reservoirs in the Tennessee
Valley Authority system, and for most of the similar projects on
the Columbia and Missouri. The 308 Report work benefited from
pump-priming money in both the Hoover and Roosevelt administrations, and the reports quickly paid for themselves in making
possible faster starts on various New Deal projects. They were
the first full commitment by the Engineers to the inescapable
reality of multipurpose reservoir construction, and they were
invaluable in advancing the idea of coordinated river basin development and improvement.

The Corps' navigation program also benefited by emergency relief appropriations during the Hoover administration, leading the way to the present Inland Waterways System, instead of the old chaotic system of local improvements evident before World War I. The Corps of Engineers had passed through one of its worst periods and was beginning to measure up to its responsibilities for federal water development as the New Deal arrived.

CHAPTER XI

Muscle
Shoals

1

More than one hundred years ago President Monroe and his Secretary of War, John C. Calhoun, laid Muscle Shoals like an un-
wanted child, on the doorstep of Congress. Ever since the day of
its entry into this body it has been a most perplexing, persistent
and pestiferous guest. During the past century Muscle Shoals has
consumed the time of legislators, marred their parliamentary programs, deluded those who have desired the distribution of its
power, and bitterly disappointed every farmer who has ever hoped
to enrich his impoverished soil with the fertilizer which could be
so cheaply made by a proper utilization of its potentialities. . . .
Muscle Shoals has proved to be more vexatious and expensive to
the American people than the plagues of the frogs and the flies
and the locusts and the lice were distasteful and disastrous to the
ancient Egyptians who endeavored to perpetuate the bondage of
the children of Israel.

Senator Matthew M. Neely of West Virginia

The shoals of the Tennessee River were known to the Indians
throughout the South, and they became equally familiar to white
settlers after the first group attempted to move west by the route
of the Tennessee River. Nobody knows whether they were named
"Muscle" because of the strength necessary to take river shipping

through them or whether the spelling is merely a corruption of the word "mussel," the shellfish common in the Tennessee. The preliminaries to the Muscle Shoals fight have been touched on already in this book, but the whole story throughout the 1920's is worth telling in detail. It is probably a classic exposition of the differences between the tactics of private exploitation and those of public-interest conservationists.

Plans to use the legal authority which Cotton Ed Smith had provided for the production of atmospheric nitrogen in a plant to be owned and operated "solely by the government" began well before American entry into World War I. A committee named by the National Academy of Science and the American Chemical Society, at the request of Secretary of War Baker, recommended construction of a hydroelectric station to supply power for nitrogen production. After a series of reports, President Wilson announced on September 28, 1917, that the first plant would be at Sheffield, Alabama, near the Muscle Shoals on the Tennessee River.

In December the War Department signed a contract with the American Cyanamid Company to build the nitrate plants, with a capacity of 40,000 tons per year. The dam to supply power for the plants was not authorized until February 23, 1918. Since it obviously could not be constructed in time to serve the nitrate plants upon their completion, a contract was negotiated with the Alabama Power Company for the interim power supply.

The nitrate plants were completed in October, at a cost of $68 million, but they were not put into operation because of the imminent end of the war. The dam was not complete, but contracts had been let which allowed construction to continue at a slower pace until 1921. The War Department tried in 1919 to find a private business willing to buy and operate the nitrate plants but could develop no serious interest. Therefore, Secretary Baker proposed that a government corporation be set up to operate the plants and had legislation introduced to authorize it. The legislation was given hearings, but the Congress in 1920 was more interested in campaign issues. A subcommittee of the House Select Committee to Investigate Expenditures in the War Department attempted to prove that all the millions put into the nitrate plants were nothing more than a giant waste, with perhaps some graft thrown in.

The investigation made a few headlines, but got nowhere after Bernard Baruch testified that the project, merely by being started, had saved at least $300 million by enabling the United States to buy Chilean nitrates at better prices. The unused facility had been no more wasteful, he said, than the unused men in the army and the unused supplies made available for them. Baker's government corporation plan was piloted through the Senate by Senator James Wadsworth of New York, but it died in the House Military Affairs Committee. The Harding administration inherited the chore of disposing of the surplus property.

Harding's Secretary of War was John W. Weeks, the former Massachusetts congressman who had sponsored the Weeks Act, the federal authority for acquisition of national forest lands. He was faced with Muscle Shoals when construction funds ran out in 1921 and the Congress refused to vote additional construction money. Weeks said he was ready to entertain bids for leasing the nitrogen plants if the government could get a fair return. The Chief of Engineers checked with various southern power companies about possible bids on Wilson Dam, but none of them appeared interested in proposing firm or realistic bids. Their public explanation for the reluctance was uncertainty about a market for the power. The intimation that they might be more interested if the government would be willing to write off most of the cost as a war loss indicated the possibility that they hoped to acquire the facility in the future at a vastly discounted price.

2

The pace of interest was enlivened considerably by an electrifying prod on July 8, 1921, when Henry Ford submitted a bid for the entire Muscle Shoals project, including the nitrate plants and power dam. What Ford actually offered is still the subject of dispute, because the proffered commitments were conditioned on additional government expenditures and some carefully guarded terms regarding the operation of the nitrate plants for the production and sale of fertilizer. In round numbers, he proposed a hundred-year lease, with an option to renew, for a project which, when completed to his specifications, would cost the government at least $132 million. For this lease he proposed to make an annual payment of approximately $1,700,000.

Secretary Weeks asked the Federal Power Commission and the Corps of Engineers for a report on the offer. After a preliminary report from the Power Commission staff, Weeks announced that the offer was unsatisfactory because it was predicated upon the government's guaranteeing 600,000-horsepower generation at Wilson Dam, an impossibility because of the irregular flow of the Tennessee. There were other minor points that were unsatisfactory, but they could be modified, the Secretary added. He proposed a conference with Ford after additional reports. Despite the "unsatisfactory" label, Weeks' announcement sounded as though a bargain could be reached. Two days after his preliminary rejection of the offer, the Chief of Engineers, General Lansing H. Beach, recommended its acceptance with a few minor adjustments.

The Ford offer was not to be accepted or rejected on the basis of engineering adjustments and business bargaining, however. Ford had made it clear that he counted on public reaction as his biggest persuader when the announcement of his offer included the information that the whole endeavor was to be a sacrifice on his part in the interest of the national welfare and the American farmer.

National press reaction to the offer was largely favorable. The New York Times was pleased that Mr. Ford was ready to take a "white elephant" off the hands of the government, and it ridiculed an attack on the proposal made by Gifford Pinchot, declaring that the terms of the lease "had about as much to do with the Rooseveltian conservation program as it has with the inclination of the ecliptic." The power industry did not welcome Mr. Ford into its fraternity, however, and the *Chicago Tribune* spoke up in opposition. A *Tribune* reporter uncovered the interesting fact that J. W. Worthington, executive secretary of the Tennessee River Improvement Association, was apparently working full time for Ford, or at least in behalf of the Ford offer. Claudius H. Huston, a Tennessee promoter and politician, former head of Worthington's organization and now Assistant Secretary of Commerce, had joined with him and Gray Silver, the Washington representative for the American Farm Bureau, in working out a plan to sell Congress on the idea, which would require special legislation. According to the *Tribune*, this group would emphasize that Henry Ford's operation of Muscle Shoals would ensure cheap fertilizer for the farmers, and farmers all over the country would push the offer through Congress. The *Tribune* quoted from a Worthington letter to Silver, warning him not to mention Ford's "plan to manufacture aluminum" at the Shoals, for fear it would arouse the wrath of Secretary of the Treasury Andrew Mellon and the Aluminum Company of America, and turn the administration against them.

When negotiations on the offer got under way in earnest in September, Worthington turned out to be one of Ford's negotiators, along with William B. Mayo, his chief engineer. The bargaining reached a stalemate on the added construction costs the government would have to pay to provide the amount of regular water supply necessary to meet Ford's terms. Ford himself came to Washington for the conferences in November but refused to make any concessions. The government representatives found ways to assume some of the additional costs, but they did not go far enough for the car maker. He suddenly shifted to public pressure again by announcing a dramatic personal inspection tour of Muscle Shoals in the company of Thomas A. Edison.

Ford and Edison made a nonstop trip to the Shoals by special train, turning down dozens of invitations to meet with various chamber of commerce and farm groups along the way. En route, however, Ford talked readily to reporters. Edison, he said, was along to evaluate the nitrate plants for cheap fertilizer production. Ford expected to use the surplus power at Muscle Shoals to manufacture aluminum, cloth, steel, and automobile parts. After an enthusiastic ovation at Florence, the largest of the three towns at the Shoals site, Ford explained the broader purpose of his plans. He was out to defeat the international bankers of Wall Street.

Ford proposed to use the financing of the Muscle Shoals project to demonstrate the value of a new basis for an international monetary system, the "energy dollar." He said, "It is very simple when you analyze it. The cause of all wars is gold. We shall demonstrate to the world through Muscle Shoals, first the practicability, second the desirability of displacing gold as the basis of currency and substituting in its place the world's imperishable national wealth. . . ." The way to destroy the "money sellers" who controlled the world supply of gold, he declared, was for the United States to finance the completion of Muscle Shoals by issuing paper money based on the potential wealth of the project. The results would be so salutary "that the government would never again need to borrow interest-bearing bonds for internal improvements, but instead it would merely issue currency against its imperishable natural resources."

Edison followed with an endorsement of the energy dollar the next day, describing the plan as "flawless," which meant that "the game is up" for the "interest collectors." Ford enlarged upon his indictment of international bankers by explaining that the whole system was controlled by Jews. The Jewish financiers had not only been responsible for the World War, he told his Alabama audience, but they were also to be blamed for the Civil War.

A large crowd gathered at the railroad station to see him off on December 6, and the car maker handed them the challenge. "We have made our offer . . . ," he said. "All I ask of Congress is to give me the opportunity. And I am going to leave that to you, if you wish me to come down here, to see that Congress does." From his Detroit office on January 12 came a press release that raised another wave in the tide of the Ford boom sweeping over the Tennessee Valley. Mr. Ford was not only going to provide cheap fertilizer for the southern and midwestern farmer, but he was going to build a metropolis, 75 miles long, centered around the Tennessee River and the Muscle Shoals district. It was not going to be one huge city, but a series of small towns, because "this is in line with the manufacturer's view that men and their families should live in small communities where the benefits of rural or near-rural life would not be entirely lost." Mr. Ford had spent most of his time since returning from Muscle Shoals working out the plans for the huge development, which would begin as soon as Congress approved his offer. Upon completion, the whole project would be turned back to the people of the area, or to the Federal government, in such a way that neither Ford nor his heirs could make a personal profit from real estate speculation. More than this, however, once the practicability of the Muscle Shoals idea had been demonstrated, the project would be merely one of a whole series which Ford would eventually build in various sections of the country.

The heady intoxication of the Ford dream-boom swept over the central Tennessee Valley and over most of the Southeast. Ford was a magic name to begin with, from the tin lizzy itself to the five-dollar-a-day pay. It is worthy of note that Ford's anti-Semitic doctrine and his *Dearborn Independent* coincided with the virulent revival of the Ku Klux Klan.

The coming bonanza was to remain only a dream for most of

the citizens of the area, but for some of the landowners and a
great many real estate speculators, the boom got under way in
January 1922 and continued for more than two years. The resulting activity can only be compared with the south Florida
real estate boom of a few years later. Many tracts changed hands
dozens of times during the period. Special trains were organized
for prospective purchasers of lots, shares of development companies, or corner buildings in one of the new towns.

There was frenzied real estate speculation, but the most important Ford fervor was spread over the southern farm country
and parts of the Midwest. The postwar collapse of cotton had
struck hard at the South. The only hope for a prosperous operation left for most cotton farmers was sharply increased production without heavy fertilizer costs. Most southern cotton land
was already so depleted that yield was certain to be low without
fertilizer. Natural or manufactured fertilizer had always cost too
much, and any hope for a cheap supply was worth grasping.
The farm organizations fell quickly into line behind the Ford
offer, and southern congressmen eagerly began to assert their
support.

Ford had been identified as a Democrat when he ran for the
Senate in Michigan in 1918, and his attacks on Wall Street and
the gold standard marked him in the Populist tradition for both
the Democratic heirs of Bryan and the Republican progressives
from the Midwest and western states. With widespread farm and
southern regional support being rallied for his offer, the prospects
of congressional action to get rid of a white elephant looked
promising.

There were to be many slips to finally spill the cup, but the
strongest was the operation of the seniority system in the United
States Senate. Legislation having to do with fertilizer production
was subject to action by the Senate Agriculture Committee,
whose chairman was the progressive Republican from Nebraska,
George W. Norris. His adamant opposition to the Ford offer

was to be the main reason it never received congressional approval, partly because of his clear-sighted presentation of the weaknesses in the proposal, and partly because of his careful political maneuvering to take advantage of every weakness in the political coalition aligned behind Ford. The influence of individual attitudes on American history has never been more clear than in the career of George Norris and the Muscle Shoals issue; his fight to block a windfall giveaway of natural resources gradually evolved into a dedicated struggle to bring to reality a slowly developing plan for the coordinated development of those resources.

In the long list of political leaders, in and out of office, who have fought the battle for the conservation and development of America's natural resources, the name of George Norris will always stand at the top. The great monument to this giant of a man from Nebraska is in Tennessee, fittingly symbolic of the spirit of a senator dedicated to all the United States. He summed up his creed in his autobiography, after his defeat and shortly before his death during World War II:

> I am sure that, from among America's fighting men and others, warriors will appear to fight the unending battle for good government. I am sure that, so long as there are men, there will be knights to lift their swords and press their shields against the enemies, corruption and evil.
>
> Liberalism will not die.
>
> It is as indispensable to life as the pure air all around about.

There were other barriers, in addition to George Norris, which helped to block what might have been otherwise quick congressional action in favor of Ford. One of them was the stubborn effort by Secretary Weeks to make Ford squeeze out a cent or two more than the nickel or dime he was offering for the government's dollar. Weeks had been directly involved in the negotiations for some six months when Ford broke loose with a personal attack on the Secretary's position, demanding that he answer

yes or no. Apparently it was a calculated plan by the Ford
negotiating team, which hoped that if the demand could not force
Weeks to concede one more point and say yes, it would give
them a chance to win in Congress without the Secretary's support. The Ford offer was thus reduced to a signed contract, with
some clarifications but still considerable vagueness about the obligation to produce large quantities of fertilizer. Weeks refused
to accept for the government but submitted the offer to Congress
on February 2. Although the Harding administration had rejected
the offer, its submission to Congress carried the implication that
the administration would accept whatever agreement on it came
out of congressional action.

Senator Underwood, eager to promote the Ford offer in the
interest of Alabama, moved to submit the Muscle Shoals report
to the Agriculture Committee, on the theory that farm interests
dominated the committee and that its members would be most
responsive to Ford. His great mistake was not first discussing the
idea with Chairman Norris, who had more influence with his
members than did Gray Silver, the Farm Bureau representative.
In the House the plan was submitted to the Military Affairs Committee. J. W. Worthington lined up an impressive assortment of
witnesses in favor of Ford from throughout the South and the
Mississippi valley. A bill to accept the Ford offer, with some
modifications, was approved by the House committee in June by
a 12-to-9 vote, but it stalled in the Rules Committee. Some reports
were that Secretary Weeks had persuaded Majority Leader
Mondell to delay the bill until adjournment, and others that the
Ford promotion campaign had neglected to include the Republican leaders. The fact that the most outspoken Ford supporters
were men like Finis J. Garrett of Tennessee, the Democratic
minority leader, certainly helped encourage a stall by the Republican leaders.

At any rate, the bill had been turned down by a 9-to-7 vote
of the Senate Committee. Norris had maneuvered carefully to

see that every question mark in the Ford offer was raised before his committee and to make sure that they knew about the orgy of real estate speculation at the Shoals:

> These real estate speculators are organizing a wonderful propaganda in favor of the acceptance of Mr. Ford's offer. . . . They have flooded the country with their letters and circulars, particularly among the farmers, in which they falsely represent that Mr. Ford has agreed to make fertilizer at one-half its present cost, and thus they have brought to the aid of their real-estate speculations thousands of honest farmers throughout the country. . . . If their propaganda is anywhere near true, there will be, if Mr. Ford gets this property, a city spring up there which will make New York look like a country village. Why a warranty deed to the capitol at Washington is not included in this great transfer of property . . . has never been explained. . . . Notwithstanding this apparent neglect, the transaction still remains the most wonderful real-estate speculation since Adam and Eve lost title to the Garden of Eden.

In the midst of the hearings before his committee, Norris introduced his first Muscle Shoals bill, and thus began the evolution of what was to become the Tennessee Valley Authority Act eleven years later. This first bill authorized the completion of Wilson Dam and another listed in the Corps plans as Dam No. 3 (the present TVA Joe Wheeler Dam, thirty miles upstream from Wilson). The completed dams and the nitrate plants would be operated by a government corporation which would manufacture a complete fertilizer to be sold to farmers at cost, with the surplus power to be sold under a preference system to states, counties, and municipalities. Although a survey of the entire Tennessee for power development was authorized, no reference was made to flood control or navigation, or to general ideas of economic development, nor was there authorization to construct transmission lines for delivery of the surplus power to the preference customers specified.

The Ford offer was not acted on before the 67th Congress ended, but the delays it encountered were not abnormal for a controversial legislative item on which the administration presented a confused position. The first months of 1923 saw a growing increase in farm support for Ford's fertilizer idea. Although the Hearst press was the offer's chief source of newspaper support outside the South, pro-Ford factions were hinting or sometimes flatly predicting that the offer contained all sorts of unofficial extra attractions. There is an intriguing similarity between some predictions of the bonanza which would come with Ford and some of the goals and actual achievements of the TVA, created ten years later. The pro-Ford newspapers and congressmen usually stressed the value of the Ford program as a tool for economic reclamation for the South, and a demonstration of regional economic improvement which would be a lesson for other regions of the nation. Worthington said, "Mr. Ford has stated that he felt a river ought to be taken up as a whole and completed in its entirety," and that he intended "to make Muscle Shoals and the Tennessee River an example of what our power resources on our rivers will do for the people of this country." There was talk of a complete navigation system, a resurgent agriculture, and all the new industries that would inevitably result from a combination of Ford's and Edison's genius with cheap electricity, nitrogen, and navigation.

The public concept of the value of coordinated development of the Tennessee River was first built in the projections of the value of the Ford development to the Tennessee Valley, and the ideas from Ford and his partisans undoubtedly contributed to the broadening base of Senator Norris's own legislative proposals for Muscle Shoals.

Throughout 1923, Henry Ford was the most talked about potential candidate for President in the country, sometimes even more than the obvious candidate of the Republicans, Calvin Coolidge. Most of the talk was that Ford would become the candidate of LaFollette Progressives in a third party. Ford never proclaimed himself a candidate, but he did not disavow the Presidential support of the Hearst newspapers when it was announced in May. The Ford Motor Company prepared special biographies of its founder for distribution by Ford dealers throughout the country. Some observers said that the Ford Muscle Shoals offer was a part of his Presidential campaign, while others maintained that the Presidential boom was a result of the offer. On December 3, Ford conferred with Coolidge about the Shoals offer, and on December 4, Ford ran a bad loser in Democratic and Farm-Labor Presidential preference polls in South Dakota. On December 6, Ford ordered canceled a nationwide Ford-for-President rally scheduled for Dearborn. On the same day, Coolidge sent a message to Congress which suggested that it establish a joint committee to negotiate with bidders for Muscle Shoals, with the inference that agreement could be reached on the Ford offer. On December 19, Ford announced his unequivocal support of Coolidge for re-election.

Ford-for-President workers were disillusioned, most of them assuming that their hero had traded his support of Coolidge in return for Coolidge's support of his Shoals offer. The Muscle Shoals development boosters were elated for the same reason, because they believed the last barrier to congressional approval had been overcome.

The House hearings on the Ford offer in 1924 introduced a new element of opposition which had never fully developed before. The Alabama Power Company was now actively interested in acquiring Wilson Dam. A group of southern industrialists, represented by Nashville Lawyer Dan McGugin—who also doubled as the football coach at Vanderbilt University—began to talk about the loss to southern industry that would result from the low-cost Tennessee River power if it were monopolized by Henry Ford. Neither group was able to influence votes in the House of Representatives, where Southerners voted almost solidly for the Ford offer in tandem with midwestern Republicans and other strays collected by the Farm Bureau and the Hearst newspapers. A bill to accept the Ford offer for Muscle Shoals passed the House on March 10, 1924, by a vote of 227 to 143.

The momentum of the heavy majority in the House appeared to be enough to win the day for Ford in the Senate. Senator Norris was still as strongly opposed as ever, but few other senators were genuinely committed to defeat the proposal. The shadow of the Teapot Dome scandal, then very heavy over the country, was the one major indeterminate factor. A commentator in *The New Republic* voiced a common doubt: [The proponents of the Ford offer] "use precisely the same arguments which led honest men at one time to accept the Teapot Dome leases as legitimate."

In the hearings before his committee, Norris explored every lead that might show that a bargain had developed between Ford and Coolidge, to such an extent that, at one point, Coolidge had to specifically deny that any bargain had been reached. Whatever had in fact occasioned Ford to mount the Coolidge bandwagon, the defensive effort necessary to establish that there had been no sellout unquestionably strengthened the hand of Secretary Weeks in holding out for a fair return from Ford. Teapot Dome obviously paid some unexpected early dividends.

Norris must have smiled when he found southern industrialists, apparently lined up by McGugin, defending the public interest in the Federal Water Power Act, and joining with Pinchot and James R. Garfield in saying that the potential for public power had to be preserved. The National Fertilizer Association rounded out the picture by insisting that the Ford offer was really pure socialism. The Union Carbide Company came up with an offer for the property and was given a full hearing, along with the private power offer made by the Alabama Power Company. Late in May, the committee turned down all the purchase offers and voted out the Norris bill, 11 to 4. The pro-Ford senators, led by Edwin F. Ladd of North Dakota and Tom Heflin of Alabama,

submitted a vigorous minority report. They claimed confidence
in winning in the full Senate, but Norris's delaying tactics prevented them from getting the bill on the floor before the adjournment for the 1924 Presidential campaign. An agreement was
reached, however, that the Norris bill, with an opportunity to
substitute the Ladd bill accepting Ford's offer, would be at the
top of the calendar when the Senate met in its lame-duck session
in December.

The campaign took the political headlines away from the Ford
controversy. Then, without any advance rumblings or warnings,
on October 13 Ford withdrew his entire offer, with no reason
other than the implication that he had given up because he could
not buck big business. "Wall Street doesn't care to have the power
trust's strangle-hold broken," he said.

Whether Ford actually believed that he faced a defeat in Congress or a veto of the bill by Coolidge, or whether he had simply
become bored with the Muscle Shoals idea, will probably never
be known. Norris and his group of progressives who fought the
plan were certainly not confident of victory at that stage. Whatever the reason, the Ford Muscle Shoals balloon suddenly burst.

There are still remnants of the Ford mirage at Muscle Shoals.
Even though the TVA stimulus increased the population of the
Shoals urban area from 23,000 in 1930 to 58,000 in 1960, there
are still hundreds of acres of empty lots, some with weed-grown
roads and sidewalks, that were sold during the days of real estate
speculation. A half dozen brick store and bank-type buildings in
the small-town style of fifty years ago can be found at strategic
road corners over the still-undeveloped area, vestiges of the evidence built to show the prospective lot-buyers that the boom
was already under way.

Perhaps the chief irony is that one of the major industries of
the present-day Shoals is the Reynolds Aluminum Company.
Next door is an engine assembly plant of the Ford Motor Company, where the blocks are molded with aluminum fresh from

the Reynolds pot lines. This happens to be only one of the ways in which the reality of the TVA system has proven the worth of Colonel J. W. Worthington's forecasts, in behalf of Henry Ford, of economic development through the river's potential. Worthington attained his greatest prominence as promoter for Ford, and later his services were available to the American Cyanamid Company, but his real love through the years was the development of the Tennessee. Undoubtedly his rose-colored visions of the economic development which could come to the valley through Muscle Shoals helped evolve the concept of full development by TVA, and helped to persuade the people of the valley that it was possible.

3

While the Ford supporters were still in shock, the Alabama Power Company moved to revive its offer to purchase Muscle Shoals. Senator Underwood stepped forward as the company champion, and worked out an agreement with Secretary Weeks that was given the official blessing of President Coolidge. The Underwood bill, offered now on the Senate floor as a substitute for the Norris bill, provided for a fifty-year lease of the entire Muscle Shoals property at an annual fee of only 4 per cent of the government cost of Wilson Dam alone. The lessee would agree to produce 40,000 tons of nitrogen fertilizer from the chemical plant within five years after taking over, and there would be no control on the resale price of either the power or the fertilizer.

With the power companies offering to produce fertilizer, Norris worked out with Senator Kenneth McKellar of Tennessee a change in his bill obligating the government to produce 40,000 tons. McKellar was to prove a tower of strength to Norris in the critical days of the fight against sale to the power company, for he became the chief bridge to support from southern senators under pressure to go along with Underwood. McKellar's drive, and the ready acknowledgment that the Norris bill offered far more hope for cheap fertilizer than did the Underwood bill, kept the Southerners in line.

Voting on amendments began in mid-December, and critically close votes continued through early January in a flurry of substituting, tabling, and amending. The White House had announced that Coolidge would sign the Underwood bill if it passed. On one vote, every Southerner joined Norris except Underwood and Shields of Tennessee, and his bill was kept alive by a vote of 40 to 39. Underwood managed to switch some votes when a new chance came to offer his plan as a substitute, and he won final passage by a decisive margin on February 14. The fight now was whether the conference could be completed and final action taken before the Congress expired on March 4.

The conferees reduced the already imperfect fertilizer guarantee in the Underwood bill, partly because the power companies were afraid of the commitment, and partly as a result of pressure from the fertilizer industry. This weakening of the main attraction for most of the southern senators gave Norris enough strength in the Senate to prevent the conference report's ever coming to a vote. When he announced that a filibuster had been organized and was waiting to start, the Republican leadership conceded and took the report off the calendar.

4

Jones of Washington had supported the idea of a Presidential commission to submit a plan on Muscle Shoals as a compromise between the Norris and Underwood bills. When it became known that Norris had blocked the Underwood bill for the session, the commission idea was revived in the House, and a resolution authorizing the President to appoint one cleared the Congress on March 2. The commission was a mixed bag, with none of the five members favorable to the idea of government operation, and its report turned out to be a recommendation for

a plan similar to the Underwood bill, with more specific requirements about fertilizer production. Its most significant finding was
in a minority report signed by the chemical engineer Harry A.
Curtis, questioning the value of the Cyanamid process.

So far as Norris was concerned, the Commission meant he would
have the time he needed to build support for government operation of the power generation facilities and research in fertilizer
at the chemical plants. National sentiment for public operation
was gradually growing. There were no federal hydro facilities
anywhere in the country, and Southerners looking for economic
development were being reminded of the fantastically low rates
offered in Ontario as a result of the entirely government-owned
hydro development there.

The Muscle Shoals fight took place in the years before the
Congress began to supply itself with a reasonable amount of
staff assistance. Norris's chief help during the whole controversy
was a lawyer-lobbyist named Judson King, who was probably
during this period the best-informed man in the country on the
subject of public power. King was director of the National Popular Government League, formed by a group whose leaders included Pinchot and Norris, to lobby "for the people" in contrast
to the always-represented special interests. In its first years, the
league worked primarily in behalf of initiative, referendum, and
recall provisions in state constitutions, in direct connection with
the LaFollette wing of the progressive movement. As this particular crusade faded, membership in the league also declined.

The Popular Government League lived only through Judson
King and his wife. Born in Pennsylvania, King's first contact with
public issues was as editor of a weekly paper in Denison, Texas,
in 1902. From Texas he went to Toledo, Ohio, to work for the
famous reform mayor, Brand Whitlock, and from that time on
he was never out of the progressive crusade. The declining membership in the league was not enough even meagerly to support
its director, but Pinchot and other veterans of the conservationist

crusade came through with contributions that kept things going. For many years King and his wife would drive in from their home in Takoma Park, pick up Senator Norris at his home, and take him to the Senate office building before going to the league office, where Mrs. King was the sole office staff. They usually took the senator home in the evening, as well, and these commuting conferences were the source of much of the day-to-day strategy in the Muscle Shoals fight.

Age and the death of Senator Norris eventually limited Judson King's activities, but he joined in some fashion in every TVA fight until his death on July 4, 1958. He liked to consider himself one of the creators of TVA, and at his request his ashes were scattered over the waters of the first reservoir that TVA built, Norris Lake.

Missionaries like King were taking the case for public development of the Shoals to every possible interested group. Two potent sources of support, the American Federation of Labor and the League of Women Voters, were helpful in making clear Norris's position that the national interest was involved, at a time when President Coolidge was commenting, "The problem of Muscle Shoals seems to me to have assumed a place all out of proportion with its real importance. It probably does not represent in market value much more than a first-class battleship. . . ."

The Coolidge administration began again the effort to dispose of Muscle Shoals by backing a resolution by House Majority Leader Bertrand H. Snell of New York for a joint congressional committee of six members to seek bids on the installations. The commission resolution passed, but Norris and his group managed to include an amendment sponsored by Senator Thaddeus Caraway of Arkansas, which provided that any buyer or lessee of the power had to guarantee equitable distribution over a broad geographic area. Ideas about what might be accomplished with Tennessee River power were spreading throughout the South.

The joint committee majority recommended acceptance of the

offer of the power companies, again made through the Alabama Power Company, and a bill to accomplish this was introduced by two administration Republicans. Southern farmers were not happy about what this might mean to fertilizer, and began to talk to their congressmen. The American Cyanamid Company and the Union Carbide Company had both presented bids to the joint committee, to keep alive the idea that the facilities could still be used primarily for fertilizer production. Privately the two companies had agreed that if the Cyanamid offer was accepted, they would pool their operation.

During most of 1927 and 1928 the Shoals issue in the Congress was a running dispute between Norris and the Cyanamid Company, whose spokesman was usually Chester Gray of the American Farm Bureau Federation. Norris was convinced that the Cyanamid process was impractical and uneconomical for large-scale fertilizer production at the Shoals, and that the real purpose of the chemical company offer was to acquire control of Wilson Dam power. Gray tried to make the case with southern congressmen that the Norris plan would be of no value in getting cheap fertilizer, and a large group of southern farm papers, replete with Cyanamid Company advertising, supported him. The most responsible and by far the most potent farm publication in the South, however, was the *Progressive Farmer*, edited by the highly respected Clarence Poe. The *Progressive Farmer*, with editions in every southern state, endorsed the Norris plan for government operation and helped keep alive southern support for Norris.

The first Norris bill to pass the Congress was far short of a plan for unified development of the Tennessee River. It provided for public operation of the Muscle Shoals installations for power production and fertilizer research and for public distribution of the surplus power produced at the dam. The Senate, tired of the long fight and confusion, adopted the Norris bill on March 13, 1928, by a vote of 48 to 25.

In the House, the bill went to the Military Affairs Committee, where it found a greater interest in mass production of fertilizer than it had in the Senate. One amendment the committee adopted provided that the board of directors of the corporation established to administer the program "shall be persons that profess a belief in the feasibility and wisdom . . . of producing fertilizer under this act." The committee also listened to good advice from the Corps of Engineers, who pointed out that Wilson Dam would be far more valuable with a storage dam on Cove Creek of the Clinch River in upper east Tennessee, and included authorization for the dam in the bill they approved, a major step toward making Muscle Shoals a full Tennessee River project.

The House bill, sponsored by John M. Morin of Pittsburgh, the committee chairman, passed in May by a vote of 251 to 165. Most of the votes in favor were from the South or farm areas, but there was a significant handful of city members following the leadership of Fiorello LaGuardia, who was involved in all the debates and committee hearings. In conference, Norris was pleased to accept the Cove Creek amendment, and the fertilizer changes were in favor of research and experimentation. It now developed that potent Tennessee interests were opposed to the Cove Creek provision, because they were convinced that the state was entitled to exclusive jurisdiction over the power produced there. Senator McKellar caused a brief flurry with a one-man filibuster against the report. He could not stop its approval, but his break with Norris had to be overcome for the future.

Coolidge got the bill on May 26, 1928, three days before the adjournment of Congress. It was not a *sine die* adjournment, but the President allowed the ten days which meant a pocket veto to pass without his signature. There was no statement as to the reason, although most newspapers friendly to the administration said it was because of his opposition to the principle of government ownership. Norris provided this explanation: "To have offended this great [power] trust by approving the Muscle

Shoals bill would have dried up the sources of revenue that we
must have in the great campaign just ahead of us."

5

Norris supported Al Smith for the Presidency in 1928, basing
his endorsement entirely on the comparative records of the two
candidates on the power issue, even though Republicans in Tennessee had managed to get from Hoover a back-handed statement
in favor of federal development of Muscle Shoals. The Federal
Trade Commission investigation of power company propaganda
activities had helped pass the Norris bill earlier in the year, and
public power advocates hoped that it would propel the issue into
the Presidential campaign. There were some interesting revelations, such as the fact that the president of the National Federation of Women's Clubs had also been on the payroll of the National Electric Light Association, and that power companies,
through an organization called the Appalachian Power Conference, had subsidized two engineering professors from the Uni-
versities of Tennessee and North Carolina in their studies to show
the impracticability of public power in the southern mountains.
The effect on the Presidential campaign was nil, but the investigation registered in delayed action in the Congress.

As far as Muscle Shoals was concerned, the real meat of the
private power lobby investigations was one conducted by Senator
Caraway as chairman of a Judiciary subcommittee early in 1930.
The Caraway investigation destroyed what chance might have
existed for the American Cyanamid Company to lease Muscle
Shoals in conjunction with Union Carbide. It brought the revelation that the Cyanamid Company had underwritten the cost of
most of the lobbying that Chester Gray had carried on for the
Farm Bureau. Senator Frederic C. Walcott of Connecticut, a director of Union Carbide, had written the Senate Agriculture
Committee minority report opposing the Norris bill. The Ten-

nessee River Improvement Association, the J. W. Worthington
operation so recently part of the machinery of the Ford offer,
was now in full tilt for Cyanamid. Huston, the Tennessee Association president, became chairman of the Republican National
Committee when Hoover became President. The records revealed
that Huston solicited a $36,000 contribution from Union Carbide
to promote the Cyanamid bid, then used the money for his own
personal speculations. Huston's political ally, Representative Carroll Reece of Tennessee, was the most active promoter of the
Cyanamid bid in the House, where he had brought out a bill
favorable to the company by calling a disputed rump session of
the Military Affairs Comittee.

In the vain hope that the Court might rule his bill was now
law, Norris delayed reintroducing his own Muscle Shoals plan
until the Supreme Court acted on the legality of Coolidge's pocket
veto. The bill, in substantially the same form, was introduced and
brought out of committee in May 1929. The Senate passed the
measure in April the next year without a major fight; the Caraway
investigation, plus the growing doubts about the value of mass
production of nitrates by the Cyanamid process, were factors in
its increased support. The two Alabama Senators, Heflin and
Hugo Black, supported the Norris bill, and McKellar was once
again a strong supporter, thanks to a provision granting compensation to Alabama and Tennessee for loss of the states' rights
to develop the facilities. Arthur H. Vandenberg of Michigan
and Alben Barkley of Kentucky protested against this amendment, asserting that the two states would receive more than
adequate compensation through the flood control, navigation,
and power benefits that would come their way.

In the House, regular Republicans were now in firm control
of the Military Affairs Committee, and Representative Reece
became their spokesman on Muscle Shoals, with the help of a
well-leaked secret: that President Hoover had told Chester Gray
he favored action through a commission that would authorize

a lease designed to develop a chemical industry at the Shoals. Reece introduced a bill along this line, and it was approved by the committee.

New champions of the Norris plan, now that the lines were more clearly drawn, were two southern members of the committee, Percy Quin of Mississippi and Lister Hill of Alabama. They denounced the Reece plan as one more effort to delay action, and charged that its eventual goal was to turn Muscle Shoals over to the power trust. Their effort to substitute the Norris bill failed on the House floor, but they did accumulate the solid support of virtually all the southern members. The Reece bill was passed on May 28 and sent to conference.

The conference had trouble meeting, because Congressman Reece, its chief House member, was busy trying to put down a revolt at home. East Tennessee was now anxious for construction of Cove Creek dam by the government. A Republican committed to the Norris bill, Samuel R. Price, was attracting wide support over Reece's district in upper east Tennessee, while Reece was attacking the Norris bill as "socialism." One of his chief supporters, Guy L. Smith of Knoxville, a newspaper editor and party leader, joined with John Q. Tilson, the Republican leader of the House, in denouncing Reece's opponents as "the Alabama Power Trust and red radicals." Reece managed to hold off the power company-radical combination in the primary, but the returns were so close that a nominal Republican, Oscar B. Lovette, entered the November general election as an independent candidate. The Democrats did not enter a candidate in the rock-ribbed Civil War Republican district, and Lovette defeated Reece by a decisive margin.

The election of 1930 indicated the first national reaction to the depression, but it was also significant for the defeat of Reece and victories for all of the outspoken supporters of public power in the Congress. Norris won despite an early effort to eliminate him in the primary by qualifying a grocery clerk named George

W. Norris as an opponent in a race where there was already stiff opposition. When this effort, which involved both the Nebraska Power Company and the Republican National Committee, failed, the same groups tried to purge the senator with Congressman Gilbert M. Hitchcock, a Democrat who published the *Omaha World-Herald*. Norris won with a solid majority.

During the lame-duck session which followed the election, the conference committee read the election returns and finally brought out a bill generally favorable to Norris's position, after the House conferees deserted Reece. For the first time there was a provision for publicly owned transmission lines, although there was also authorization for the President to seek the lease of the chemical facilities for private fertilizer production. The big question was whether the House would take a bill so different from the one it had originally passed. Reece, bowing to public opinion back home, gave a reluctant endorsement to the conference report, but some of his colleagues still decried the result as "socialism" and "communism." Quin responded that the opposition was speaking only for "predatory wealth" against the interests of the masses of the American people. The House voted approval, 216 to 153.

The bill went to the White House accompanied by mixed hopes about its signing. Hoover had carried both Tennessee and Alabama in 1928, and many of his newspaper supporters in those states predicted he would sign the bill, but they were whistling in the dark. The President vetoed the bill on March 3, 1931. His veto message cited a long list of objections to the project and provisions of the bill, one of which was the provision requiring directors to profess a belief in the feasibility and wisdom of the project. He cited a Corps of Engineers report which predicted that the power operations would result in a net loss of two million dollars annually. His major reason for the veto was more basic: ". . . I hesitate to contemplate the future of our institutions, of our government, of our country if the preoccupation of its officials is to be no longer the promotion of justice and equal opportunity but is to be devoted to barter in the markets. This is not liberalism, it is degeneration." The Senate failed to override the veto by a veto of 49 to 34.

In the veto message, Hoover proposed again that the Muscle Shoals disposal be put in the hands of a commission. This time the commission would be named jointly by the President and the governors of Alabama and Tennessee. Hoover's appointees included Edward A. O'Neal of Florence, Alabama, national president of the Farm Bureau, who had been active in support of the various fertilizer proposals while head of the Alabama Farm Bureau. All nine of the members named to the commission were described as being opposed to governmental operation of Muscle Shoals, although one of them, W. A. Caldwell of Nashville, resigned in protest over the failure to consider any plan for the multipurpose development of the Tennessee River.

The commission report proposed operation of the Shoals facilities primarily for the purpose of fertilizer production. Representative Hill introduced a bill on behalf of the House Military Committee based on this plan and incorporating some aspects of the Norris bill. It passed the House on the vote of the same basic coalition of Southerners and farm area Republicans.

Norris had reintroduced his vetoed bill when the new Congress met, but he did nothing to bring it to a vote, despite many pleas that the more liberal new Congress might be more likely to override a veto. The Nebraskan was looking beyond the Congress to the Presidential election, and the chance to have a much broader bill passed with Presidential support. He gambled that it would be worth waiting out 1931 for November 1932.

CHAPTER XII

Built for the People
of the United States

1

Norris's instincts couldn't have been more sound. Those twelve
years of struggle over Muscle Shoals, and the intermittent activity
which had proceeded for a century before that, were a good basis
for his judgment. The worn-out land and the sometimes worn-
out people contributed to the general feeling over the valley
that it would be a fine thing for the government to step in and
do something for their river. But it was the knowledge that the
Tennessee Valley was the most poverty stricken of all the major
river basins of the country that fired the imagination of Franklin
Delano Roosevelt, and the special interest of F.D.R. brought
about the unique genius of TVA.

In the 1932 campaign, Roosevelt endorsed the Norris Muscle
Shoals bill. During the busy period between election and inaugu-
ration, the President-elect worked out a trip into the valley as
an excursion en route to Warm Springs, and invited Norris to
join him. At Chattanooga, Tennessee, and Decatur, Alabama, they
were joined by practically all the members of Congress within
range of the Tennessee Valley, and there was long conversation,
and some speeches, about what could be done for the river. "Is
he really with you?" someone asked Norris when the senator returned to Washington. The old man from Nebraska, who had

fought so long for Muscle Shoals, was still in a trance from the vision of the man from New York. He answered, "He is more than with me, because he plans to go even farther than I did."

On April 1 and 7, Roosevelt met with Norris, Representative John Jackson McSwain of South Carolina, chairman of the House Armed Services Committee, and Representative Hill of Alabama to talk about the plan and to give them a preview of his Tennesee Valley Authority message. The message of April 10 was masterful in its directness, emphasizing his own idea of the most important value in conservation, planning for comprehensive use:

> The continued idleness of a great national investment in the Tennessee Valley leads me to ask the Congress for legislation necessary to enlist this project in the service of the people.
>
> It is clear that the Muscle Shoals development is but a small part of the potential public usefulness of the entire Tennessee River. Such use, if envisioned in its entirety, transcends mere power development: it enters the wide fields of flood control, soil erosion, afforestation, elimination from agricultural use of marginal lands, and distribution and diversification of industry. In short, this power development of war days leads logically to national planning for a complete river watershed involving many States and the future lives and welfare of millions. It touches and gives life to all forms of human concerns.
>
> I, therefore, suggest to the Congress legislation to create a Tennessee Valley Authority—a corporation clothed with the power of government but possessed of the flexibility and initiative of a private enterprise. It should be charged with the broadest duty of planning for the proper use, conservation and development of the natural resources of the Tennessee River drainage basin and its adjoining territory for the general social and economic welfare of the nation. This Authority should also be clothed with the necessary power to carry these plans into effect. Its duty should be the rehabilitation of the Muscle Shoals development and the coordination of it with the wider plan.
>
> Many hard lessons have taught us the human waste that results

from lack of planning. Here and there a few wise cities and counties have looked ahead and planned. But our nation has "just grown." It is time to extend planning to a wider field, in this instance comprehending in one great project many States directly concerned with the basin of one of our greatest rivers.

This in a true sense is a return to the spirit and vision of the pioneer. If we are successful here we can march on, step by step, in a like development of other great natural territorial units within our borders.

Support for it was such that Norris did not even have to have hearings on the administration bill in the Senate, but the House committee gave the power companies of the area a chance to protest. "I can see no market whatever for this power," said E. A. Yates, a vice-president of Commonwealth and Southern, who was destined twenty years later to have a more prominent role in another TVA power controversy.

The House committee voted out a version of Hill's bill, modified to limit the construction of new dams and transmission lines, but even this faced some rough oratory on the floor, where Charles A. Eaton of New Jersey called it a Russian idea. "The development of power in that particular locality of the nation, or of fertilizer for that matter, can be of no general good," declared a young member from Illinois named Everett M. Dirksen. Roosevelt intervened in favor of the Senate version when the bill went to conference, and it was essentially the Norris bill which he signed on May 18, 1933.

The bill's preamble mentioned all the purposes in Roosevelt's message, then set up a government corporation with broad powers for resource development as a coordinated effort. The specific enabling language was sometimes too restrictive to purposes of navigation, flood control, and power, but even this joint recognition of the multipurpose concept was revolutionary. The old language from an earlier House bill was still carried, requiring the board of directors to affirm their belief in the wisdom and feasibility of the TVA Act.

The day the bill was signed was a proud one for George Norris. "It is emblematic," he said, "of the dawning of that day when every rippling stream that flows down the mountain side and winds its way through the meadows to the sea shall be harnessed and made to work for the welfare and comfort of man."

2

On June 16 the board of directors met for the first time in an improvised Washington office. Despite the overwhelming vote passing the TVA Act, there was already an undercurrent of criticism about the three men chosen to direct the Authority— two college presidents and a law professor, to use one of the derogatory descriptions. The most common measurement, however, was one of high regard for a good balance of experts in the public interest.

Arthur E. Morgan, 55, was president of Antioch College, but he was best known as an engineer with a social conscience. After disastrous flooding at Dayton, Ohio, in 1913, he had provided the engineering and organization ability to establish the Miami Conservancy District's series of dams and reservoirs for flood control on the river. The work on the Miami proved relatively effective in the 1920's and was pointed out as an example of how flood control could be achieved without the Federal government. Other conservancy districts were established in Ohio, and the whole system was eventually given massive federal aid in the 1930's.

Morgan was chosen president of Antioch College in 1920, and his school became known as an outpost of an idealist educational preparation for men and women to learn how to remake society by remaking both the natural and the human environment. His obvious dedication to the oldtime moralist fervor made him an impressive spokesman for the cause of human as well as environmental conservation. Some of his associates said his righteousness was sometimes self-righteous, but his patent honesty made the criticism seem frivolous at the time.

Roosevelt had known of Morgan's reputation both from the Miami and Antioch, and it seems that he had decided upon him to head up the TVA experiment well before it became law. Roosevelt was primarily responsible for the selection of the other two board members as well, although he gave Morgan the job of scouting both and passing on their qualifications.

Harcourt A. Morgan was president of the University of Tennessee, formerly dean of its college of agriculture. Transplanted from Louisiana, he was a veteran of the growth of the land-grant college program under the steady assistance of increasing federal funds. He filled an obvious need for a member of the board who would be representative of the Tennessee valley area itself, yet removed enough from the normal political channels not to be labeled a political placement. He was already 66 years of age, but his solid reputation as a soil scientist appealed to Arthur Morgan.

The third member of the Board was chosen for his reputation as an uncompromising champion of public utility regulation who was capable of carrying his points with his own solidly built legal case. David E. Lilienthal was the son of a small-town merchant in Indiana, who struggled to send his son to DePauw and Harvard Law School. Felix Frankfurter recommended the young lawyer to Donald Richberg in Chicago. After helping Richberg draft the Railway Labor Act, Lilienthal began to specialize in public utility law and was on the brink of an obviously promising career in that field when Governor Phillip LaFollette asked him to become chairman of the Wisconsin Public Service Commission. The idea of direct public service and the recognition that went with the state office were too appealing to turn down. By 1932, after a Democrat had defeated LaFollette for re-election, the telephone companies were out in force to prevent Lilienthal's reappointment. The TVA post was a timely challenge.

At that first organization meeting, part of the agenda was a letter to the board from another Indiana lawyer who had gone into the utility field, Wendell Willkie, president of Commonwealth and Southern, the holding company which included most of the southeastern electric utilities. Willkie wanted a discussion of "common problems." When the TVA Board began to discuss these common problems, as Lilienthal recorded in his journal, "there was some difference of opinion as to tactics and strategy expressed as between myself and Chairman Morgan, with Harcourt Morgan acting as a mediator. This will require a good deal of working out."

These were days of rapid action, building, and planning ahead, but it rapidly became apparent that there were differences about power between Arthur Morgan and Lilienthal. The new chairman had told Judson King a few days after his appointment, "I want to tell you one thing, I am not going to fight the power companies." The difference on this issue was to be the heart of the first great TVA crisis that simmered three or four years before breaking into the open.

Meanwhile, TVA began to move into vibrant life. The much-discussed Cove Creek dam was the immediate major construction project. TVA took it over in its planning stage from the Corps of Engineers, enlisted design help from the Bureau of Reclamation, and began to build the dam that was to be named Norris. Thanks to Arthur Morgan, assigned direct responsibility for engineering and construction, it was more than just a construction job. The laborers out of the Cumberland Mountains were to learn technical productive skills for the first time, and to get a taste of a new life in the construction village. They were to build more than a dam and would be more than casual laborers.

Harcourt Morgan was assigned supervision of the fertilizer and agricultural program. He turned immediately, and naturally, to the land-grant colleges and their extension services as his work-ing partners in the fertilizer use and land improvement program. The step served as a fine introduction for TVA to a conservative group suspicious of government operation. The close association would also create handicaps in the years ahead. In the meantime, in the first formative period, Harcourt Morgan steered TVA toward a realistic approach to the two nitrate plants whose value to the American farmer had been oversold for twelve years. One of the plants proved capable of producing nitrates through the Cyanamid process; the other appeared impractical for any im-mediate purpose. The value of Norris's prolonged effort to take the emphasis away from mere fertilizer production and to place it on research instead was immediately obvious.

Lilienthal was given the responsibility for organizing and oper-ating the TVA power system, and put in charge of legal affairs. His immediate job was to find a market for the power already available from Wilson Dam and to determine a system of dis-tributing it. A vital early decision was to stay out of the retail business, to become a wholesale supplier for other public agencies who would handle the distribution through nonprofit organiza-tions patterned after the public municipal systems common throughout the country. Tupelo, Mississippi, John Rankin's home town a hundred miles southwest of Wilson Dam, was the first to sign up, and the much smaller town of Muscle Shoals, Alabama, came in at about the same time. The Alabama Power Company had been retailing, for about 5 cents per kilowatt-hour, power it had bought at the Wilson Dam bus bar for 2 mills. The new residential rate, which averaged 1.5 cents per kilowatt-hour, im-mediately brought home the advantage of TVA power.

His particular combination of personal experience was the reason for Lilienthal's assignment to TVA law, and it became extremely useful. The court challenges to the constitutionality of the TVA Act were largely based on opposition to its power program, and they grew thicker as the Supreme Court began to rule against other New Deal measures.

As the three directors went about their initial assignments with too little comprehension of what each of the others was doing, excitement and exhilaration were the order of the day with the people they brought into Knoxville to help them. (Knoxville was chosen as the temporary headquarters, because it was closest to the first construction job, Norris Dam, because it was the most convenient large city in the valley to Washington, and because Harcourt Morgan already had a nice home there, furnished by the University of Tennessee. Through the ramifications of politics, it is still the headquarters.)

The symbol of TVA as the first great American social engineering job attracted some of the best minds in America. In 1934, the mere existence of a fair supply of new jobs in engineering, agriculture, chemistry, and a dozen other fields for specialists in natural and human resources made it possible to skim the cream of the field. The TVA merit system made it possible to require that belief in TVA and its program was a prerequisite for employment, and this was no problem for most of those who applied. From the start there was an *esprit de corps* unrivaled in any government agency. Technicians came from throughout the country, but the bulk of the work force came from the Southeast, to begin a tradition of TVA-trained labor that was to spread throughout the region and become a major by-product of the Authority. Norris and every other dam and steam plant carries the prominent inscription: "Built for the People of the United States."

3

A stockholder of the Alabama Power Company named George Ashwander was the man whose name was on the suit which tested the constitutionality of the TVA power distribution system. During the three years Norris Dam was being built, the fate of the entire idea lay in the *Ashwander* case. A district court in Alabama not unexpectedly ruled against TVA, and during the appeal no new expansion of the power system could begin. In February 1936, the Supreme Court held, in an 8-to-1 decision, that TVA could dispose of Wilson Dam power in any appropriate way, because the dam had been properly built for purposes of defense and navigation. It was a narrowly based victory, so dubious that all 18 power companies then operating within 150 miles of any TVA installation filed another suit alleging that the agency was involved in a conspiracy primarily to produce power while claiming its facilities were being built for navigation, flood control, and defense. In a 1938 decision, a three-judge district court in Tennessee decided every factual issue in favor of TVA. The next year the Supreme Court, which had survived the packing fight, refused to hear an appeal on the ground that there was no standing to sue. On that basis the TVA constitutionality has rested, although other cases since have more fully upheld the right of agencies of the United States to generate and distribute power.

After the Ashwander suit failed, the TVA opponents placed their faith in the 1936 election. When it was over, they began to put their hopes of blocking the agency in the reports of dissension within the board of directors. There was no question by now that the great experiment in unified resource development was in danger because of irreconcilable division among its board.

Part of the problem was an unworkable division of authority within the board, which had given virtual autonomy to the different divisions assigned to each director; another part was the personality of Arthur Morgan. Too much was being done by each of the directors without the full knowledge of and coordination with the others. With the lack of knowledge came suspicion and doubts about the values of the specific programs, and it was easy to move from there to doubts about the people.

Arthur Morgan had reinforced his early ideas that TVA should avoid fights with the power companies. To meet his and Roosevelt's wishes, Lilienthal worked out a truce with Commonwealth and Southern about power service areas that would hold until three months after power generation started at Norris Dam. The truce lost all meaning to Lilienthal, however, when Willkie and his company became the center of the court fight against TVA, and at the same time held out the hope to Morgan that peaceful arrangements about power could be worked out which would end the whole controversy with TVA. There was talk of power pools and territorial agreements, but in actuality the only arrangement that would have satisfied the power companies would have been the right to buy TVA power wholesale at the dam.

For Arthur Morgan, the conflict over power seemed to be merely something that got in the way of his plans for remaking the human resource of the Tennessee valley. Precisely what his plan was never became clear, but the whole TVA program was original and unfettered enough to make room for any new idea. The workmen at Norris would be rotated in different skills, because they would go back to their original mountain cabins after the job was finished. Better skills and better markets would be developed for mountain crafts and woodworking. New crops that fitted old mountain ways, like nut trees, would be developed. To help preserve this isolated regionalism, TVA might adopt a separate scrip for its currency. Norris construction village became the ideal planned community, thanks to the day-to-day interest of both Dr. and Mrs. Morgan, but natives and outsiders alike were pleased that Mrs. Morgan's idea of keeping the old mountain-type wood stoves and fires for cooking and heating was overruled in favor of electricity as a symbol of what TVA could bring. The school system was the best in Tennessee; the adult education and library program which were established ranked above anything else of its kind in the South.

Norris Village was supposed to be a showplace of what TVA could mean, but in hard reality it was little more than an idealized company town. There was no practical way either to translate or to transport Norris to the entire Tennessee valley. The State of Tennessee would be happy to have TVA take over the schooling in the TVA town, but nowhere else. There was no objection to some of the cooperative plans for both production and marketing for small groups in the Norris area, because they could be no worse than the nothing which the mountaineers had, but there was no demand and no wish to take them into east Tennessee, or through the cotton country of north Alabama and west Tennessee. In the light of hindsight, it is easy to see that most of the Morgan ideas were not working at the time, and would not work into the future, but their impossibility then was based on the plain fact that there was little interest in them among the people of the Tennessee valley, and no way to develop that interest through the use of the limited powers established in the TVA Act. A newspaper comment at Muscle Shoals was typical of valleywide reaction: "A kindergarten for Appalachian hill-billies may be a fine objective, but it is hardly what the people of the Tennessee Valley had in mind."

The first and lasting difference between Arthur Morgan and the other two board members was over power policy, but within a couple of years more and more decisions were being made by a 2 to 1 vote, with the chairman in the minority. From a not-unnatural idea at the start that his ideas should prevail because he was the chairman, Morgan quickly began to believe that there were sinister personal motivations behind the opposition. Under a provision by which the term of one of the three directors would expire every three years, Lilienthal was up for reappointment in 1936. Morgan went to Roosevelt, Norris, Ickes, and others in Washington to try to prevent the reappointment. Roosevelt's first reaction was that he would have to go along with the chairman in the interest of harmony, but his second thought, and that of Norris, was that the fault might be with Morgan himself. A power company campaign against Lilienthal did nothing to hurt his standing with the President, and he was reappointed.

The reappointment did not change Morgan's attitude. Those few whom he managed to convince that the whole humanitarian aspect of TVA policy was being sacrificed for power were often the same people who were also losing fights in Congress for even more practical programs in the height of New Deal prestige. Morgan apparently believed that only a dishonest or immoral person could have ideas about policy differing from his, and consequently opposition to his ideas could properly be called dishonest and immoral. In this way, the Morgan self-righteousness began to delineate very broad definitions of dishonesty and immorality. "Morgan was an authentic descendant from the witch burners," said Harry Hopkins, "and his piety was sure to catch up with him." Like many another zealot, he confused policies with principles, and his self-proclaimed refusal to compromise principles meant that he could not bother to review his policies.

After Morgan's charges began to be made public, Roosevelt and Norris both repeatedly asked him to document them, or at least to list any substance that he had for his statements. Morgan refused to do so; during one period he repeatedly refused even to show up at the White House for a confrontation about the charges. After a long exercise of patience, Roosevelt ordered Morgan's removal as a director for "contumacy." The Morgan charges against his fellow directors, combined with the increasing velocity of the power company opposition, were naturally echoed in Congress. The inevitable result was a full-scale congressional investigation, which came in the form of a joint committee headed by Senator Vic Donahey of Ohio. Although none of the Democrats on the committee were TVA partisans, and the committee had the benefit of whatever recriminations were available from Arthur Morgan partisans on the TVA staff, no hint of scandal or corruption developed from months of investigation and testimony. The majority report was a clean bill of health, and the minority fell back upon the traditional opposition to government in the power business.

Roosevelt designated Director Harcourt Morgan as the new chairman, and filled the vacancy with Senator James Pope of Idaho, a New Dealer recently defeated in the Democratic primary because he had made the mistake of being a premature internationalist from a state still represented in the Senate by William E. Borah. H. A. Morgan's age and personal inclination made him reluctant to assume the most active role in representing TVA in Washington, and thus Lilienthal became the most prominent member of the board during the remainder of his service with TVA. He became chairman in 1941, when H. A. Morgan voluntarily asked to be relieved of the responsibility. The administrative machinery was repaired in 1937, with the designation of a general manager, appointed by the board of directors and responsible for all operations of the agency. Only minor adjustments have been made since that time, with the board restrained to a policy-making role.

4

During the board controversy over exactly what the power policy should be, and the massive court battle against any power program, TVA moved cautiously in investment in transmission lines and other distribution facilities. With its permanent ability to serve them in doubt, the agency was in no position to sign up many large power customers. The entire picture changed in 1938 and 1939, when the congressional investigation ended and the favorable court decisions were made. TVA decided to offer wholesale electricity to any municipal or cooperative distributor in the Tennessee valley watershed, or within economic transmission distance of TVA generation.

The obvious next step was to purchase the facilities of the private power companies in the region owned and controlled by

Commonwealth and Southern. Duplicating facilities would be wastefully expensive, but they would obviously be constructed wherever nonprofit agencies asked for TVA service and the power company was not willing to sell. A major part of the cost for the Commonwealth system would be the local distribution facilities which the company owned; under the TVA system, they would be owned and operated by the various municipalities and cooperatives. Dozens of towns and cities had to decide whether they would come into the TVA system, and then vote the bond issues necessary to buy their share of the existing facilities. TVA itself had to get authority from Congress to issue bonds against expected revenue for its share of the purchase.

Willkie, of course, by now had attained national prominence as the chief utility spokesman against TVA, and he kept up the role in the highly publicized negotiations of the sale to TVA. The TVA staff people wanted Lilienthal to make a short speech on the virtues of TVA for the benefit of the newsreel cameras, on the day when the Tennessee properties changed hands at the First National Bank in New York, and Willkie was to accept the check in behalf of the utility companies, but Lilienthal would not accept the advice on the grounds that it would give Willkie the chance to open up a public power debate. (TVA's part was $44 million, with the local distributors furnishing the remaining $34 million of the $78 million purchase price.) Lilienthal handed over the check from TVA; Willkie looked at it quizzically, then said, "Dave, this is a lot of money for a couple of boys from Indiana to be handling."

This particular newsreel clip reached a bigger audience than any ever before for Willkie, and from it came most of the public impression of the power company executive. It was an image of a friendly businessman, accepting with good grace the onslaught of the government juggernaut, and it had a lot to do with making Willkie the Republican nominee the next year.

5

Other aspects of the TVA program had been moving along without the problems of obstruction in the courts. Harcourt Morgan had been one of the many soil nutrition experts who shared Senator Norris's doubts about the value for fertilizer of the nitrogen plants at the Shoals. The process was outmoded, but, more important, southern farmers needed phosphates more than nitrogen. Phosphates could renew the worn-out land; nitrogen was primarily a one-time crop booster. Dr. Harry Curtis, the chemical engineer whom President Coolidge had appointed as a member of the commission on disposition of the Shoals, had had ideas about the best use of the facility ever since that time. He was brought in and told to put the ideas to work, and the result was an adaptation of electric furnaces to refine the various phosphorous compounds.

Through the years since then, TVA at Muscle Shoals has been the chief center of fertilizer research in the world. Wilson Dam and the chemical plants could never have been held for public ownership and operation without the hope that they would be the source of vast quantities of cheap fertilizer for the southern farmer, but the means of assuring that low-cost supply has been changing through the years, in line with the statutory requirement for fertilizer research. During the early years, TVA provided large-scale mass production of concentrated superphosphate to the Agricultural Adjustment Administration for distribution to farmers as part of the soil conservation program of that agency. Gradually, however, distribution has been built around a system using the fertilizers to induce farmers to follow better soil-building and farm management practices. Test-demonstration farms have naturally been more common in the Tennessee valley, but they have also been utilized in a total of forty states. The test-demonstration farms have proved to farmers that fertilized pastures and forage crops are usually more valuable than the soil-destroying row crops, and they have literally changed from brown and red to green the face of the countryside in the Tennessee valley.

Perhaps the most important technique TVA has demonstrated is the value of high concentrates of nutrients in fertilizers in cutting shipping and distribution costs—the closer the actual farming operation to the dilution with inert material or other mix, the lower the cost. County agents and the other levels of land-grant college-extension service personnel are still used for some types of educational work with farmers, but over the years the TVA agricultural personnel have learned that the average farmer has greater reliance on his fertilizer dealer's advice than on any other source. Most new TVA fertilizers, consequently, are demonstrated by offering the product through regular dealers, who receive a small discount to cover the cost of the educational promotion involved in the process. All TVA fertilizers become public patents, and any private company can secure without charge a license to produce them. Once a new fertilizer goes into general commercial production, TVA halts its own production.

Thanks largely to the impetus of the TVA program, fertilizer is the one major farm cost that has declined instead of increased in recent years. The goal of low-cost fertilizer for the farmer, which was half of the inspiration for the fight for Muscle Shoals, has been more than realized.

6

TVA's value for flood control was tested and proven during the first year after the completion of Norris Dam. The full storage capacity of the new reservoir, more than 600 miles from the Ohio, was used to hold back waters from the Ohio and Mississippi floods of that year, and the damages immediately averted were a sizable portion of that part of the dam's cost allocated to flood control. Flood control on the Tennessee includes afforestation, soil conservation, and flood plain zoning; but for the massive controls with benefits measurable far down into the Mississippi, the control has come primarily through high dams. Most TVA dams include flood storage, but the major flood control capacity comes from the highest dams on the tributaries. This same tributary dam storage system is a principal source of balanced flow for hydro power generation, and it is measured to ensure maintenance of the navigation channel on the Tennessee from Paducah to Knoxville. In occasional emergencies, TVA storage is utilized to help provide minimum navigation channels on the lower Mississippi.

TVA acquired Wilson Dam from the Corps of Engineers and Hales Bar Dam, near Chattanooga, from Commonwealth and Southern. Seven other dams with navigation locks were built on the main stem of the river. Norris was the first of a dozen tributary dams. Arthur Morgan's Miami River project was famous as a single-purpose flood control project, but the engineering team he introduced to TVA was the first to prove that multipurpose dams worked, and that failure to utilize them was wasteful.

In the construction of multipurpose facilities, costs must be allocated among the several resulting benefits. The TVA Act limited multipurpose construction to flood control, navigation, and power. TVA opponents attacked the cost allocations as stacked to lessen the burden on power. In actuality, however, both the navigation and flood control features have yielded returns much greater and much faster than even the most optimistic estimates for them. The first TVA Board, like some of the national supporters of TVA, tended to downgrade the flood control and navigation values in discussing TVA plans over the Tennessee valley, but the people of the region itself soon stopped the downgrading. Primarily because of local insistence, the dam-building schedule was prepared on a plan of one tributary dam to be followed in tandem with one run-of-the-river or main-stem dam. The old dreams of the Tennessee River Improvement Association were not to be denied.

The river control utilized for the dams was the first experience anywhere in coordinated control. Flood control operations receive priority, of course, along with the minimum navigation channel. The skill and science involved are in determining proper releases to achieve the essential flood control with a minimum of spilling through the flood gates of water then lost to the power turbines. When the power system was chiefly dependent upon hydro generation, there were a number of crises during periods of drought. In today's operation, the fullest employment of hydro is primarily a means of cutting generating cost averages.

Even before the engineering competence of the TVA dams was recognized, the beauty of their design and the accompanying landscape architecture had been widely acclaimed. Chief credit should go to the authority's first architect, Roland A. Wank, but he shares it with top officials all through the agency. So it was that TVA added an aesthetic value to the other services of the dams.

7

After the beginning of World War II in Europe, Lilienthal was quick to point out that vastly increased TVA power capacity would be of vital importance in the American mobilization for defense. In Washington he ran into some of the usual bureaucratic hassles and delays, but the first big problem was to avoid the program's being blocked by the representatives of private power who naturally dominated the power policy decisions of the Defense Advisory Commission. Despite an inevitable distrust, the dollar-a-year power men were impressed with TVA's ability to come up with specific plans and timetables for putting energy on the line. Before many months, Gano Dunn, president of General Electric, and Charles W. Kellogg, president of the Edison Electric Institute, were unhesitatingly rubber-stamping plans for added TVA capacity.

The breakthrough for TVA's defense role was not easy, however. Lilienthal's access to Roosevelt helped cut down the barriers
in the defense committees, and his private power support cleared
the way for emergency appropriations for a dam and a steam
plant in 1940. The steam plant was a new departure, although
essential for a balanced power system (two had been built by
the Army as co-adjuncts for Wilson Dam), and would have encountered fierce resistance at any other time. The step-up in
TVA appropriations enabled the agency to play a major role
in the defense effort. Two thirds of the elemental phosphorus
used in wartime munitions came from Muscle Shoals, but a more
important contribution was the electricity for the vastly expanded aluminum industry in the valley, from which came a
large part of the planes used during the war. The supply of
electricity was the basic factor in the precise location of Oak
Ridge, Tennessee, and its gaseous diffusion plants to make en-
riched uranium.

During one period, TVA had twelve separate dams and one
steam plant under construction at the same time, all fitted into
the river control system, but all for the immediate basic purpose
of more energy for war production. Construction records were
broken right and left, and there were no slipups on the basic
schedules given at the time of the appropriation requests.

During the construction of Fontana Dam in western North
Carolina, members of a congressional delegation inspecting work
on the dam were given a guided tour of the area; they were
shown the cabins for the construction workers, the library,
tennis courts, recreation hall alongside, and the well-stocked
kitchen and cafeteria provided for them. One of the congressmen protested that, even if they were in an isolated mountain
area, and unable to drive to their homes on weekends, the workers
were being pampered too much.

"Mr. Congressman," Fred Schlemmer, the construction superintendent, answered, "all of this pampering gets you the cheapest concrete being poured anywhere in the country today."

The wartime dams were not built without one bitter fight that was to leave a ten-year scar. One of the dam sites chosen as a quick power producer was Douglas, on the French Broad River, thirty miles northeast of Knoxville. Building the dam would take out a fertile stretch of river valley largely devoted to raising vegetables to be sold to the Stokely Canning Company. Senator McKellar roared up in defense of the canning company, with the support of his colleague in the Senate, Tom Stewart, and the local congressman, Carroll Reece. They were bolstered by the University of Tennessee. The resulting anomaly of the chairman of the Senate Appropriations Committee opposing a dam in his own state was both unique in its occurrence and unique in its outcome. McKellar managed to delay it, but Douglas Dam was built. It was convincing evidence of the TVA prestige developing in the Congress, but the victory would not have been won without the all-important contention that the dam was needed for power for war production.

The battle over Douglas Dam was the first head-on conflict between TVA and a congressman from the area. When the agency first adopted a policy of ignoring political recommendations in hiring personnel, there was some grumbling; but most of the members from the TVA area accepted the idea as less bothersome in the long run and went on to make a political asset out of supporting "TVA free from politics." McKellar, however, growing old and unreasoning in his post of immense power, could not conceive of such a refusal to accommodate political patronage. In addition, he believed TVA should look to him for policy guidance. McKellar developed an issue of personal prestige between Lilienthal and himself, and it was his prestige which suffered. He liked to point out that Lilienthal was a Jew from Wisconsin, but Lilienthal proved a better politician in both the

Tennessee valley and Washington, by rousing the friends of
TVA at home and over the country to resist "political interference in TVA." McKellar attempted several times to add a
rider to the TVA appropriation bill requiring Senate confirmation for all employees above a medium salary grade, but each
time he was defeated. His personal vendetta continued after
Lilienthal was nominated as the first chairman of the Atomic
Energy Commission, and gave the TVA Chairman the chance
to make his great impassioned outburst in defense of democracy
that will always be a classic among American congressional in-
quisitions. After hours of bullying questions from McKellar about
such subjects as the birthplace of his parents, Lilienthal was provoked to a spontaneous oration when McKellar asked for his
views on communism:

> My convictions are not so much concerned with what I am
> against as what I am for—and that excludes a lot of things auto-
> matically.
> Traditionally, democracy has been an affirmative doctrine
> rather than merely a negative one.
> I believe in—and I conceive the Constitution of the United
> States to rest, as does religion, upon—the fundamental proposition
> of the integrity of the individual; and that all Government and all
> private institutions must be designed to promote and protect and
> defend the integrity and the dignity of the individual; that that is
> the essential meaning of the Constitution and the Bill of Rights,
> as it is essentially the meaning of religion.
> Any forms of government, therefore, and any other institutions,
> which make men means rather than ends in themselves, which
> exalt the state or any other institutions above the importance of
> men, which place arbitrary power over men as a fundamental
> tenet of government, are contrary to this conception; and there-
> fore I am deeply opposed to them.
> The communistic philosophy, as well as the communistic form
> of government, falls within this category, for its fundamental
> tenet is quite to the contrary. The fundamental tenet of com-

munism is that the state is an end in itself, and that therefore the powers which the state exercises over the individual are without any ethical standards to limit them. That I deeply disbelieve.

It is very easy simply to say one is not a Communist. And, of course, if despite my record it is necessary for me to state this very affirmatively, then this is a great disappointment to me. It is very easy to talk about being against communism. It is equally important to believe those things which provide a satisfactory and effective alternative. Democracy is that satisfying affirmative alternative.

And its hope in the world is that it is an affirmative belief, rather than simply a belief against something else, and nothing more.

One of the tenets of democracy that grow out of this central core of a belief that the individual comes first, that all men are the children of God and their personalities are therefore sacred, is a deep belief in civil liberties and their protection; and a repugnance to anyone who would steal from a human being that which is most precious to him, his good name, by imputing things to him, by innuendo, or by insinuation.

And it is especially an unhappy circumstance that occasionally that is done in the name of democracy.

Lilienthal concluded with a heartfelt "This I deeply believe." The spectators responded with spontaneous applause, and Mc-Kellar's attack was doomed.

8

TVA personnel policy was partly laid out in the TVA Act, which required a merit system but gave full authority to the board of directors to handle all employment outside the Civil Service System. The board was required to pay prevailing wages by the law, and in 1935 it adopted an employment policy position requiring collective bargaining with employees, more than 25 years before similar action was taken for the government as a whole.

One of Arthur Morgan's first decisions about construction, fully supported by a unanimous board, was that TVA construction would be by force account—done by TVA's own employees instead of by the traditional governmental construction system of letting the work by contract. The system has worked well from a standpoint of cost alone, but also from the contribution it makes to the morale of a permanent construction corps. Contracting is now occasionally used for jobs outside the normal pattern of TVA construction, but most TVA work will continue to be homemade.

Perhaps the key to maintenance of high morale among TVA workers in the sustained effort to instill a sense of achievement in carrying forward the TVA program. TVA's early program of management-labor cooperative conferences, also adopted temporarily in many industries during World War II, has been continued as a major part of TVA's organized employee-relations program. The conferences are carried forward on each job and at each working level. Some of their suggestions have provided major improvements in efficiency, working conditions, and general economies. More important than this, they have served to make it clear that each employee is a working partner in an over-all operation that can be fully successful only with his help.

As an example of the policy's mutual benefits, it was the alertness of the TVA purchasing division, which includes a good sprinkling of people who often know more about the business of the people they buy from than the sellers themselves, which made possible the government case that cracked the price conspiracy in the electrical equipment field.

Gordon Clapp, who came to TVA in the first days fresh out of Lawrence College at Appleton, Wisconsin, and worked his way up through the personnel division to General Manager and then Lilienthal's successor as chairman of the board, is entitled to important credit for the agency's general administrative efficiency. The chief credit, however, should go to a permanent policy of encouraging full participation at all levels—of team operations throughout, with no search for either heroes or scape-goats. The TVA spirit of public service usually bestowed recognition upon its ablest practitioners only in the form of the high esteem of their fellow workers in TVA, but some measure of the quality of people the agency attracted and trained can be found in a partial listing of some who left eventually for other opportunities in government—James Lawrence Fly, Julius A. Krug, John B. Blandford, Jr., C. Girard Davidson, Henry H. Fowler, Adrian Fisher, Joseph C. Swidler, Lee White, and James T. Ramey.

TVA carefully avoided head-on confrontation with the southern pattern of segregation in the valley. It did successfully resist pressure in the early days to establish separate wage scales for Negroes, but otherwise generally accommodated to local practice. At a time when even its "separate but equal" doctrine was far ahead of other federal agencies, it still could have accomplished more. In the years since World War II, TVA's record has been well ahead of the government in general, an added tribute to its capacity for working out community problems within the community, in a geographic area where the progress has been inevitably more difficult to achieve.

9

Lilienthal and the first TVA officials helped sell TVA both to the valley and to the nation as the vibrant example of grass roots democracy on the march. It was an idealized overdramatization of the impact of TVA upon the Tennessee valley, but it was basically a correct interpretation. Most of the TVA programs could have worked better, but the success of all of them has been achieved primarily by a system of largely voluntary cooperation with local groups, either parts of local government or simply unofficial local organizations.

The power contract has been a weighty tool to use with local

power distributors in working for improved efficiency and lower
rates, but in most other programs involving agreements or close
working relationships with local groups, the carrot of anticipated
results has usually been the only tool available to help achieve
the necessary cooperation.

The TVA forestry program is an example of the change from
the concept of an action agency to one of guidance and advice
to local and private forest services. A chief forester, E. C. M.
Richards, was appointed, and he entered actively into a tree-
planting program with the Civilian Conservation Corps in 1933,
but did not present a full-scale plan of action until 1937. His
proposal included increasing the public forests in the valley from
12 to 50 per cent, with half a million acres to be retained by
TVA as a demonstration of scientific forest management and
an experiment in the development of forest-supported communities. Privately owned forests would be subject to public regulation.

As part of the Arthur Morgan controversy, the board rejected
the policy, hired a new forester, and adopted a program roughly
comparable to the general cooperative policy of the Forest Service. For a number of years, TVA nurseries supplied a major part
of the seedlings planted in the valley, but this service became
unnecessary as cooperative state-U. S. Department of Agriculture
programs were able to handle all that were needed. TVA forest
research is to some extent the equivalent of a regional service for
the valley, but it is generally much more extensive than that
available for other parts of the country, and much more adaptable
to area economic development needs. Thirty years after the determination of TVA forest policy there is still an underplanting of
trees in relation to the quality of land in the valley, but the di-
versity of responsibility between the Forest Service, TVA, and
state forest agencies makes it impossible to pinpoint the reasons
for failure to achieve the essential goals. The large acreage in the
valley in small, private tracts will probably never be utilized to

the fullest without either some kind of public regulation, or a system of incentives that will be its equivalent.

Thanks to TVA pioneering efforts, most of the valley developed the basic state fire protection and reforestation services at a more rapid pace than they normally would have come. Today, TVA's greatest service to forestry can probably be in the field of improved management and utilization and research in forest species.

The enormous recreational opportunities which developed with the TVA lakes was a surprise by-product to almost everyone concerned. In the hard times of 1933 there simply was not enough awareness of the added value of shorelines to recreation, as well as to the coming increase in fishing, boating, and swimming. TVA more than met the challenge, however, at a time when the Corps of Engineers and the Bureau of Reclamation were slow to act. There was no provision for recreation in the TVA Act, and not much likelihood that the Congress of the day would appropriate money for the purpose, but TVA gave its division of reservoir property management a responsibility for recreation that helped bring about wide utilization. The Authority built demonstration parks, donated shorelines to state and local governmental units for parks, and quickly put the Tennessee valley states ahead of most of the rest of the country in providing public recreation.

State planning agencies were absolutely essential to full use of the opportunities available to the states through the TVA programs. Some of these were established in the TVA region only through direct TVA subsidies. The cooperation of TVA's local governmental relations staff has been a major asset to all these agencies, although it is not as important to their existence today, when so many federal agencies have to work through them.

Although there has been an adaptation to cooperation with most state and federal programs which have come into being since TVA, the performance has not always been good. The chief failure was the early working relationship with the Soil Conservation Service. At the start, the problem was TVA's close ties with the land-grant colleges and the extension services, at a time when SCS was something of an orphan in the Department of Agriculture. For two agencies with such related goals, halting erosion and rebuilding the soil, it should have been possible to have worked out a better basis for joint work in the Tennessee valley. There are no major conflicts in the basic programs today, and a better effort is being made to coordinate the small watershed programs being developed by both TVA and SCS.

The best example of TVA's grass roots democracy approach can be found in the story of Decatur, Alabama. Decatur was a passed-over railroad junction cotton town on the river in 1935, when Barrett Shelton, a local publisher whose chief activity is building his town, arranged a meeting between Lilienthal and the local business leaders.

"What can TVA do for us?" the director was asked.

"TVA won't do a thing for you, but we'll help you do something for yourselves," Lilienthal replied.

Today Decatur is one of the prime examples of the economic growth of a community within the Tennessee valley—growth without the benefit of government payrolls. Shelton says he is regularly asked by visitors "Wouldn't this all have happened without a TVA?" His answer to one and all is, "It didn't!"

The "Decatur" system has worked throughout the valley, wherever there has been a real local effort, and when TVA has been free enough from its national fights for survival to respond to the request.

Lilienthal believed mightily in TVA's unique position as a regional agency operating with relative autonomy outside Washington. He had to learn his way around the Washington jungles, however, to beat back repeated attempts by Ickes to make TVA part of the Interior Department. Thanks to Lilienthal's counterpressures, none of the schemes ever reached the Congress, but they sometimes got as far as reorganization plans submitted to

Roosevelt. The TVA argument against combination was always the value of being able to approach problems without the regimented solutions of bigger agencies.

10

In the race to generate the energy for war, TVA completed all the major hydro power sites available on the Tennessee River watershed. The demand for power did not slacken; in line with the general postwar boom and shift in defense needs to atomic energy for nuclear weapons, it rose. The combination of fierce opposition by the power companies and a superabundance of caution by the TVA Board and power staff about expanding service had virtually confined the TVA power system area to Tennessee, large slices of Alabama, Mississippi, and Kentucky, and very small parts of Georgia, North Carolina, and Virginia. To meet normal load growth even for this area, with balanced generation at lowest cost, TVA had to start on a program of coal-fired steam generation, and in steam generation TVA opponents among the private utilities, and their voices in the Congress, sensed a new weapon that could eventually choke the TVA power system to death. Despite the steam plant acquired at Wilson Dam and the much larger plant built during World War II, the opponents became concerned about what they called a new departure in a governmental gargantua. Only a full-scale mobilization of every possible vote by the congressmen from the TVA territory, aided by the first flush of strength in Harry Truman's Fair Deal, made it possible to pass an appropriation item allowing TVA to build a nonwartime steam plant at New Johnsonville, Tennessee.

The New Johnsonville steam plant fight had boiled down to an almost straight party line affair in the Congress, but TVA was not an issue in the 1952 Presidential election. With a telegram to the Knoxville *News-Sentinel*, General Eisenhower pledged TVA support in a carefully hedged commitment. Apparently, however, TVA was the classic creeping socialism that the professional army officer felt he could never accept, in keeping with a philosophy of free enterprise. Emmett Hughes told of a private Presidential reaction at a 1953 cabinet meeting: "By God, if ever we could do it, before we leave here, I'd like to see us sell the whole thing, but I suppose we can't go that far." The *News-Sentinel* telegram made it impossible for the Eisenhower administration ever to take a position of open hostility to TVA, and that may have been the difference between life and death at several times during the next eight years.

The first Eisenhower budget cut TVA's operations to the bare bones. Steam generation units, started without congressional opposition during the Korean War, were allowed to be completed, but virtually all activities apart from power and basic water control were eliminated. TVA was saved from emasculation by a masterful rear-guard action in the Senate led by Lister Hill. The young Representative from the Alabama Black Belt, who had become the House sponsor of Senator Norris's bill, had moved up to the Senate in 1935. After Senator Norris's defeat, he soon became identified as TVA's most effective congressional champion. His persuasion of the Republican Senate to restore TVA nonpower developmental funds in 1953 was one of the agency's great crucial victories.

On the surface the victory looked very small, for at the same time a specific request for funds to start construction of a new steam plant on the Mississippi River a few miles north of Memphis near Fulton, Tennessee, had been turned down by both appropriations committees, and defeated in amendments offered from the floor. The Fulton plant, or some other similar increase in generating capacity, was essential if TVA was to meet the growing civilian power demand in the valley and at the same time fulfill its contracts to nuclear energy installations within the area.

The Eisenhower administration was determined not to approve funds for a new TVA steam plant, yet it could not escape the responsibility for electricity to power the gaseous diffusion units which were part of the process of building the hydrogen bombs. Given this problem, Joseph M. Dodge, the new Budget Director, was unwilling to accept advice from either TVA or his regular budget staff. George D. Woods, chairman of the board of the First Boston Corporation, the largest underwriter of private utility bonds in the country, suggested that he could make available for a TVA power study one of his vice-presidents, Adolphe H. Wenzell.

The eventual result of the Wenzell study was a recommendation that the Atomic Energy Commission contract to buy power from private sources for resale to TVA for purposes of supplying Memphis. The private source would be the Mississippi Valley Generating Company, to be formed for that purpose by Middle South Utilities and the Southern Company, which owned the power companies to the south of TVA and were headed by Edgar M. Dixon and Eugene Yates. The agreement became known as the Dixon-Yates contract. It was both awkward and costly, and also directly contrary to the federal conflict-of-interest laws, for the Dixon-Yates proposition was to be underwritten by the First Boston Corporation, the employers of Adolphe Wenzell.

TVA was being required to buy private power to supply its customers, but instead of being told to negotiate directly for it, the purchasing was to be done by the Atomic Energy Commission, to avoid the odium of the action being directly ordered by President Eisenhower. The Dixon-Yates steam plant was planned so hastily that the first designs would have built it inside the Mississippi River levee across from Memphis, an area subject to regular overflow. The president of the Mississippi River Commission, General John R. Hardin, was chastised as being uncooperative when he pointed out this discrepancy.

The revelation of the Dixon-Yates plan unleashed an uproar throughout the Tennessee valley which echoed in Congress and from Democratic orators all over the country. Wenzell's role in the arrangements went unknown during the period of the contract's first consideration by the Congress, but broad charges of sellout and corruption were nevertheless leveled by some of the members. With the help of a specific directive from Eisenhower, AEC Chairman Lewis Strauss gave the contract the blessings of a majority of his commission, but TVA resisted all the way. Gordon Clapp's term expired in the midst of the fight, but Harry Curtis, now a board member by appointment of Harry Truman, spoke up vigorously for himself and the other member, Raymond R. Paty.

A Democratic Congress elected in 1954 kept the issue alive into the next year, but there were enough Democratic defections against funds for the Fulton steam plant that the House in effect gave approval to Dixon-Yates. Even the Senate failed to provide any funds for the plant. Mayor Frank Tobey and other officials of the City of Memphis had already made it clear that Memphis would build its own plant before it would become dependent upon unregulated power from another state, but the White House wrote off their statements as part of the political bluff involved in the congressional fight. When the city officially notified TVA that it would not renew its power contract after it expired in 1958, Eisenhower asked to see the mayor. After he had heard the Memphis plans directly, he ordered the Dixon-Yates contract canceled.

There was one final unhappy note. The Dixon-Yates Company was refused termination costs by the government after its contract was canceled. When suit was brought in the Court of Claims to collect, the Justice Department opposed the claim because of the Wenzell conflict of interest, and it was eventually denied by the Supreme Court. Memphis built its own generating plant but returned to the TVA system in 1965.

Clapp's resistance to the Dixon-Yates plan eliminated any possibility that he might be reappointed as chairman of the board. With some consciousness of the snub involved, Eisenhower turned to the Corps of Engineers, and not even to one of its senior officers, in choosing the new chairman. Brigadier General Herbert D. Vogel, after he was rid of the yoke of Dixon-Yates, carried out his job in keeping with the best qualities of a Corps officer. Within the limitations imposed by the Eisenhower administration, he turned out to be a good administrator for TVA, proud of TVA's achievements and increasingly conscious of the agency's role.

The Dixon-Yates contract was not forced on TVA, but neither were any congressional appropriations for much-needed new steam plants. The failure to receive steam plant appropriations even after the unsavory aspects of the Dixon-Yates plan had been aired made it apparent that appropriations might not be forthcoming even under a Democratic President and Congress. By 1956 it became obvious that a direct self-financing plan was essential for the power program.

A plan under which TVA could finance its new power facilities through bonds sold on Wall Street, subject to the same taxation and other competitive factors involved with private power company bonds, was drawn up by the TVA staff and introduced in Congress by Representatives Cliff Davis of Memphis and Bob Jones of Alabama. The Eisenhower administration opposed this plan, and offered amendments which would have had the effect of giving the Bureau of the Budget veto power over any bond sales. The bill was the subject of bitter controversy in the House Public Works Committee for nearly three years. Most of the Bureau of the Budget ideas were defeated, but an unrealistic limitation of $750 million on the bonding authority had to be accepted.

A much more bitter pill had to be swallowed to get the bill passed on the floor. A one-way wall, which barred TVA from serving any new areas more than five miles removed from areas where TVA was the principal source of power in 1957, had to be accepted. The amendment was offered by the veteran Representative Carl Vinson of Georgia, who acted in behalf of the power companies surrounding the TVA territory. Vinson spoke for a bloc of House votes that could pass or defeat the financing bill. After Davis and Jones counted noses, they had no choice but to agree to the amendment. The Vinson group then stood by its promise and helped pass the bill, which came through the Senate in substantially the same form, guided by Senator Robert S. Kerr of Oklahoma.

A last minute cliff-hanging session still lay ahead. President Eisenhower began to talk about vetoing the bill, and there were nowhere near enough votes to override his veto. Fortunately, the 1952 telegram to the Knoxville *News-Sentinel* still had its effect. Chairman Vogel made perhaps his most important contribution to TVA when he and A. R. Jones, another Eisenhower appointee, defended the bill in a meeting with the President. After he had secured a verbal commitment from Speaker Rayburn to pass a minor amendment to the act once it had become law (to eliminate a provision involving a direct report to Congress), Eisenhower signed.

There may be minor adjustments on the fringe, but the basic TVA power service area will probably remain as it is for quite a while, political reality being what it is. The 800 square miles served by TVA get the most efficient power service in the country. Retail rates are the lowest in the nation, except for some parts of the hydro-rich Columbia valley. TVA and its distributors pay local and state tax equivalent to the average payments of private power systems. TVA has for several years been repaying into the Federal Treasury, on a scheduled installment basis, the federal funds invested, through appropriations, in the power system. In addition, each year TVA pays into the Federal Treasury a dividend amount equal to the current interest rate the government would have to pay if it were borrowing the money to finance the balance of the investment in power. The basic tax difference between TVA and the private power systems is that TVA, operating on a nonprofit basis as a part of the Federal government (its profit on the power operation is required to be plowed back into the system), pays no income tax. The private companies pay income tax on their profit, but they are free to decide for themselves the extent to which they will put profit back into their systems.

TVA competition does not seem to trouble the power companies which operate adjacent to TVA. They rank among the most efficient and most profitable private power systems in the country, with relatively low rates. Perhaps their proximity to TVA and their successful operation are no coincidence.

The TVA achievement in keeping down power costs has been primarily due to a willingness to pioneer in larger and larger generation units and transmission facilities, plus a general dedication to efficient operation. G. O. Wessenauer, the Manager of Power, has earned the grudging respect of the country's private power executives during his 23 years of running a system which is twice as big as any other in the nation. His annual budget runs more than $375 million, and his annual salary is several times smaller than that of most private power company top executives.

11

TVA had to fight hard for its very existence, both during the initial crisis of the board of directors' controversy, and the attempts at a takeover by Harold Ickes. For five years, its whole effort had to be submerged as a vital part of the war effort. The fight for survival had to be resumed in the Eisenhower years. Even today, its future is by no means politically invulnerable, as the views of Senator Barry Goldwater demonstrated during the 1964 election. In view of the scars and bruises of such struggles, it is not surprising that the authority has failed to live up to some of the high hopes of its founders and supporters. Even with these limitations, however, it is still the greatest success story of the New Deal.

Even with the help of the TVA, the Tennessee valley as a
whole ranks only with the average economic indices of the South.
A better measure might be what much of the valley might have
been without TVA, and a comparison can easily be made. In
1933, southeast Kentucky had much in common with eastern
Tennessee—both areas were Appalachian mountain country grub-
bing very little out of coal, timber, and tobacco. Individual in-
comes were far below the national average—36 per cent in Kentucky and 45 per cent in Tennessee. East Kentucky is outside the
TVA territory, and most of east Tennessee is in it. After a generation of TVA, income in the east Tennessee counties is now
68 per cent of the national average; in southeast Kentucky, it is
39 per cent. Many factors are involved in this picture, but no one
can argue away TVA's significant contribution to the difference.

Power has always been the major TVA controversy, and in
saving and perfecting the power program, there has sometimes
been too much of a tendency to avoid controversies in other
areas. Concern about power was probably the principal reason
for failure to accept responsibility, as a conservation agency, for
the destructive methods employed in strip mining coal for TVA.
The responsibility had to be assumed reluctantly, instead of being
actively sought. There has been a reluctance to take on the role
of telling the TVA development story to the underdeveloped
world, at a time when American leadership in this field should be
an all-important national objective. Operation of any governmental action agency under the limitations of the Eisenhower
years was hardly conducive to the development of bold new
ideas and initiatives.

Except for power, TVA's programs are financed by annual
congressional appropriation, and new ideas need new dollars.
Under Kennedy and Johnson, the annual budget has steadily
improved, but not with major breakthroughs. With some obvious
notable exceptions, congressional representatives from the TVA
area have drifted into the notion that the agency is without major

legislative problems, with little political sex appeal remaining, and thus worthy of little extra legislative effort.

In the years immediately ahead, TVA's programs offer the prospect of exciting challenges in a new concept of total resource development. The tributary area development program, just getting under way as a full-scale operation over the entire valley, holds the best possible chance—working with some of the other general agencies of the Great Society—to help local people on their own initiative to eliminate poverty and build a new local economic life in some of the back corners of American geography. There are new possibilities in recreation facilities and complete pollution control. An amendment to the basic TVA Act, lifting the restriction on the allocation of benefits to flood control, navigation, and power, and making possible a reallocation based on all the new concepts of water and water-oriented facilities, can bring to TVA a new opportunity to pioneer in completely integrated resource development.

« « « » » »

CHAPTER XIII

F.D.R.

1

The Tennessee Valley Authority was the most sweeping and the most successful of the natural resource programs developed during Franklin Roosevelt's Presidency, but it was by no means the only one. Even without the stimulus of striving to bring the country out of the depression, F.D.R. would have pursued the same goals, if not by the same means, for no Democrat had been so strong a supporter of Theodore Roosevelt's conservation program as had his young cousin at Hyde Park. The family estate on the Hudson was the basis of his knowledge of the land and the history of how it had fared in the years of American stewardship. F.D.R.'s attachment to the land was not the result of the passion for outdoor physical activity that was the theme of T.R., but was born instead of the gentleman farmer's concept of the role of land in the family history, and the obligation to preserve it as part of the family heritage.

Young Roosevelt found records which showed that Hyde Park produced prize corn as late as 1840, but when he took over its management in 1910, the soil was apparently too far gone to be restored as farmland. It probably could have been restored with the use of the conservation practices that were to be demonstrated by the Soil Conservation Service, and the application of the fertilizers and soil-building practices that were to be developed by the Tennessee Valley Authority, but Roosevelt was without these technological tools, so he began to turn it into forest as the best potential land use. "I am putting it into trees in the hope that my great grandchildren will be able to try raising corn again—just one century from now," he said.

Planting the trees and watching them grow was part of his own method of restoring his physical strength and mental outlook during the first hard years after his crippling attack of polio. The trees gave Roosevelt more than the pleasure of looking over sweeping green glades down to the river—he conceived them as an essential part of an intricate balance of nature to which the stewards of the land were obligated to make a contribution. Part of his pleasure was identifying each variety of pine, poplar, and hemlock to the visitors at Hyde Park as part of the conducted tour in the special-model car equipped for his driving. The depth of his feeling is obvious in an excerpt from one of his speeches: "The forests are the 'lungs' of our land, purifying our air and giving fresh strength to our people."

Conservation issues had a reality for Roosevelt far beyond the newspaper headlines of the Progressive Era, or the philosophy of the gentleman farmer. He had been chairman of the New York State Senate Forest, Fish, and Game Committee at a time when many of the fights were breaking out on the state level. Some of the fights he helped develop himself. At his suggestion, the committee invited Gifford Pinchot to inspect the state forests and to make recommendations for legislative action. The resulting bill which he sponsored included a revolutionary provision regulating the cutting of timber on private property, but it had to be dropped before the committee reported the bill, in the face of angry protests from lumbermen and farmers. Most of his committee actions were on the side of the wildlife preservationists, and he liked to tell these groups that he was one of their number as a member of the American Ornithological Union, and a member since boyhood of the American Museum of Natural History.

After his re-election as a state senator in 1912, in the brief time before he went to Washington as Assistant Secretary of the

Navy, Roosevelt was promoted to the chairmanship of the Committee on Agriculture. One of the themes of his speeches was that the liberty of the community was sometimes more important than the liberty of the individual—in practical terms, there was the possible necessity of the government compelling the farmer to put "so much lime or so much fertilizer on every acre." "Conservation of our natural resources," he said, "was the first lesson that points to community freedom."

In Washington, he maintained contact with the conservation groups, and discreetly joined in some of their campaigns to influence other agencies or the Congress, but he resisted the effort to involve himself in the fight against Hetch Hetchy, declaring that there was another side to the issue. On a trip to New Orleans he became involved in the discussion about how to control Mississippi floods, and told a local partisan of the "levees only" theory that reforestation and reservoirs would help supplement the levee system. His acceptance speech upon receiving the Democratic nomination for Vice-President in 1920 included a better conservation paragraph than any he was to use twelve years later:

> The day of "pork barrel" is gone. Every dollar of our expenditures for port facilities, for inland waterways, for flood control, for the reclamation of swamp and arid land, for highways, for public buildings, *shall be expended only* by *trained* men in accordance with a *continuing* plan. [Italics by F.D.R.]

As governor, Roosevelt had attempted to breathe life into the New York State Power Authority, to provide some of the blessings of low-cost hydro power for the people of the state. New York shared a long common boundary with Ontario, and the power companies of the northern part of the state found it impossible to camouflage the success of public power operation in that province. They mustered enough strength in Albany, however, to prevent any effective organization of a similar power body for New York State, even though there was no argument about the point that half of the benefits of the international boundary waters belonged to the United States. Some of the New York State Power Authority opponents said only the Federal government could exercise ownership of boundary waters. In the day when only the states proposed doing anything about public power development, the private companies spoke in favor of federal development; after Governor Roosevelt became President, all the talk shifted to the rights of the states for development.

The skirmishes in New York were F.D.R.'s introduction to the power companies, and the arguments used there became the more or less permanent battle line for TVA, REA, the utility holding company death sentence, and dozens of other public power battles. Roosevelt was convinced that only a federal program could adequately develop and distribute the Niagara and St. Lawrence power, and he committed his administration to this policy. The St. Lawrence Seaway was to become a massive public power project as well as a navigation channel.

F.D.R. was well aware of the lack of coordination in federal conservation programs. "Unlike most of the leading Nations of the world," he said, "we have so far failed to create a national policy for the development of our land and water resources." T.R. had given the first Presidential blessing to federal conservation, and even if F.D.R. was to fail to achieve the coherent, coordinated national policy that he realized the need for, he succeeded in instilling the whole federal effort in this field with a sense of urgency that was the hallmark of the New Deal.

2

The great landmark programs like TVA and projects like Grand-Coulee were started without much delay, but even before their arrival, the new values of conservation on the American land had been established in the Department of Agriculture. Although the immediate emergency was to save the American farmer,

Henry A. Wallace knew too that he had to save the land. Wallace had been introduced to Roosevelt by Rex Tugwell, the Columbia professor who was to be Undersecretary of the department. A good part of the public of that day, and some interpreters even to this one, painted Wallace and Tugwell's AAA as an ogre which killed little pigs and plowed up growing acres. The permanent value of the new program was that the farmer was directed toward planning with his neighbors, not just for his own farm but for the improvement of farming in general. A hard look might be necessary to discover the value of a system which paid the slowest cooperators in the economic system to learn that general improvement was in their own self-interest, but the value was there to be found.

When the Supreme Court struck down the Triple A, it was natural to substitute for it a program not only better thought out and planned, but one that was better geared to general public acceptance: the Soil Conservation and Domestic Allotment Act of 1936. Under it, farmers received their benefits not for curtailing production but for restoring soil fertility. The burdensome surplus crops were also the crops that depleted the soil, and the theme of the Wallace program for the future was building instead of destruction.

Most of the New Deal conservation programs were based on the people's relationship to the land. Some of the most spectacular failures, such as Tugwell's Resettlement Administration, were really permanent successes in that they established public responsibility in the field.

3

In his eight years out of public office, 1920 to 1928, Roosevelt carried on his private reforestation program at Hyde Park and was involved in a half-dozen efforts to promote private financing for large-scale forest farming to prove the value of sustained-yield management. As governor, he continued to promote tree planting, private and public. In 1931, as about-to-be-candidate Roosevelt, he received a letter from a lumberman in Gloster, Mississippi, F. A. Anderson, with a "plan for relieving unemployment and replenishing forest growth." Anderson proposed to put 40,000 young men to work in each of the thirteen southern states, planting trees on 400,000 acres of cutover timberland acquired for that purpose. The tree planters would be paid one dollar per day and be enrolled in a "forest reserve department" of the Army. Other similar suggestions were made a little later. In his Chicago acceptance speech, F.D.R. proposed to put a million men to work in forestry programs over the nation. The Civilian Conservation Corps came from that.

Louis Howe, Rex Tugwell, and Frances Perkins put the plan into legislative form, and it went to Congress before the end of March. Agriculture and Interior would prescribe the various work projects, all with conservation value and not limited to simple tree planting. The men would be recruited by the Labor Department, and the War Department would administer the program.

Congress passed the bill in a week's time, but even in that week there were outcries over the precedents that its adoption would break. William Green, president of the American Federation of Labor, called it fascism, Hitlerism, and sovietism, and the Communist party said it would "establish and legalize a system of forced labor." The echoes of these charges lingered longer than the soon familiar one of "boondoggle." It took a while for the pedantic students of unemployment, like John Dewey, to realize how quickly 300,000 boys were off the streets and into the woods. The thousands of unemployed and underemployed reserve officers, eager for work or a living wage themselves, were the most obvious administrative officers for the camps. Thirty dollars a month might sound like a low wage, but the biggest pay was abundant food, with barracks and work uniforms thrown in. Health was a major by-product of the good food and hard work outdoors, and there were few serious complaints of military atmosphere.

Six weeks after the bill passed, more than 1,300 camps had been designated and were in the process of being built by the first recruits. The enrollment reached 300,000 in July and climbed as high as 500,000 in 1935. Before World War II ended the experiment, more than two-and-a-half million unemployed youths had been enrolled in the CCC. They planted more than two million acres of trees and thinned out the overgrowth in four million more acres. Countless thousands of other acres in the national forests were saved by the half-million miles of fire trails, breaks, and forest roads which they built and repaired. Many of the national parks have never had as much attention, and dozens of state and county parks blossomed from land they prepared.

The economic dividends, in the generation since the work began, have probably equaled the cost of the program, with a good part of them paid directly to the Federal government in the form of increased yields from federal forests. A 1963 sampling of privately owned lands planted by the CCC in the Tennessee valley showed that they were yielding their owners a net of better than twenty dollars an acre more per year than similar untreated lands.

The human dividend was obvious from the start. Alumni of the CCC were among the most valuable members of the military services a few years later, and they are sprinkled across the top today in places of leadership in business, labor, and government.

The Forest Service was the most active agency in the operation of the CCC, and the service was immediately given dozens of other jobs in the first year of New Deal planning. Major R. Y. Stuart, the chief of the service, broke down from overwork, but his successor, Ferdinand Silcox, was equal to the challenge of serving under Forester Roosevelt.

Most of F.D.R's attention as a private citizen conservationist had been devoted to plans for forestry, public and private. As

President, he kept the Forest Service busy planning several projects for vast new acquisitions; although he never sent the projects to the Congress because their over-all cost was too great, he still added vast acreages to the national forests by purchase. It was the one period when large sections of timberland were available at a reasonable price, and a President willing to give rein to the Forest Service in acquiring it was a wonderful coincidence.

The shelterbelt tree planting program on the Great Plains was one of F.D.R.'s special interests. It was oversold to the public at first as a cure for dust bowls, but the planting program, handled largely with relief funds, ranks as a major achievement of the Forest Service. Because the President wanted direct legislative authorization for this program after the relief system became impractical, he supported Senator Norris and Representative Wall Doxey of Mississippi in passing a law which provided federal assistance for both public and private tree planting, and which established technical advisory services for the private tree farmer.

Special government services for tree planting, possibly through some permanent type of organization like the CCC, were part of F.D.R.'s plans for a postwar America that did not get beyond the talking stage. He wanted the lungs of the land to always be available to give fresh strength to the people.

4

In the early days of the Public Works Administration, while its administrators still were looking for useful projects instead of being buried under applications, Harold Ickes allocated five million dollars for terracing projects to check farm erosion. Tugwell reported that the best expert on erosion was in the Department of Agriculture, a longtime government geologist named Hugh Hammond Bennett. After he heard Bennett's ideas about what could be done, Ickes set him up in the Interior Department as head of a new bureau, the Soil Erosion Service.

Bennett had learned soil problems firsthand, growing up in the hard struggle for existence on a well-cared-for, but still worn-out, farm in the Pee Dee Basin of North Carolina. After working his way through the University of North Carolina, he had gone to work for the old Bureau of Soils. He was assigned to prepare a survey of Louisa County, Virginia, where he first defined sheet erosion after studying fields where the original eight or nine inches of topsoil had been gradually washed off after each rain through long years of cultivation.

In later years he liked to talk about this simple discovery of how constantly cultivated land had gradually washed away in miniscule sheets, while adjacent fields containing the same soil characteristics, but left uncultivated in woods, were virtually intact. "The red, yellow, and black colors of floodwater running away to the sea are no reflection from the sky," he said, "the color of such floodwater is produced by the color of the soil material in suspension. This material comes from the surface of the ground, the best part of our fields, and thus impoverishes the land."

In Fairfield County, South Carolina, in 1911, Bennett surveyed and reported on 136,000 acres of once-good land, destroyed by gully erosion or by deposits of erosion debris washed off higher land. He made surveys in most of the major farming areas of the country, but mostly in the South. The people knew the land was worn out and growing worse each year, but they had never before had anyone to tell them how it had happened, or why. In 1918, he was promoted out of the field surveys, and from a desk in Washington had a chance to both write and talk about the extent of erosion and what to do about it.

Bennett's crusade against erosion did not get formal support until 1928, when the USDA gave its official imprint to his paper, "Soil Erosion, a National Menace." In the House of Representatives, John Buchanan of Texas, whose family had moved west from a worn-out South Carolina farm, listened and produced an amendment appropriating $160,000 for a national program of research in soil erosion. For four years the Bennett program proceeded primarily under Buchanan's sponsorship (Buchanan was ranking Democrat and later chairman of the House Appropriations Committee). Most of the experimental work was in Texas, but it went forward with the zealous effort that was part of everything Big Hugh Bennett did.

The dust bowls of 1934 and 1935 brought home the Bennett message better than anything he had ever said. In 1935 Roosevelt transferred his bureau to the Department of Agriculture, where it was named the Soil Conservation Service. Bennett shepherded the Soil Conservation Act through the Congress, establishing soil conservation on every acre of farmland as part of the national conservation responsibility. Buchanan was followed by dozens of other congressmen potent in the field of agricultural legislation or appropriations, who grudgingly or lavishly acceded to the Bennett programs. The Bennett record was backed by Bennett's skill in telling his story and presenting his evidence. A hearing on the Soil Conservation Service bill before the Senate Public Lands Committee that included Carl Hatch and Carl Hayden was proceeding one day, with Bennett testifying, when the Capitol building itself was almost blacked out by a dust storm which had originated two thousand miles away. It was Bennett luck, but also Bennett strategy, for he had helped time the hearing for a period when the winds were supposed to be bringing the dust east.

Bennett always made it clear that there were no magic answers to the problem, that the farmer had to do most of the job himself, through terracing, crop rotation, contour plowing, fertilizing, and sometimes wholesale moving to grasses, but that his service would be ready to give him help. The old Triple-A approach was to evolve into incentive payments for carrying out conservation practices, and SCS fieldmen were to be based in every rural county. The Farm Bureau-Extension Service hierarchy at first resisted a separate SCS with roots down to every county, and eventually, but too often unfortunately, the SCS became part of it. The SCS program, working through farmer-chosen soil conservation districts, was a refreshing innovation from the start, however, and helped carry into practice the New Deal theory of a community responsibility in the farmer.

5

Edward T. Taylor had come to the House from Colorado in 1909 as an avowed enemy of Pinchotism. The popular doctrine for most Colorado officeholders during the period was state control of the public domain and even of the national forests. Taylor joined in the clamor that was demanding freedom from Washington. For most of his rancher constituents, freedom from Washington usually meant the right to graze their cattle and sheep on the public domain without effective regulation, and without fee. Taylor through the years helped preserve this freedom, and, in the process of establishing seniority on the House Appropriations Committee, became the most influential House member from the public lands states.

Conservationists of the Pinchot-Garfield era had warned against overgrazing, but the stockmen had answered that the domain would never give out. Pinchot persuaded them to accept regulated use of the national forests, but no law on grazing in the domain was passed after 1897. The predictable deterioration of the range was accompanied by a deterioration of the cattle industry. Taylor gradually realized that only effective regulation of the public range could save it from destruction, and that such regulation also would stabilize and save the livestock industry.

In 1932, President Hoover's Departments of the Interior and Agriculture asked for a regulatory bill but got no results. The next year, Taylor, the former leading opponent of regulation, introduced the bill to allow the Interior Department to regulate grazing and collect fees. A Grazing Service was established within the department to administer the act. Interior and Agriculture were traditional rivals for the right to handle the program, but both Secretaries Wallace and Ickes lobbied vigorously for the Taylor bill, which F.D.R. pronounced part of his program.

The Taylor Grazing Act became law in 1934, and is still the basis for administering grazing on the public domain. During the first twenty years of its life, conservationists had to be mobilized from time to time to resist attempts to weaken it, but they won all of the big fights. The law stands as a fairly permanent reminder that, upon occasion, the most rugged opponents of conservation programs can be converted when they see the light of intelligent self-interest.

6

When F.D.R. became President, only one American farm in ten had electricity. Most of the nine farms without it had to get by with coal oil lamps and hand pumps, if they were lucky enough to have them, for water. Electricity meant more than lights; it meant running water. Nine out of ten farms also had no bathtubs, and nearly as many were dependent upon privies. The power companies did not believe that rural electrical service would pay a greater return than the cost to build and maintain the facilities, and, except in the most thickly settled and prosperous rural communities, they simply were not built.

Occasionally, in the twenties, when electrical service was being completed for the small towns of the country, a voice would be raised about an obligation for rural service, but the effective answer had always been that rural service would have to mean higher rates in the towns and cities. When Governor Gifford Pinchot made his Giant Power Survey in Pennsylvania in 1923, the fear of increased city rates killed the chance of any implementation of the survey recommendations, which included the idea of rural electric systems as well as an over-all grid connection that would make all electric service more efficient and less expensive.

Morris Llewellyn Cooke was an Ivy League conservationist in

the same tradition as Pinchot. He was a Philadelphian who described himself as a management engineer by profession, and who had started out as Director of Public Works for Philadelphia more attracted by the social implications of management than by its technical details. Pinchot had suggested that he adapt his ideas to improvements in electrical service with the Giant Power Survey, and Roosevelt used him for consultation with the New York Power Authority. Cooke's first job in the New Deal was to direct the Mississippi Valley Survey, paid for by a Public Works Administration grant. The result was an imaginative outline which accepted the necessity for coordination of physical and social resource development, but which had been worked out largely without local participation or awareness of its far-reaching potential; with no local base for political action, it was destined to be honored largely by being ignored. The Mississippi valley report did stress, however, the opportunity and the need for a federal rural electrification program.

F.D.R.'s message to the Congress in January 1935 mentioned rural electrification as a task for the relief works program. By Executive Order on May 11, he established the Rural Electrification Administration with Cooke as administrator. Before the month was out Cooke had solicited and received a rural electrification plan from a committee of private power companies. The private power plan amounted to little more than a suggestion that most of the hundred-million-dollar allocation given the REA program be turned over to them to underwrite the cost of rural transmission lines and connections. Cooke rejected the plan, for it included nothing that would lead to expansion of electrical service throughout entire rural areas.

During the next few months, the REA headquarters on Massachusetts Avenue (located in an old mansion that had once belonged to Frederick Westinghouse) became something of a reviewing stand for a parade of ideas on how to achieve rural electrification. Relief workers could not do it—too many engineering and technical skills were needed. The existing cooperative movement could not handle it, partly because some of its leaders wanted no dependence upon government finance. Municipally owned power systems could not be expanded to serve the national rural need, because they were hemmed in by local restrictions and state laws. The power companies were not interested in low-interest loans, if they carried government requirements for a low-cost area service.

The solution eventually arrived at was a combination of all three of these approaches. TVA had helped organize and finance a local distribution system for Alcorn County, Mississippi, to supply the first rural customers for power at Wilson Dam, and this demonstration served as the model for the nationwide system of rural cooperatives financed with low-interest REA loans from Washington. The Executive Order had to have the implementation of specific law, and there were two ready sponsors available. Sam Rayburn of Texas and George Norris of Nebraska were liberals primarily because they believed the intervention of the government was necessary to relieve the grinding, monotonous poverty and labor of rural life. Rayburn's parents had migrated to east Texas, seeking to escape the rural poverty of post-Civil War east Tennessee. As an old man, he was to tell about bleak days of boyhood on that Texas farm—walking down to the road to try to escape the loneliness, so that he could look out down that road that must lead to something that was better. And George Norris remembered how "I could close my eyes and recall the innumerable scenes of the harvest and the unending, punishing tasks performed by hundreds of thousands of women . . . growing old prematurely; dying before their time."

In the House, Rayburn was joined in sponsorship of the REA legislation by John Rankin of Mississippi, a Southerner in the radical-populist tradition of Tom Watson. Although destined to end his career in bitter, ugly anti-Semitism, he was unchangingly dedicated to public power. Rankin wanted to ban REA loans to private corporations, but his efforts were important in establishing a firm principle of preference for nonprofit cooperatives.

The power companies began to realize the propaganda value of rural service when the REA bills passed both Houses without even the necessity of a roll call on final passage. Bitter battles began to head off the formation of well-based cooperatives when the power companies started skimming off the cream of the rural neighborhoods. Cooke and his protégé and successor, John Carmody, found that they had to step up the extent of assistance from Washington to get some of the co-ops organized. There was a flurry in 1939 when Carmody resigned after REA was made an agency in the Department of Agriculture, but the new administrator was Harry Slattery, the long-time Pinchot associate who had been the spark plug of the National Conservation Association and the foremost fighter for such conservation causes as the Teapot Dome investigation.

7

Rural electrification, now virtually complete over the nation, will probably always rank as the greatest transformation government ever brought to American life. The miracle of electricity has revolutionized the daily pattern of all life, but TVA and REA showed that it did not have to be denied to the most primitive American existence.

One reason for the relative ease with which the REA bill passed was that it came on the aftermath of the savage fight to destroy utility holding companies. No matter what role they might have played in the "death sentence" fight, most congressmen were anxious to make it clear that they were not opposed to electricity for farmers. The fight over the Rayburn-Wheeler bill to eliminate the holding companies was the first major mobilization of the entire financial community of the country against the New Deal. Its marks are still visible a generation later, for it was also the point at which anti-New Dealism began almost automatically to include the identification of anti-public power. The holding company struggle came at a time when Democrats were at their peak of numerical power in the Congress, and it was more a fratricidal fight among Democrats than it was between parties. As the Republicans in Congress began to resurge, however, they almost automatically adopted all anti-New Deal postures.

The collapse of the Insull Empire revealed that a vastly watered nonproductive structure of immense interlocking overlay had been built on the private power system, and that the money was to be made in financing the system rather than in selling power. The exposure produced major public incentive for federal law to cleanse the system. Samuel Insull, London-born, had been secretary to Thomas A. Edison. He established one of the first large electric utility systems in the country, based in Chicago, and then he moved on from selling electricity to selling stocks in a vast public utility holding company combine. It was valued, at its inflated height, at more than three billion dollars. The complicated structure of interlocking directorates collapsed in 1932, leaving the electric companies at the base of the paper pyramid to struggle out from under the burden of superfluous capital cost. Insull fled to Greece. He was eventually acquitted of embezzlement charges, but the general view of the operation he had built was probably characterized in a comment by N. M. W. Splawn, counsel for a House investigation, when he said, "These holding companies manufacture nothing, so far as I can find out, except securities."

Senator Burton K. Wheeler introduced the bill which passed the Senate, including clauses providing for elimination of utility holding companies and one allowing the Federal Power Commission to establish regional interties of power companies for increased operating efficiency. The power grid clause had to be watered down to a permissive version which was destined to have practically no effect, but the holding company clause, popularly called the "death sentence," became the first legislation to mobilize the financial structure of the country for the task of saving the American economic system. Testifying against it, a long string of power company executives warned, like the president of Electric Bond and Share, that the bill would "nationalize these industries just as sure as I am standing here." John W. Davis, the noted lawyer who was the Democratic nominee for President in 1924, identified the bill as "the gravest threat to the liberties of the American citizen that has emanated from the halls of Congress in my time." In the House, even Chairman Rayburn's influence was not sufficient to induce approval of the holding company death sentence by the Commerce Committee. The language it eventually used in compromise, however, did provide considerable power in defeating the companies. According to the Scripps-Howard newspapers, which were supporting the bill, there were more power company representatives in Washington than there were congressmen. Representative Owen Brewster of Maine, who had fought the utilities as governor of Maine and was elected to the House as a strong supporter of the Passamaquoddy tidal power project, told the House that he was going to vote against the death sentence because Tommy Corcoran, the fabled White House assistant, had threatened to kill the Quoddy project unless he voted right. A Rules Committee investigation showed that Corcoran had very likely not been so direct in his attempts to keep Brewster's vote, but the uproar that resulted was enough to make it possible for Senator Hugo Black of Alabama to begin a hard-hitting investigation of the whole utility lobby.

The Black investigation was attacked by the American Civil Liberties Union for the seizure of letters and telegrams under its subpoena power, but it was a revealing explanation of the methods used by the utilities in fighting the holding company bill. An estimated 5,000,000 letters and 250,000 telegrams in opposition to the bill had been delivered to Capitol Hill. The sponsors of the legislation were convinced that most of the messages had a common origin, typified by those received from Warren, Pennsylvania, where the manager of the town's Western Union office testified that he had orders from the local utility manager to send Representative Denis J. Driscoll one thousand telegrams a day. The names signed to the messages from Warren had been collected by a messenger boy at three cents each, or simply copied in alphabetical order from the city directory.

Despite the reaction that resulted from the Black investigation, the House still refused to vote for the outright death sentence clause. The compromise language written as a substitute by the conferees proved to be strong enough to have the same effect, however. The holding companies disappeared from the utility organization table. The change helped to bring about a general reduction in cost per kilowatt of electrical generation, although the holding company's fight established a precedent for the astronomical lobbying cost that was to continue as a major part of the total power cost.

F.D.R. found that new men and new ideas would change the outlook of the Federal Power Commission to one for initiative and action in the public interest. Leland Olds, whom Governor Roosevelt had named chairman of the New York State Power Authority, was named chairman of the Federal Power Commission, where he built a great career as a champion of power regulation in the public interest.

8

Projects do not emerge out of the pork barrel by accident. America's largest dam, the Grand Coulee, was plucked out and started on its way by Roosevelt during the first 100 days, but it owed its existence to a long, bitter, and bruising fight by a small group dedicated to an idea that it could be the one tool for economic uplift for their region.

The Big Bend country of the Columbia valley in eastern Washington State was pleasant, pretty country to see during good rainfall years. The homesteaders had begun to dribble in after the

Civil War, and they came thick and fast around the turn of the century, during the period when the miracle of small, sometimes individual, irrigation schemes were being promoted as a means of making permanent farms out of western dry lands. A few years after 1900, however, overfarming began to take its toll. A dry cycle set in, and one homestead operation after another was abandoned to bankruptcy or turned over to large grazers who could afford to wait it out. Spokane became the center of eastern Washington promotion of a giant irrigation project for the Columbia valley, through the use of gravity flow from the Columbia tributaries in Idaho and Montana.

A handful of men in Grant County, however, conceived a combination irrigation and power project through a huge dam on the Columbia that would collect the water and generate the power to pump it several hundred feet higher into the Grand Coulee, a great natural trough that had been the stream bed of the Columbia during an ice age period when the normal stream bed had been blocked. Their ideas grew out of horseback engineering and windshield surveying, but some very limited state-financed surveys gave them support. There was a great deal of talk and promotion for the project around 1920, but it faded out as it became obvious that only the Federal government could possibly assume the cost, and the government was taking on no such projects at the time.

The Grand Coulee plan revived, however, in 1928 when word got around that the Army Engineers were evaluating the idea as part of their 308 survey of the Columbia basin. The new interest coincided with the return to Grant County, which he had left to go back to his native Michigan after going bankrupt in 1920, of James O'Sullivan, one of the original Grand Coulee boosters. O'Sullivan had first come West as a lawyer, tried his hand at teaching, and then gone broke at farming before going back to Michigan, where he was a small-town contractor. His great talent, however, was promotion, and Grand Coulee today is the monument that his hand was the largest in building.

O'Sullivan was for four years the Columbia River Development League. There were a dozen or so knowledgeable and faithful leaders of his organization, and although none were rich, in the first four years of the depression none were very busy, either, and they were able to devote valuable time to its work. O'Sullivan kept the organization alive by securing, as donations to the league, hotel and restaurant due bills which he could use in lieu of salary. Postage and gasoline came from one-dollar memberships that he individually solicited, even though he occasionally had to accept a pants pressing in lieu of that cash minimum. His letters of solicitation to the farmers who would benefit from the project brought replies like this: "You are no doubt wondering why I have not sent you the five dollars I should have sent you the 1st, but I simply haven't got it. I never have seen cash so completely stopped. I spoke to the parties on the list you gave me, and most of them said they were very short of cash."

One volunteer solicitor for memberships collected twelve dollars for the cause, and then yielded to temptation to use the money to buy groceries. He was not reprimanded, in the hope that he would eventually be solvent enough to restore the money. Such was the luxury of pork barrel promotion during the depression.

O'Sullivan kept working because of sheer fortitude, and possibly also because in the early 1930's there were no other job opportunities for even a man of his talents. Nobody opposed the idea of irrigation from the Columbia, but he had to fight not only indifference, but a well-organized, well-financed campaign for a gravity dam plan which was backed by the private power companies of the area, most of the railroads, and a state reclamation agency. He could absorb an audience with a dramatic story, however. He told of a visit to a privately owned dam, and of watching the spinning turbines . . .

. . . creating ceaseless wealth for men that perhaps never saw this power project. Then I turned and looked out along the

Columbia and watched its ten million horses racing madly to the
sea. I recalled the bitter fight that has been made by these barons
of wealth to prevent the people from harnessing just a part of
these steeds—from seven to ten million powerful horses racing
down the Columbia and serving no purpose. These horses require
no feed, no care or no stalling. They never tire and never die.
Imagine a team 250 miles long and you will get an idea of the
power to be utilized.

Then I looked over that vast desert waste of several millions of
acres and I saw the tragedy that had happened there. Thousands
had lost their all in the hopeless fight against the desert. With
courage they had remained, eking out a pitiful existence, hoping
for the day when the water would come. And I wondered if the
country of Washington and Lincoln and Jefferson would permit
greedy men to deny those pioneers the use of only a part of what
belonged to them, a right earned by settlement and made valuable
by their sacrifices in the building of a commonwealth.

The district engineer, Major John S. Butler, recommended the
Grand Coulee giant pump irrigation project as feasible; the critical
element in his decision was a favorable projection of a market for
the electricity to be generated. The Board of Engineers in Washington turned it down, however, asserting that Butler was many
times too high in his estimate of the market for power. Elwood
Mead of the Bureau of Reclamation was more sympathetic, and
was willing to adopt the project for Reclamation, but the Bureau
of the Budget refused to allow him to submit it, and Grand Coulee
prospects seemed bleak.

The year was 1932, though, and rejection in the carefully cultivated House Irrigation Committee was not necessarily decisive.
Franklin Roosevelt virtually committed himself in support during
the campaign speech he made at Spokane. Senator Wesley Jones,
chairman of the Senate Commerce Committee, had become a
Grand Coulee supporter as a result of O'Sullivan's missionary
work, but an even more outspoken supporter, Homer T. Bone, an

all-out public power advocate, swept Jones out of office in the fall voting. Clarence Dill had been a more cautious Democrat in his support, but after the election he caught fire.

Roosevelt decided to take a short cut around the still long pathway to authorization and appropriation. The public works section of the National Industrial Recovery Act allowed him to designate a comprehensive plan of public works and allocate funds to it from a lump sum appropriation. He allocated $63 million to start the Grand Coulee Dam project, to be built by the Bureau of Reclamation.

A few weeks earlier a new state administration in Washington had established the Columbia Basin Commission to represent the state officially in promoting the project and to act in liasion with the federal agencies during construction and operation. Jim O'Sullivan was named secretary of the state agency, but it turned out to be a temporary job. During most of the time when he continued to carry forward the fight for Grand Coulee appropriations, he still had to worry about his next meal. Ultimate recognition came for O'Sullivan in 1948, when Senator Warren Magnuson pushed a bill through Congress which specified that one of the Grand Coulee tributary dams be named the O'Sullivan Dam. A month after the then-Potholes Dam became the O'Sullivan, Jim O'Sullivan died.

Grand Coulee is still the largest and most majestic of all the dams in the United States. Its total cost has exceeded $200 million, but in the economic life of the Pacific Northwest it has paid constant dividends; Major Butler's power market estimates proved conservative instead of inflated. When F.D.R. pulled Jim O'Sullivan's project out of the pork barrel, he set the stage for a long line of journalists and opposition politicians to prove themselves worthy successors to scoffer Proctor Knott.

9

From his observation post in New York State, Roosevelt was well aware of the repeated failures of the Biological Survey. His solution was to appoint the most widely known amateur game and fish conservationist in the country as the new head of the agency. Thanks to *Literary Digest* reprints, Jay N. "Ding" Darling was probably the country's best-known newspaper cartoonist, but his hobby of wildlife promotion had made him a leader in various organizations in the field. Roosevelt gave him the chance to put his theories into action.

The theories were fine, but most of them involved more money for ducklands and other wildlife refuges than could be conjured up. The administration-sponsored 1934 Duck Stamp Act provided about $700,000 a year, but nowhere near enough for the Darling program. Darling sought funds from PWA and other emergency relief allocations, but never received what he regarded as a fair share. By campaign time in 1936 he was back in his Republican cartoon harness, and making speeches for Landon in addition. Darling's chief complaint was the failure to stop hunting completely for a year, as demanded by the Audubon Society, but the public in general paid little attention to his relapse to Republicanism, assuming that old habits were too strong.

In 1937, Senator Key Pittman of Nevada and Representative A. Willis Robertson of Virginia put through a bill providing for a tax on sporting arms and ammunition, which has been the basis of financing cooperative programs with the states in wildlife research and management. With the Duck Stamp, the Pittman-Robertson Act has been the basic source of revenue for wildlife programs since that time. The Duck Stamp fee has twice been raised, and now all Duck Stamp revenue is required to be used in the purchase of migratory bird sanctuaries.

A 1939 Roosevelt reorganization plan transferred both the Biological Survey, then still in the Agriculture Department, and the Bureau of Fisheries of the Commerce Department, to Interior. The next year, the two bureaus were merged into one unit: the Fish and Wildlife Service. This merger was undone to an extent in 1956, when a new law created a new U.S. Fish and Wildlife Service and divided it into two bureaus: Sports Fisheries and Commercial Fisheries.

The most important postwar legislation in the field was the 1946 Coordination Act, which improved upon a similar bill passed in 1934. It wrote into law previously informal requirements that all new federal water projects include provisions to prevent or minimize damage to fish and wildlife at the project site. The means of achieving this was a requirement that all such projects be referred to the Fish and Wildlife Service for comments on their effect on wildlife values, and its recommendations to eliminate damage. In 1958 the law was affirmatively amended to change the emphasis from preventing damage to one of improving the wildlife resource as a part of the project. The stimulus provided by the former chairman of the New York State Game and Fish Committee has not been lost.

Most of the New Deal's innovations and achievements in the conservation field had been begun by the time the first term came to a close. Most of them are standard landmarks a generation later, but the undying contributions were the new spirit and attitude among those responsible for conservation, and the wider and clearer realization that the government conservation programs would protect and develop the land and water for the benefit of the people.

«« «« «« »» »» »»

CHAPTER XIV

Labored
Progress

1

Roosevelt's selection of his Secretary of the Interior had been almost an afterthought. He first offered the post to two western senators who turned it down, and after that considered it unnecessary to continue the western monopoly on the post. Harold Ickes, a Chicago lawyer, had hoped to be appointed Commissioner of Indian Affairs. When Roosevelt checked into his background, he found all the credentials of a full-fledged Bull Moose Progressive. With very little fanfare, Harold Ickes became Secretary of the Interior.

Ickes was the son of a local politician in Altoona, Pennsylvania, sent to Chicago for an education after the death of his mother. He went from the University of Chicago into newspaper work and politics at the same time. Both as a newspaperman and as an avid spectator and participant in Chicago politics, he got a close view of corruption in operation. The era of the Democrats, when the Carter Harrisons, father and son, both served terms as mayor, kept him a Republican without qualms, but after he came really close to some of the local Republican operations, he had no choice but to be a Progressive Republican and stay on the outside. He dropped newspapering and took up law, and was free to continue his political crusade on most of the issues of the day, local or national. After 1912, he was one of the most consistent of the Progressives, never getting national attention but always in touch with the Progressive names over the country. In 1932, he tried to organize a campaign backing Gifford Pinchot for the Republican nomination. After Hoover's renomination, he joined the switch to Roosevelt.

Ickes' 1932 effort for Pinchot was probably his closest touch with the conservation crusade of the progressive movement. Most of his progressive motivation was based on his stand against political corruption. He was destined to be Secretary of the Interior for thirteen years, but for the first eight years his most important role was as head of the Public Works Administration, dispensing the vast sums poured into the New Deal recovery program with the hope that they would also be of permanent value to the country. Whatever reputation he earned for bellicosity and extravagant rhetoric, he also deserved one for pugnacious incorruptibility. That reputation was a major asset to the Roosevelt recovery program, and his jealous guardianship of the national interest in the massive public works programs is visible today in many of the buildings, roads, and other works still rendering useful service to the nation.

Ickes was quick with his tongue, but slow and cautious in exercising his own initiative. He was vainglorious, self-righteous, and suspicious; and these traits left him few close friends either in the New Deal bureaucracy or along the other avenues used to evoke the favorable public opinion needed to support the empire-building within the Interior Department which became his goal. He fully supported the Roosevelt-Pinchot conservation doctrine, but he mastered it so slowly that he was in no position to push for the kind of enlargement and reorganization of his department that could have given it a bigger role in the first years of the New Deal.

Thanks to his personality traits, all streaked with stubbornness, Ickes lost what should have been valuable years of conservation development in vainly pursuing foredoomed fights over reorganization and procedure. The wasted hours and years of agency infighting and heightened rivalries between agency constituency interests were to some degree inevitable, but a more realistic Secretary of the Interior could have salvaged much more out of them.

From the start, Ickes had a reputation among the New Dealers as a man with an eye out for agencies to add to Interior. Once Roosevelt sent him to Florida on a fishing vacation with Harry Hopkins, and must have thought a telegram from Hopkins enough of a dividend from the trip: "WHEN HAROLD GOT A STRIKE THE OTHER DAY . . . FIRST THE ROD AND REEL AND THEN HAROLD WENT OVERBOARD AND WE HOPED FOR A BRIEF MOMENT THAT WE HAD LOST THE BEST FISHERMAN IN THE CABINET. BUT NO LUCK. HE CAME UP WITH A COUPLE OF HENRY WALLACE'S BUREAUS."

Ickes' first attempt to enlarge the scope of his department involved no agency reorganization; it looked like nothing more than a title change. Interior would become the Department of Conservation and Works. Roosevelt gave him the go-ahead to have the bill introduced, but never either officially endorsed it or barred other administration officials from actively opposing it. Once Ickes told the President that the bill would pass if he would only lift his little finger, but F.D.R. never lifted it. It did pass the Senate in 1936, but only with the general expectation that it would be allowed to die in the House, which it did.

The renaming of the department might have been managed rather simply if Ickes had not preceded it with definite rumblings about the necessity of putting the Forest Service back in Interior. Pinchot, who had engineered the Service's shift to Agriculture thirty years before, was quickly aroused, and the jealous antagonism of the forestry people was to haunt Ickes for the rest of his time in office.

In the early days of the Public Works Administration, Ickes had called back to government service Louis Glavis, the Land Office martyr of the Pinchot-Ballinger episode. Ickes made him a sort of inspector-general of PWA and gave him a free hand to root out any sign of corruption or irregularity. But Glavis was too suspicious even for the man who had made his Chicago career out of pointing to signs of dishonesty. "These investigators have become persecutors, man hunters, and they are just as eager to hunt and drag down members of my staff as they are lobbyists and crooked contractors," he said. In his reaction against both Glavis and Pinchot, Ickes turned to his questionable vindication of Ballinger as a persecuted public servant.

2

A good part of the history of F.D.R. and water development programs was the struggle to bring national planning into the picture and to establish administrative control over the Corps of Engineers. The same effort continued through the Truman administrations. Considerable progress was made toward both goals, despite the fact that the fight rarely received the full attention of the President, and that his administration was usually represented by a weak agency with no legislative base, the National Resources Committee.

Roosevelt apparently paid little attention to the activities of the Corps until prodded into action by Senator Norris, who put through a resolution in February 1934 requesting a report from the President on "a comprehensive plan for the improvement and development of the rivers of the United States; with a view to giving the Congress information for the guidance of legislation which will provide for the maximum of flood control, navigation, irrigation, and development of hydroelectric power." The resolution was the result of all the requests for action on river basin development plans "like TVA." Roosevelt used the request to come forward with a National Resources Board with Ickes as its nominal chairman. The board was financed by a grant from PWA funds, and Ickes was determined to prevent the board's becoming an independent agency. This identification with Ickes, already out to build his Conservation Department, was to be a severe handicap in Roosevelt's effort to give the board the legislative power to coordinate water resource development.

Frederic A. Delano, uncle of the President, was the most distinguished city and regional planner in the country, but his advanced age made it difficult for him to keep the board unified after he was named its chairman following its reorganization as the National Resources Committee in 1935. His age was also a handicap in building support in Congress, where the name Delano was a healthy target for those still afraid to attack F.D.R. direct. Charles E. Merriam of Chicago was the most forceful member of the committee, but some of his very force and personal differences with his colleagues made him as much a divisive influence as a contributor.

In 1934, the Resources Board set up a water planning committee, including a representative of the Corps of Engineers, to submit a preliminary planning report as the first step in response to the congressional resolution. Doubts expressed by Secretary of War George H. Dern, speaking for the Engineers, are worth noting for the provincial view at so late a date:

> . . . putting an end to stream pollution seems to have little or no connection with improving the streams for navigation, flood control, power or irrigation, because it is chiefly a matter of the construction of sewage disposal plants, which so far has been a municipal question. . . . And so it goes. Each of these activities is a special problem to be handled by a special group of experts if satisfactory results are to be obtained. . . .

The most interesting part of Dern's letter to the President, however, was his reference to the Corps of Engineers "as an agency of the legislative branch." Somehow this particular sentence must have escaped the attention of the President.

Senator Royal A. Copeland of New York, chairman of the Commerce Committee, introduced the legislation proposed by the

President to establish a permanent National Resources Board. The bill was reported out of committee but did not reach the floor before adjournment in August. The same bill was introduced and then tabled in the House Public Lands Committee the next March. It became obvious that normal procedure would not get it through Congress, so in May, Carl Hayden joined Copeland in offering the plan as an amendment to the 1936 Flood Control Bill. Joseph O'Mahoney of Wyoming moved to send it to the Public Lands Committee, stating that he was fearful that the plan might interfere with Secretary Ickes' plan for a Department of Conservation. The O'Mahoney motion carried, and the plan for the board went to the Lands Committee, where it died. O'Mahoney's action is indicative of the confusion that prevailed and of the lack of urgent administration support for the plan. The Wyoming senator, elected in 1934 from a subcabinet position, was no defender of the Corps of Engineers. A dozen years later he was to be the vocal champion of the Hoover Commission plan to transfer the Corps to the Interior Department.

The 1936 Flood Control Act was a milestone despite the loss of the National Resources Board. For the first time, federal responsibility was assumed for flood control work; the step was inevitable after the Mississippi Valley Flood Control Bill of 1928. Thanks to the direct intervention of Roosevelt, the bill was amended to include legal recognition of the complementary relationship between the improvement of waterways and the prevention of erosion on the watersheds. It established the improvement of watersheds as a policy of Congress, with investigations of watersheds and responsibility for soil-erosion prevention to be under the direction of the Secretary of Agriculture. This placed a specific responsibility for flood control in small watersheds in the Soil Conservation Service.

The watershed amendment was a direct result of a pamphlet entitled "Little Waters," by H. S. Person, prepared for the joint use of the Soil Conservation Service, Resettlement Administration, and Rural Electrification Administration. The three bureau chiefs, Bennett, Tugwell, and Cooke, promoted it widely among conservation groups, and Roosevelt was a convinced reader. It was the most successful effort since W J McGee to demonstrate the social significance of every aspect of flood control.

In 1937, the House Flood Control Committee picked up a resolution introduced by Representative John McClellan and Senator Hattie Caraway of Arkansas calling for the Chief of Engineers to submit to Congress a national flood control plan for all the streams of the country. The House committee added direction for a report from the Department of Agriculture for watershed flood control and sent the bill toward passage. It was a logical and far overdue improvement in the long record of congressional and Corps indifference to national planning in the field of waterway development, but it contained two fatal flaws—it ignored the executive department, and it confined the purpose of waterway control to flood control. Roosevelt pleased his Uncle Fred by vetoing the bill.

Congress completed action on a general reorganization bill for President Roosevelt in 1939, but pointedly omitted his request for a National Resources Board. A specific provision of the bill exempted the Corps of Engineers from any reorganization plan the President might submit to Congress under the powers given him in the bill. The National Resources Committee struggled as Roosevelt's rather limp arm in coordinating water development under a new name, the National Resources Planning Board, but Congress killed it outright in 1943 by rejecting entirely his appropriation request.

After the death of the planning board, the Bureau of the Budget took over the task of administrative coordination in the field, with considerably more powers but with neither an adequate staff nor an adequate orientation on goals and policy in the field of waterway development. This role continued for some twenty years, until the Kennedy and Johnson administrations came back to the idea of a White House water resources planning unit.

In the meantime, significant improvements were made in spelling out federal responsibilities and improving Corps of Engineers procedure in the flood control acts of 1938, 1941, and 1944. The 1938 act provided for much broader powers in acquiring rights-of-way and reservoir land at federal expense, for it had become obvious that some of the most imperative work would never qualify under the earlier restrictive authorization. The pre-eminence of multipurpose development was fully established, not only for flood control and navigation, but, after 1944, for irrigation and hydroelectric power. Full federal payment for reservoir costs was written into the law through the joint efforts of House Majority Leader John McCormack and Flood Control Committee Chairman Whittington. McCormack believed that only by this means could dams be built on the Connecticut and Merrimack Rivers, and Whittington had already established full federal costs for Mississippi valley flood control. McCormack persuaded Roosevelt to agree to the language as a step toward public power installations in New England. Ironically, the power companies managed to block any effective New England flood control system until the destructive floods of 1955.

The 1938 Flood Control Act authorized the Engineers, upon recommendation of the Federal Power Commission, to put penstocks for eventual power turbines in some dams, but no direct authority for the production and marketing of hydroelectric power was given the Corps until the 1944 act. Direct intervention by the President and some heavy fighting on the floor of both houses were necessary to attain the complete multipurpose authority. It would probably not have been approved at all but for the fear that further blocking of this authority for the Engineers would lead to passage of valley authority plans for the Columbia and Missouri.

Under the power amendments, the cost attributable to power would be repayable to the government, but under no specific time-table. The power would be marketed by the Interior Department, with the same provisions for preference customers, and authority to build transmission lines to take the power to load centers. These powers have been limited sharply for specific projects and areas, but the basic preference system has stood up despite some heavy attacks.

The broad new authority and responsibility given the Corps in the three major flood control bills led to vast building programs after World War II. Specific basinwide planning had been di-rected and authorized for a number of rivers, and the Corps pro-ceeded on a coordinated plan of development more advanced than in any previous works. The pork barrel system for water pro-grams had been successfully defended, but in the process some of its worst transgressions were being slowly and painfully mini-mized.

3

After TVA survived its first court tests and began to sell power from its new dams, nationwide interest in similar regional agen-cies developed, and in at least half a dozen river basins there was active promotion for development through an agency similar to TVA. After some months of behind-the-scenes discussion, argu-ment, and delay, Roosevelt sent a message to Congress on June 3, 1937, urging, in effect, six additional TVA's. George Norris and John Rankin promptly introduced bills to put the plan into action.

The proposed machinery for the new operation was shaky, however. The exact organization of the new regional agencies (the Missouri valley, the Atlantic seaboard, the Great Lakes and Ohio valley, the Arkansas, Red and Rio Grande valleys, the Colo-rado River valley, and the Columbia River valley) had to be ob-scure in the first draft, to allow for compromise on the specific details that some of the regional boosters undoubtedly would seek.

Part of the delay in perfecting the legislation was a result of Ickes' insistence on over-all Interior Department authority, including an unsuccessful effort to take over the TVA. The proposal ran head-on into overwhelming opposition from the power industry, now mobilizing against any new loss of territory like that represented by TVA, from the Corps of Engineers that claimed it could do the job better, and from the Department of the Interior and its Bureau of Reclamation, who thought the plan might be acceptable only if it were all a part of Interior. The bills were never given serious committee consideration, even though the scare they raised is still occasionally thrown up at utility company stockholders on appropriate political occasions.

A young congressman named Clyde Ellis came to Washington in 1939 on his election theme of an Arkansas River authority. He successfully urged the idea upon Congress, President Roosevelt, and the State of Arkansas, and was making progress with all three until he made the mistake of testing the issue in a statewide senatorial race. After Ellis lost and left the Congress, he became one of the organizers and chief Washington representative of the National Rural Electric Cooperative Association, the spokesman for the REA cooperatives of the country.

Governor Culbert Olson of California talked repeatedly with Roosevelt about an authority for California and asked David Lilienthal for detailed plans. Olson's reluctance to consider a program that might be dominated by the Interior Department eventually deflated the whole idea.

In 1949, President Truman's plan for a Columbia Valley Authority received a hearing before the Senate Public Works Committee, but the only river valley authority proposal which received full-scale attention was the one outlined for the Missouri valley. The active sponsorship by James Murray of Montana was enough to get that plan before the Senate, and a crusade in its behalf by the *St. Louis Post-Dispatch* kept the proposal before the country.

The rapid progress in building up the responsibility and authority of the Corps of Engineers in the 1936 and 1938 Flood Control Acts brought about amendments to the Reclamation Act in 1939 which gave the Bureau of Reclamation much the same multipurpose authority. Most of the Missouri and its tributaries were in the reclamation states, and one of the motives behind the support for MVA was the need to head off wasteful duplication and rivalry between the two agencies. The financial restrictions of World War II kept most of the development at the planning stage for several years.

Colonel Lewis A. Pick, division engineer at Omaha, drew up one of the first basinwide plans for the Missouri in 1943, spurred by the regional interest in a plan for postwar construction activity. The Pick plan naturally emphasized flood control and navigation, for it evolved before the Corps had authority to plan hydroelectric development. W. G. Sloan, assistant regional director for the Bureau of Reclamation stationed at Billings, Montana, had been working on a detailed plan for the Missouri and tributaries on the basis of the 1939 authority given his agency. After the Pick report was publicized, Sloan quickly issued a draft of his report. Missouri valley senators saw the possibilities involved in both programs, and began to move to authorize them in the Flood Control Act of 1944, already pending.

To head off this uncoordinated authorization, Roosevelt in September, asked the Congress to create a Missouri Valley Authority. When it became clear that the MVA would not pass that year, Roosevelt tried to make the best of the situation. He ordered the Corps and the bureau to meet and reconcile the two plans. The resulting shotgun wedding was no more than the sandwiching of the two plans, but it was the first joint planning by any two major federal resource agencies for a basinwide program. In brief, the Pick-Sloan plan would have the Corps build the larger dams on the main stream of the river, for flood control and power, with some navigation and irrigation features in the lower and upper stretches of the river. The bureau would build most of the tributary dams for power, flood control, and irrigation, but with all the structures by both agencies meshed for the best use of waterfall and stream flow. The plan was written into the 1944 Flood Control Act.

In 1945, Roosevelt again submitted the MVA plan to Congress, and its supporters severely criticized Vice-President Truman for referring the bill to the Commerce Committee, considered to be strongly against it. In the long run, however, the referral was not too important, for there simply were not enough votes in the Senate as a whole to pass the bill. After Truman became President, he made clear his support, with no difference in the result.

After the failure of the MVA, better basin coordination was achieved with the creation of the Missouri Basin Interagency Commission, which consisted of representatives of six federal agencies and the governors of the five states that chose to participate. The Interagency Committee is cumbersome, with little real power, but it is a step forward in regional planning, even for those who decry the idea of "outside" planning. It is a formal assurance of agency consultation in basin development, and adequate reporting of its meeting gives the region possibly the only full picture of programs and plans. The interagency idea is now used in some form for most of the major river basins. Senator Robert Kerr secured the adoption of a similar interagency program for the Arkansas-Red River. For the Missouri basin, presently authorized programs for the Bureau of Reclamation and Corps of Engineers alone exceed more than two billion dollars. MBIC planning is a vast improvement over previous lack of coordination procedures.

4

Harry Truman's major statement of conservation policy was in a section of his special postwar policy message of September

1945. He said, "Conservation and development of the national plant must proceed according to an intelligent and coordinated design. The watersheds of this nation are not utterly independent, one of the other; our irreplaceable wealth of minerals, land and timber is not composed of segments which can be dealt with separately. . . ."

The holdup on major development programs and an all-out assault on public power by the Republican 80th Congress gave Truman a ready-made issue for his 1948 campaign. The election results in the western states show how successfully he exploited it. The Korean War and the conservative 82nd Congress prevented a lot of potential progress in the conservation field, but Truman proved a loyal supporter of the major concepts of the Roosevelt conservation programs. Perhaps his greatest achievement was civilian control of atomic energy development, at heart a conservation issue even though it is a topic not attempted for consideration in this volume.

Truman vigorously supported Mike Straus, Commissioner of Reclamation, in his back-to-the-wall defense of the 160-acre limitation (actually 320 for man and wife) for federal irrigation, first established in 1902 by the Newlands Act. The 160-acre limitation, along with aspects of the public power argument, was part of the bitter struggle during the 1940's between the Bureau of Reclamation and the Corps of Engineers over the Kings River development in California. The Kings River fight was a classic example of how two agencies can be wastefully self-defeating in rivalry that eventually becomes pointless. Some political scientists have used the Kings River story to demonstrate the administrative insubordination of the Corps of Engineers. The Corps obviously transgressed, but usually under the direction of its traditional authority: congressional committees. The blame should probably rest on the White House for not exercising more discipline when it had power to do so. The Kings River area was the big loser, thanks to both agencies, as a result of the long-delayed development.

The fact that postwar government was costing more than prewar government shocked the Congress, and one of its out-growths during Truman's time was the Hoover Commission on economy and efficiency in government. The commission proposed transfering the civil functions of the Army Engineers to the Interior Department. Widespread lip service to economy plus the regrown prestige of Herbert Hoover might have put the plan across as part of a reorganization act, if the same Hoover Commission had not called for vast cutbacks in all federal con-servation and water development programs, all at the same time. Opponents of the change charged that the commission's recom-mendations would mean the end of water programs, and this general fear resulted in a sharp limitation of the reorganization power. The Corps of Engineers was not specifically exempted from the reorganization authority, but it was unofficially ex-empted by silent agreement.

Truman-appointed commissions wrote two highly valuable reports: the William S. Paley Commission on Materials and the Morris L. Cooke Study on Water Resources. Neither, unfortu-nately, produced new laws or programs, but both have provided rich fields for research and ideas.

CHAPTER XV

From Pause
to Movement

1

Dwight Eisenhower's campaign for the Presidency had included few specifics on conservation. He came to the office with strong commitments about economy in government, but few promises for resource development programs.

The Eisenhower budget officials were left a good working tool for their economy policy by one of the last official acts of the outgoing Truman budget director, Frederick J. Lawton, when he signed what was to become the famous budget circular A-47. The circular was designed to provide a uniform procedure for the Budget Bureau's use in evaluating requests for funds from the water development agencies, but it was also designed to give the bureau additional weapons in denying requests, especially for projects that included power. The Eisenhower budget officials not only accepted A-47, but strengthened its restrictive interpretations.

A-47 was a helpful supplement to the new administration's policy barring the starting of any new water project construction. After being rigidly adhered to during the first year, it was modified to include approval of such major programs as the Upper Colorado River and the St. Lawrence Seaway, where there was overwhelming local Republican support. Eventually,

routine water projects were cleared if they met A-47 specifications, but during the Eisenhower years most of the new starts
for any multipurpose program that included power were passed
by Democratic congresses over administration objections, even
after the Eisenhower "partnership" system had been allowed to
wither and die.

The partnership idea was an attempted compromise between
river basin development and the ideology that opposed government generation and sale of electric power. Under the partnership plan, the government would pay the portion of the cost of
a multipurpose dam allocated to navigation, flood control, and
other nonreimbursable benefits, but would allow private power
companies to pay for and take title to the power generation
portion of the structure. It was a modification of the old Hoover
Dam idea, where separately owned turbines had been installed
in the dam. The administration defended the plan as supporting
private enterprise and cutting capital costs to the government,
and opponents assailed it as a direct subsidy to the power companies at the expense of the taxpayers. The basic premise in
multipurpose development was that shared costs on the whole
project would make it less expensive for all beneficiaries. Giving
the power companies part-ownership in the projects was so obviously detrimental to comprehensive basin development that
few partnership systems were ever approved and built.

The partnership policy spelled the end of hope for public
power in many long-planned projects like the Kings River in
California, and for comprehensive multipurpose development for
the Snake River in Idaho. Hell's Canyon was the site of the high
dam on the Snake planned by the Corps of Engineers as part of
its over-all program for the Columbia basin. The Idaho Power
Company proposed to build three smaller dams without irrigation or water storage values, and had the support of the administration. Democrats kept the Hell's Canyon plan alive by passing
an authorization bill in the Senate, but the bill always lacked a

vital vote or two for clearance in the House Interior Committee.

Even after the Federal Power Commission granted a license to the power company, the Hell's Canyon supporters fought desperately for the high dam. In 1956, a bill by Senator Wayne Morse of Oregon to authorize the Hell's Canyon dam was defeated on the Senate floor 51 to 41. In that same year Eisenhower's Secretary of the Interior, Douglas McKay, left the Cabinet to run against Morse. After soundly defeating McKay in an election which had been made a referendum on Hell's Canyon and the Eisenhower conservation and power policies, Morse brought the same bill to the Senate and passed it, 45 to 38. Then Hell's Canyon died in the House Interior Committee with the close of the 85th Congress.

The Upper Colorado River project, involving major dams for irrigation and power, was authorized under the Eisenhower administration, but power was not a part of the controversy. The Interior Department proposed to include a dam at Echo Park, which would have damaged some of the best scenery in the Dinosaur National Monument, and wildlife and conservation groups split sharply with public power advocates in opposition. When most of the Democrats in the House who normally supported power projects refused to go along with Echo Park, the plan was amended to drop the idea, and the Upper Colorado became an important victory for the park preservationists.

The one important victory for public power during the Eisenhower administration was brought about by a rockslide at Niagara Falls. After a treaty ratified in 1950 made it possible for both Canada and the United States to develop the long-discussed hydro potential at Niagara Falls, the Truman administration endorsed a plan for federal construction of the American facility. Representative William E. Miller of New York proposed instead that five private companies in the area build the plant and sell the power. In 1953 his plan was rammed through the House by an overwhelming vote, but Senator Herbert Lehman of New York managed to keep the bill from the Senate floor by vigorously pointing out that it was a violation of the 1920 Federal Power Act preference provisions. In May 1956, Lehman's bill to have the facilities constructed by the New York State Power Authority passed the Senate and was approved by the House Committee. The Democratic leaders of the House Public Works Committee were reluctant to take the bill to the House floor, however, because their count indicated that the Miller plan would be adopted as a substitute. On June 1, 1957, a massive rockslide destroyed the Niagara Power Company's 365,000-kilowatt generating capacity plant at the falls. In the resulting emergency, the power company agreed to accept public power at the site, if the New York Power Authority would be required to guarantee the company 445,000 kilowatts for thirty years. Lehman still preferred a direct federal program, but accepted the compromise for New York State development after it had been worked out by Senator Kerr and Judge Sam Rosenman who represented the state authority. Even with the compromise, many congressmen who had been supporting the private power position decried the "sellout to socialism."

The New York State plant at Niagara Falls, with a two million kilowatt capacity, is second in generating capacity only to Grand Coulee among American hydro generating stations. Under the authorization bill, half of the power is required to be sold subject to the terms of the federal preference clause, with at least one fifth available for neighboring states. The state authority is also required to include in its sales contracts with private companies provisions for maintaining low generating cost benefits for ultimate consumers.

2

The signal success of the Eisenhower administration in the resource development field was the authorization of the St. Lawrence Seaway in 1954, sixty years after the idea first gained widespread attention. Fighting against the Seaway project for some thirty years was a profitable lobbying industry, and the final victory will be one of President Eisenhower's permanent landmarks, even though he brought about passage of a narrower project than the original one worked out during the Roosevelt administration.

When Grover Cleveland appointed a study commission in 1896, the idea of a waterway for ocean shipping from Duluth, which Proctor Knott had derided, to the Atlantic by way of the Great Lakes and the St. Lawrence River was already bubbling. Concrete plans began to emerge after World War I, promoted by a combination of business interests on the lakes and in the Midwest and visionary resource developers. Under Franklin Roosevelt, a treaty was negotiated with Canada which provided not only for the deepwater navigation, but for a new dimension: joint development of power from the Lachine Rapids west of Montreal.

The treaty was given a bare majority vote in the Senate in 1934, considerably short of the required two thirds. After that effort the St. Lawrence project was always presented to the Congress as an authorization bill, to avoid the two-thirds problem. The leading Seaway support came from the western Great Lakes states—although the railroads always managed to keep this support from being unanimous—and the wheat-producing states of the northern Great Plains. The only nonregional support came from public power advocates, along with the inveterate resource developers who could not resist the attraction of the 2,300-mile link between Duluth and the Atlantic with a massive power development along the way. The opposition consisted of all the railroads in the country, the lake carriers, the East Coast and Gulf shipping interests, and all the elements of normal opposition to public power, including the coal industry.

The pre-World War II opposition sometimes sounded like the 1830's instead of the 1930's. Great alarm was voiced concerning the dangers of a thousand-mile stretch of water from the Atlantic to Montreal, all surrounded by land controlled by Great Britain. England had been our enemy once, and might be again. The opposition to the power development was just about as realistic. "There has been enough hydroelectric power already developed in that region, however, to satisfy all needs for half a century to come," said William E. Woollard, president of the New York State Waterway Association in 1936.

In March 1941, Roosevelt concluded an executive agreement with Prime Minister MacKenzie King of Canada in which the two countries agreed on a plan for joint construction of the Seaway. A 27-foot navigation channel would be provided all the way, and the two nations would share the power generated at the International or Lachine Rapids. Most of the construction would be in the stretch from Montreal west to Ogdensburg, New York. Senator George Aiken of Vermont came to the Senate as a champion of the Seaway. He attempted its authorization as a part of the 1944 Rivers and Harbors Bill, but lost by a heavy vote.

No President tried harder for the Seaway than Harry Truman, especially after the Canadian Prime Minister, Louis St. Laurent, told him that his country was going to build the navigation facilities alone unless the United States acted. Truman had made Lewis Pick, the co-author of the Pick-Sloan plan, his Chief of Engineers, and Pick set an historic example as an engineer chief working in behalf of administration policy. He was an imaginative officer dedicated to resource development as a major economic development tool, and the Seaway should be one of his credits, even though it came after his retirement.

The major obstacle to Truman's success with the Seaway was the House of Representatives, and he performed minor miracles in the fight to overcome opposition there. Representative Charles Buckley, chairman of the House Public Works Committee, was from New York City, historically solidly opposed, but Truman persuaded him to become an active backer. The President himself promoted a switch in the committee assignments of three Democrats who opposed the Seaway. Unfortunately, the only Republican House vote for the Seaway was a member from Detroit, thanks largely to a rigid policy of the House Republican leadership that made opposition to the Seaway a prerequisite for appointment to the committee. Despite the best efforts of the President and the chief Seaway supporter on the committee, John Blatnik of the Duluth district, they failed by two votes. After the bill also failed in the Senate, Truman acceded to a Canadian request and approved a plan for joint power development by Ontario Hydro and the New York State Power Authority, regardless of the fate of the Seaway.

Important iron ore deposits were found in Labrador around 1950, and the M. A. Hanna Company of Cleveland became the chief operator in this field. George Humphrey, chosen by Eisenhower as his Secretary of Treasury, was head of the Hanna Company, and known as one of the most active business supporters of the Seaway when he came to the cabinet. After the Eisenhower endorsement, Republican votes appeared, and the Seaway was authorized by a comfortable margin. Queen Elizabeth came to help Eisenhower dedicate it in 1959.

Even though now, seven years later, the Seaway is still icebound for four months out of the year, those opponents who blocked it for so long with cries about the waste of taxpayers' money might be interested in the fact that the eastern port groups are now organizing a campaign to establish a more "realistic" (higher) schedule of tolls on the system.

3

Partly to offset the lingering bad taste of Teapot Dome, there was some talk in the 1920's about federal conservation policy for oil and gas and other minerals, but it was little more than talk. "Conservation," as far as it relates to oil and gas, doesn't mean much more than state and federal regulations designed to help large oil producers control production. Conservation regulations are essential for any properly controlled producing area, but the term has been too often mixed with mere production restrictions.

The first federal action in the field was an amendment to the NRA Act of 1933 sponsored by Senator Tom Connally of Texas, unsought by the Roosevelt administration. The Connally "hot-oil" amendment, later passed as a separate law, forbade the interstate shipment of oil produced in excess of state quotas or regulations, and was designed to bolster the price of oil by helping to regulate production. An interstate compact, applying also to natural gas, has supplemented this regulation since 1935, and has been renewed regularly by the Congress.

President Eisenhower's 1952 campaign partially hinged on the most hard-fought federal oil issue since Teapot Dome, and he had to make a decision in a major legislative controversy over natural gas. The discovery of oil and gas in the "tidelands" between the low-tide mark and the historic offshore boundaries of California, Louisiana, and Texas, brought an immediate campaign to give title to these submerged lands to the states, even though the Supreme Court had ruled them the property of the Federal government. To counteract this campaign, Senator Lister Hill proposed legislation to keep the tidelands in federal ownership and dedicate the oil and gas revenue to a program of federal aid to education. President Truman's veto threat had prevented the enactment of the bill to give the land to the states, and left the issue for decision in 1952.

Republican candidate Eisenhower announced himself in favor of state ownership. For coastal states with offshore oil and gas or hopes of it, the issue was simply whether they or the Federal government got the money. Potential producers of the oil and gas wanted state control also, and they managed to convince many of the interior states that a basic question of states' rights was involved. Texas Governor Allen Shivers tried to persuade Democratic candidate Adlai Stevenson to endorse state control. When Stevenson refused to do so, Shivers declared himself for Eisenhower for President.

The tidelands bill giving title to the states quickly became law in 1953. The next year the Congress did pass a bill establishing federal authority over the mineral deposits under the outer continental shelf.

From 1947 through 1954 a series of Supreme Court decisions established the authority of the Federal Power Commission to regulate natural gas rates. Various proposals to exempt natural gas from this authority were pushed in Congress, and President Truman vetoed one which passed in 1950. A bill for gas exemption was narrowly passed in the House, 209 to 203, in 1955. The fight shifted to the Senate with the assumption that Eisenhower would sign the bill.

In February of the next year, Senator Francis Case of South Dakota told his colleagues that a lobbyist employed by the Superior Oil Company of California had offered him a campaign contribution of $2,500 if he would vote for the natural gas bill. Case voted against the bill, which passed the Senate 53 to 38, and his revelation brought a veto from Eisenhower because of the "arrogant" efforts of some of the supporters of the bill who were "creating doubt among the American people concerning the integrity of governmental procedure."

Another bill slightly less sweeping in the exemptions it provided gas producers was worked up for House action in 1957. It cleared the Rules Committee but was put over until 1958. Before the bill came to a vote that year, the House Republican Leader, Joe Martin of Massachusetts, was the speaker at a Lincoln Day dinner at Houston. In selling tickets for the $100-a-plate affair, the Texas Republican National Committeeman, Jack Porter, mailed out a solicitation to oil and gas men, saying, "It will be up to Joe Martin to muster at least 65 per cent of the Republican votes in order to pass the gas bill this year. . . ." Martin knew nothing of the letter, but when it was published by the *Washington Post*, the natural gas bill was dead. The shadow of Teapot Dome still serves the national interest.

4

The upstream water control theory publicized in "Little Waters," which Roosevelt had presented in 1936, gradually evolved into a direct responsibility for watershed flood control in eleven river basins enumerated in the Flood Control Act of 1944. For the first time, there was responsibility for major flood control work (usually called flood prevention). It was given to the Department of Agriculture, and assigned to the Soil Conservative Service. Although authorized in 1944, no appropriations were made until after the war.

The new flood prevention concept offered many agricultural areas their first hope of respite from flooding without the price of long-delayed reservoirs inundating rich bottomlands, or levee systems so costly they might not prove to be economically justified. The program of improved pasturage and tree planting, together with a series of small reservoirs, was beneficial for the upstream and tributary watersheds of most river systems, and was eagerly sought throughout the country. One of its added attractions was considerably less demand for cash contributions by the local beneficiaries. The popularity of this program brought about the first major soil conservation legislation of the postwar era.

Senator Aiken and Representative Clifford Hope of Kansas, the Republican chairmen of the two Agriculture Committees, were sponsors of the Small Watershed Act of 1954, which provided for coordinated watershed flood prevention programs carried out by watershed districts in cooperation with the SCS. President Eisenhower made the enlarged plan an administration measure after the House Appropriations Agriculture Subcommittee had greatly increased the pilot watershed program by adding 62 new streams to the original 11. The Hope-Aiken bill allowed the watershed reservoirs to be built only for flood control and irrigation, but two years later comprehensive amendments were enacted which allow the addition of municipal and industrial water supply, fish and wildlife develoment, and recreation facilities as appropriate components of the projects, in addition to providing for larger reservoirs and easier methods of financing the local costs. In the ten years since, a number of additional amendments designed to improve the program have been passed, and the appropriations for it have steadily increased.

The small-watershed program was thus made more liberal in its allowance of project benefit justifications than the more traditional Corps of Engineers and Bureau of Reclamation projects, although liberalization for these two agencies came in the Kennedy administration. Like its parent, soil conservation, the watershed program was often oversold in terms of the total remedy it could provide for a river basin. In both programs there was talk of returning to nature's way of "holding the raindrop where it falls," and doing away with the necessity for big dams and levees. This theory conveniently ignored the fact that there were major floods in the country several thousand years prior to its settlement; it also ignored the extensive new runoff problems that changes in agriculture and urbanization bring each year. The eagerness with which so many benefits to urban life were added to the Soil Conservation watershed program merely proved that comprehensive basin development—watershed, tributary and mainstream—was essential to the fullest utilization of the river resource.

The Eisenhower administration helped provide full multipurpose development of watershed flood prevention programs, and it also gave the endorsement of law to a long-developing multiple-use program for the national forests. This was the first major change in forestry management law in this century, and it largely ratified the system of a management already in effect. That the governing law was not a continuing target for change is an effective tribute to the systems established by Gifford Pinchot so long ago.

The Forest Service began a timber resources review in 1952, though its final report was not made until 1958. The review covered all forest lands in the country, but the portion devoted to national forests was used as a basis for a long-range national forest program submitted to Congress in 1959 by Secretary of Agriculture Ezra Taft Benson. One of the results of this report, together with action by the American Forestry Association, was pressure for Congress to write into law a statement of policy for the national forests, which became the Multiple Use Act of 1960.

As first presented, and as first reported to the Congress, the new bill put more emphasis on sustained yield from the forests than on multiple use. After a group of Democratic conservationists raised the possibility of a floor fight involving the conservation issue, the bill was amended to give first priority to multiple use over sustained yield. The multiple-use goal was listed for five basic resources: outdoor recreation, range, timber, watershed, and fish and wildlife. There was a clause making allowance for future development of wilderness areas in the forests.

The law prescribed that the forests resources would be so managed "that they are utilized in the combination that will best meet the needs of the American people . . . and not necessarily the combination of uses that will give the greatest dollar return or the greatest unit output."

5

The record of the Kennedy and Johnson administrations in the conservation fields has been one of exceptional legislative achievements, but an attempt to evaluate the achievements in relation to the history of the conservation movement would be premature and would lack sufficient perspective. As with many other legislative subjects, much of the accomplishment has been the resolution of issues hanging fire from the time of Roosevelt and Truman. Under President Johnson, however, a great deal of new ground has been broken and new goals and directions laid out. An evaluation of the legislative approach used by Johnson will have to remain for the future, but his readiness to attack broader problems deserves high credit.

The true measure of President Johnson's interest and commitment is yet to be made, however. In spite of his laudable enthusiasm for natural beauty, he has not yet faced up publicly, for example, to the politically unpopular but urgent question of whether dams in the Grand Canyon are a wise or necessary part of the Colorado project. And while he effectively supported Wilderness legislation, he has apparently not been willing to lend the prestige of his support to equally worthwhile and even more urgent projects such as protection of the redwoods in the Far West, the Indiana Dunes on Lake Michigan, and the Maryland shoreline of the Potomac.

Silence on matters such as these suggests unneeded political compromise, and seems to bespeak a less than full commitment to conservation goals. Beyond the commitment itself, there is also the requirement that it be backed up by equally determined efforts to obtain the appropriations that are essential if the goals, so widely pronounced, are to be achieved. In this respect, too, there is as yet no real indication of realization of what is needed or the determination to obtain it.

A good example of an issue resolved under the Kennedy and Johnson administrations is the establishment of the federal role in the attack on water pollution. The federal role was set out on a limited basis in 1948, with enactment of a five-year program of grants to the states for pollution studies, and the establishment of a Public Health Service pollution research facility at Cincinnati, later to be renamed the Robert A. Taft Sanitary Engineering Center. The program, which also authorized a low-interest loan fund for sewage treatment works, was routinely extended for three more years in 1952.

After the administration had requested another routine extension in 1955, Representative John Blatnik, chairman of the House subcommittee handling the legislation, decided to bring out a vigorous antipollution bill. For the first time, procedures were established for federal action against pollution violations in the event that the states took no action. Research and research grants were stepped up. The administration was expected to have to accept these changes in the law without public protest, but a careful calculation had to be made as to how much would be attained in the way of federal grants to localities for sewage treatment works. Five hundred million dollars over a ten-year period was the figure settled on. President Eisenhower signed the bill but commented that the grant program went beyond his request.

In fact, the grant program proved too modest, for the cash incentive moved hundreds of communities to plan and construct sewage disposal systems as they began to meet an essential responsibility for the first time. Despite this, in his 1959 budget message, Eisenhower asked the Congress to eliminate the program. The Democratic response was to pass a bill increasing the grants from $50 million to $90 million a year. Final passage was held up until 1960, both to avoid a pocket veto and to increase the pressure for signing the bill in an election year, but Eisenhower vetoed it anyway, declaring that the responsibility for pollution control should be left with the states, localities, and private industry.

The Eisenhower antipollution veto, together with the "no new starts" policy in water projects, was a minor but persistent theme in the Kennedy campaign against Richard Nixon. The contest was so narrowly decided that any one of many issues could be credited with giving Kennedy his victory, and the Republican record on pollution control and water policy are issues which could be so rated.

The first major bill passed under the Kennedy administration was a much-strengthened version of the bill Eisenhower had vetoed. The sewage grants were stepped up to $100 million a year, research was expanded, and federal enforcement powers were again increased. In 1965, a new Water Quality Act further strengthened enforcement powers, and set the sewage treatment grants at $150 million a year. Senator Edmund Muskie of Maine had become chairman of the Senate subcommittee handling antipollution legislation, and one of the most active legislators in the field. A strengthened air pollution abatement program had also been passed, and President Johnson's 1966 plan to place all antipollution activities in the Interior Department was a logical step toward continued improvement in the program.

One of Kennedy's greatest contributions to the conservation movement was the appointment of Stewart L. Udall as Secretary of the Interior. No Secretary since Garfield has been more personally dedicated to the conservation ideal, and his efforts and achievements may eventually rank him above all others who have held the office. Udall ran head-on into a major obstacle for his department as soon as he came into office: the near impossibility of securing Budget Bureau approval and congressional appropriations for new capital investment in national parks, monuments, and recreation areas. His solution was the Land and Water Conservation Fund, based on the radical departure of a fee system for the use of heretofore free recreation areas. The fund was written into law in 1964 but has had limited success so far. Major sources of revenue from this or some other area are imperative, for both the costs of and the resistance to buying land for public purposes are growing greater each year, as are the public demand and need for greater facilities for outdoor recreation.

Another major legislative item in 1964 was the Water Resources Research Act, which established grants for research work in every state. This potential for specific inquiry into localized water problems is highly important to action on water supply and quality problems for the future. The 88th Congress passed a number of other important conservation bills, including a significant step toward a coordinated research and development program for commercial fisheries. The Wilderness Bill was the most important, of course, in terms of the long effort involved and the direction it indicated for the future.

President Johnson labeled the 88th Congress "The Conservation Congress," but he could just as well have reserved the title for the 89th, which passed a series of significant bills, including the Water Quality Act already mentioned. Important among them was the Highway Beautification Act, introducing the dimension of beauty as a national conservation goal not only for natural resource projects but for the major construction activity of the Federal government. Before the highway beautification program achieves its objectives, its scope will have to be broadened and its emphasis redirected. There will probably have to be a more clear-cut definition of federal enforcement powers and certainly a more specific commitment of federal funds, but a farsighted first step has been taken.

One of the major items in the 1965 Rivers and Harbors Act, the bill usually labeled "pork barrel," was the authorization for a multipurpose dam at the Dickey-Lincoln School site on the St. John River in Maine. A small appropriation to begin construction planning was also made. The start of this dam is noteworthy, because it is a part of the long-discussed Passamaquoddy tidal power project, but it is equally significant as the first federal public power project in New England. The amount of power generation involved is a relatively small one, but coming with the advent of nuclear steam power, it offers the best hope yet for relief from the high New England power rates.

Some commentators have called the 89th Congress the most

liberal in thirty years, but this public power project, which also saved the white water canoe route on the Allagash River in Maine, was approved only after a major legislative fight that required the full resources of Senator Muskie and Representative Bob Jones.

The 1965 bill that heads the list, however, was the Water Resources Planning Act. By establishing the long-fought-for Water Resources Council at cabinet level, it created for the first time the instrument necessary for coordinated, comprehensive planning for the best uses for water and adjoining lands. The council program has not yet been fully implemented, and there has been no opportunity to determine whether there are major gaps in the council's power to achieve the stated aims. The basic tool so long denied Presidents has been provided, however, and Senator Newlands' ghost must smile approval.

CHAPTER XVI

Today and Tomorrow

1

In September 1964, the Wilderness Act became law after running a long course of legislative obstacles. The Sierra Club, the still active naturalist group of John Muir, had been the foremost organizational sponsor of the measure, but it had gathered support from virtually every wildlife and garden club organization in the country. The original Wilderness Bill plan involved much larger areas within the national forests and national parks, but the final law added the force of legislative as well as administrative protection for 54 areas within the national forests. The law also includes a provision whereby large roadless tracts in national parks, monuments, and wildlife refuges can be added to the wilderness areas upon the application of the Secretary of the Interior to the President and the Congress.

In the long fight for passage, backers of the Wilderness Act had to beat back the agonizing cries of western (all initial wilderness areas are in the West) stockmen, miners, foresters, and recreation business owners. Beyond that, there was the old familiar plaint that "the government already owns too much land." The opportunity for enactment came with unqualified endorsement of the Wilderness Act principle by Presidents Kennedy and Johnson, and realistic cooperation with the myriad of legislative sponsors by

Secretary Udall. Even with this support, the final bill was carefully amended by western interests to ensure that it involved no real loss of highly valuable timber or mining rights. The act should be reviewed to make certain it can achieve its basic purpose for the limited acreage involved.

A bill with related purpose, to designate a number of streams as "wild rivers" and protect them from any type of development, is now pending in the Congress. The streams designated as wild rivers are generally small, and for some of them only a portion could be so designated because of existing development. It is a practical approach to the preservation of natural rivers.

Passage of the Wilderness Act is the foremost achievement of conservation groups that have a preservationist bent instead of a developmental emphasis. They have a legitimate claim to the conservationist label, but they have no right to exclusive possession. The Roosevelt-Pinchot conservation movement, which preserved the public domain from destruction during a period when it would have been doomed without the active intervention of those who sought to preserve it for constructive use in the best interests of all the people, willed the conservation mantle to all who believe that natural resources should be protected from monopolistic greed or wasteful destruction, and who believe that they should be developed or preserved in their best use to benefit the American economic and social system.

There will inevitably be dispute and conflict over the major public interest in any resource, but recent developments have made clear that some of the emotional preservationists who would pre-empt the conservation label regard as wrong and sometimes evil virtually every change in the American landscape since the first settlement occurred. In sentimentalizing the American Indian, they have ennobled not only his environment but his every action, except his failure to enforce a restrictive immigration policy.

The American population is eventually going to reach a plateau, but it is almost certainly going to nearly double before it reaches that relatively level stage. The American standard of living, pressured by an economy that cannot survive if it remains static, and by human nature which inevitably seeks a more comfortable and physically enjoyable existence, will continue to improve. It is to be devoutly hoped that part of that improved standard of living will be an increased respect for and use of the wilderness values of open air, rugged terrain, and primitive challenges to man's deepest individual resources. At the same time, the increasing demands of the economy are going to necessitate an even more complete utilization of our available resources. Increased leisure and increased income will continue to push higher the need for recreational space that must be improved and developed for use. Preservation of the status quo will be no more practicable than it would be valid. Too much of our land can serve a more useful purpose for the majority of the people through careful, coordinated development in the general public interest.

As one small example of the large-scale action essential to meet future needs, both land and water recreational opportunities should be part of the attraction of small-town life that is inherent in the spread of American industry to the countryside. In the discussion of the great megalopolis that is growing along the eastern seaboard, too many sociologists have overlooked the shift of the American small town from an "agribusiness" to an industrial base. Agribusiness will continue to be dominant in some of the richer agricultural regions, but most American small towns are likely to follow the pattern of recent industrial growth in the South, where industrial plants have gone to the rural communities and drawn their workers from farms and small towns. The improvement of even minimum wage income over the former insufficiency of farm income may be enough to make this life attractive for the present generation, but it will be satisfactory to a new generation born to a new level of income only if there is an improved general environment.

The small watershed reservoirs pioneered in the TVA Beech

River tributary project, coordinated in their development and use by local planning groups, are an obvious part of the answer to this need. Amendment to the present law under which the Soil Conservation Service builds its small watershed reservoirs, to enable them to serve a broader community purpose, would be the simplest way for the Federal government to move in this field over the country as a whole. This type of watershed program offers so many opportunities directly to capture added community growth values that they could be readily developed by state and local bodies as well.

Water project development, like urban renewal, can easily allow a wayward bulldozer to commit transgressions against the landscape that destroy more permanent values than they replace, but these errors can be held in check with better planning and regulation. They cannot be avoided by simply barring change. The current American environment, both natural and manmade, simply cannot meet all the demands of a society growing both in numbers and in appreciation of the better qualities of life.

Too much of the preservationist-conservationist doctrine has implied a "special elite" concept which suggests that the wilderness values are to be preserved for only that small fragment of the population considered capable of proper appreciation. Too many preservationists have made this clear in their abhorrence of the great masses of people drawn to some of our national and state parks. They would like to restrict use of a major part of the public domain to only those people with the proper cultural depth or the physical hardihood to appreciate it as they do, and they have an unfortunate tendency to brush aside all arguments for popular use as "desecration." Walden Pond should have been preserved, but the Thoreaus who can appreciate it are not unlimited.

The conservation purists sometimes have pat answers to the problems which would be created by the developments they would block to maintain the status quo. An example of this can be found in a recent book of Justice William O. Douglas, in many

ways the patron saint of the cult. In *A Wilderness Bill of Rights,*
Douglas rails at dams as a source of power generation, and men-
tions alternate sources of generation: coal-fired steam, nuclear-
powered steam, and solar energy. But the same book denounces the
havoc wreaked by mining the coal to fire the steam, and there is
a solemn warning about the dangers of wholesale pollution from
the disposal of nuclear waste. There has as yet been no practical
demonstration of solar generation, which may explain why the
book makes no reference to the destructive qualities of this system
of generating electricity.

The answer to this kind of unreasoning opposition to any
change from the original is, of course, that the growth of civilization being what it is, man must utilize his environment to sustain
and improve his life. In the process of growth, the evolution of
values refines the standards that are the means by which we accept change, but the inevitability of change itself remains elemental. There simply is no perfect compromise, but the imperfect
one we can achieve must represent the least damage to irreplaceable values and the fullest utilization of the natural resources.
There will continue to be a need for power generation from all
three sources denounced by Justice Douglas, but any new source
should be one which involves the least damage to the environment.
The evils of strip mining, for instance, can be checked effectively
if there are strict enough requirements about mining methods and
reclamation, which some states are now attempting to establish.
It is unlikely, however, that there will be really effective and fair
regulation until there is a federal law covering all types of mining
and stripping. Some land is of such intrinsic surface value that it
should never be disturbed for any kind of mining. Much of the
surface above coal lands, however, is of such poor quality by any
standard of measurement that proper reclamation after stripping
will leave it in far better shape to contribute to a scenic, forestry,
and wildlife resource, even without reference to the economic
value of the coal, than it is now. Economic reality makes it un-

likely that coal stripping will be abolished, and beyond that is the
human reality to be considered—the wholesale death and injury
that are still an inescapable part of underground coal mining.

Conservation purists and their emotional allies among the preservationists have made genuine contributions to the conservation
cause in campaigns like that against strip mining and against all
types of pollution, as long as their leadership has been restrained
enough to realize that total obstruction does not necessarily provide a total solution.

Another group, or rather group of groups, which has exhibited
a tendency to pre-empt for itself the title "conservationist" are the
various organizations of hunters and fishermen over the country.
Many state game and fish departments or commissions now have
the word "conservation" in their titles, and it is natural that their
constituent groups also use the term. The over-all conservation
movement has done more than any element in our history to preserve the land and water in sufficient quality to supply reasonably
the needs of our vast numbers of hunters and fishermen. The resource development aspects of the conservation movement have
offered vast new opportunities for hunters and fishermen in the
past generation, in the form of reservoirs and slack water streams
that have greatly expanded the accessibility and opportunity for
fishing and often for hunting. Hunters and fishermen concerned
with game and fish supply have properly defined conservation of
wildlife as a major goal of government conservation policy, and
their intervention in recent years has introduced a wildlife conservation aspect to many federal projects that might otherwise
have been ignored.

Once again, however, this vital but single facet of conservation
does not qualify to be the sole or the principal criterion. Wetlands
and marshes must be preserved both as bird sanctuaries and as
breeding and feeding grounds, but some of them should not automatically merit a sacrosanct status. They may be the source of
enough economic damage to warrant replacement by other

facilities whereby man may improve upon nature. Some of these conservation groups do not exactly have outstanding conservation records, as exhibited by various campaigns to raise game limits or in general to remove restrictions which may lessen the take. In more recent years some of these same "conservation" groups have earned quotation marks for the description, because their chief interest has apparently been reduced to preventing federal regulation of the sale of firearms.

There is inevitable controversy in store for many of the decisions to be made regarding the remaining undeveloped river basins, but it is not likely that the best public purpose will be served by simple obstinate opposition to any development. Some rivers can be too wild, as some of the recent Pacific Coast floods have demonstrated. Perhaps the greater danger, however, is that the failure of coordinated public development can lead to a disuse that would inevitably result in private exploitation, the dilution or destruction of wildlife and scenic values, and the wasting of our resource potential.

A remarkable opportunity was lost when wildlife groups did not support the conservationists in the effort to authorize Hell's Canyon Dam on the Snake River in Idaho during the 1950's. The high dam proposed for this Columbia River tributary would have included features to protect fish spawning and other wildlife values that were lost when the one-purpose power dams were approved for the power companies. In another long-time public power fight, however, a victory for wild-river preservationists is being won not by them but by the public power advocates, with little help from the groups who have for so long bewailed the failure to protect the white-water canoe route of the Allagash River. Thanks to the interest of the Interior Department and the Corps of Engineers in protecting the Allagash, earlier proposals for the dam sites on the St. John River in Maine were put aside in favor of a site at Dickey-Lincoln School. After the historic fight in 1965 for authorization of this project, the first public power

plan ever approved for New England, the State of Maine acted
to preserve the wild river status of the Allagash, thanks to the help
that would now be available from the Federal government.

In the years ahead, it may be possible that the untapped reserves of coal and lignite in the Rocky Mountain area may be a
far more economical source of power than the major hydro sites
still to be considered. When the time comes for these decisions,
a choice will have to be made between reservoirs or coal mining,
either of which will involve disturbance of the landscape. But
the power will have to be made available in some fashion.

Some of the bitterest resource fights of the past have been
direct public power issues or had their roots in the private-public
power controversy. Most of the basic decisions about power supply for the country have already been made, however. Vast new
technological changes might be soothing to various ideological
prejudices, but they are not likely to come about in the foreseeable future, simply because most of them would probably be
economically inefficient. The policies of the future should be
based on achieving the most efficient low-cost power supply
under the given circumstances, without wasteful strife over
whether it will be public or private. Many of the other traditional conservation issues are being modified in much the same
fashion.

2

Most of the dams of the future, however, are not likely to include
power as their major purpose, if it is any part of their functions.
They are going to be essentially for water supply for the vastly
increased domestic and industrial demand that is expanding daily.
The water supply crisis in New York City and its adjacent metropolitan area has dramatized the nation's domestic water supply
problem, and possibly helped to provide the impetus for badly
needed action. The United States has ample water supply to meet
the vast needs of the near future, but it will be ample only if it

is saved from the present reckless and wasteful pollution, carefully conserved, and repeatedly utilized wherever possible, even when this necessitates major movement of water from one area to another.

Los Angeles pumps its water supply 250 miles across the state from the Colorado River. In Texas, water is now being pumped more than 300 miles. In the years ahead some of these distances will have to be doubled and trebled or more. Desalting processes may supply the answer for some future supply, but there is still no certainty that its cost can be brought down to a level that will make it preferable to massive piping from streams like the Mississippi River system, or from the Pacific Northwest and Canada. The most immediate advantages of the desalting process may be for brackish water instead of sea water, for local area supplies.

The predictions of doubling national water consumption in another twenty years are by no means alarmist, if we accept the concept of a continuing improvement in American productivity and standard of living. There is no need for vast new irrigation acreages in the West, but the simple rate of economic return is going to continue to increase the use of irrigation waters in existing reclamation areas, and there is going to be continued increase in irrigation to improve production in farming areas of the rest of the country. Supplemental irrigation can be of value in many farm operations where the annual rainfall is as much as fifty inches, because it can be brought in at the right time. Relatively unlimited water supply is an essential adjunct to building a great society, and part of the definition of "unlimited" should be without unreasonable cost.

To make sure that a dependable water supply is available, it will be necessary to begin within the decade the planning and construction of water projects of various descriptions. Some of them will hopefully involve new techniques for water utilization that are today little more than vague ideas in the minds of some

of those who have been involved in research and experimentation
in this field. There is no doubt, however, but that the cost will
run into totals of several hundred billions of dollars. To get
proper value for our money, to make sure that ample water con-
tinues to be available at costs not out of line with the present,
the projects and programs for the future are going to have to be
carefully planned and coordinated on a scale that challenges the
same gospel of efficient use of resources in the public interest that
motivated the progressive conservationists of the first Roosevelt
era.

3

The resource and conservation challenge for America during
the final third of the twentieth century is not limited to water
supply, recreation, or pollution (of water, land, or air). It involves new concepts of joint planning for urban growth, massive
new transportation techniques, and total acceptance of the essen-
tiality that all resource use and development is for the purpose of
improving the environment and the life of the human resource.
Is the American governmental machinery sufficiently flexible to
respond to the challenge?

Obviously, most of the response is going to have to come from
the Federal government. The basic reason, that federal money is
the only source ample enough to take care of the need, still holds
true, but there is more reason than that. State lines have not been
boundaries for resource problems in the past, and they are less
likely to be so in the future. Pollution standards simply cannot
be adequately set or enforced on the basis of governmental sub-
division boundaries. Waste and inefficiency will be inevitable
when major programs are entrusted primarily to local grants.
The costs are going to be so great that the luxury of unequal
standards and unequal enforcement of regulatory authority in
fields like pollution will simply mean duplicating costs.

In the years immediately ahead, individual states can make their greatest contribution to their role in the federal system by serving as demonstration areas for meeting some of the major conservation problems. Perhaps the major achievement of Governor Pat Brown's administration in California will be the demonstration of how effective state planning can bring major progress in water programs, partly by improved coordination, and in good part by helping to stimulate far greater federal expenditures in the state. The billion dollar bond issue which Nelson Rockefeller persuaded New York State to vote in 1965 will very likely achieve this same result in that state, with special emphasis on antipollution programs.

In a field unrelated to federal grants, Governor Edward Breathitt has set an example with the far-reaching curb on the abuses of strip mining which he pushed through the Kentucky legislature. At a time when even a general study of strip mining was bottled up in the national Congress, Breathitt managed to get the strip mining curbs adopted in a state where coal mining interests had long been recognized as sacred cows, too powerful for either governor or legislature to disturb.

TVA's experience has demonstrated that regional resource problems can be most effectively handled by a relatively independent regional federal agency. Political reality, as well as the advanced state of the physical resource development in most of the other river basins, makes any new TVA's unlikely and virtually impossible. In the past, the idea of interstate compacts has been advanced as the answer to coordination problems in river basins. Most of these compact proposals, including some which were adopted and some which never materialized, were little more than devices to block or delay federal development. The Delaware River Basin Compact, involving New Jersey, Pennsylvania, New York, and Delaware, had some of its origin in the same motivations, but it has proven an instrument for action and prog-

ress rather than delay. As evidence of its effectiveness is more
widely recognized, it may be copied in some of the other river
basins.

National planning and national action are the only answer to
most of the problems ahead. Ideally, the old concept of one single
department of conservation and resource development, responsible for all federal planning and action in the field, might still
work if it could be achieved by waving a magic wand. It simply
cannot be achieved, however, without a bloody, bone-shattering
fight, which would leave the landscape so scarred that the conservation cause would be lost in the critical years immediately
ahead. Various departments and agencies might be combined,
abolished, modified, or mangled, through vigorous action by a
powerful President, but neither the President nor his new department could eliminate the bitter, unyielding rivalries which
would have developed among the various constituent interests
served, or among the constituent committees of Congress that
would have to be responsive to make the programs work. Obvious
improvements will have to be made from time to time as their
need is recognized, but major one-sweep reorganization would
be a vast waste of energy and effort. A neater and more logical
table of organization would appeal to many conservation purists,
to theoreticians who imagine that duplicating functions are major
parts of the costs of government, and, above all, to political scientists who see organization charts as results rather than instruments.
It would not be worth the delay, however, and it certainly would
not be worth further fragmentation of the various forces which
in total are the motivation for all of our national conservation
effort.

Proponents of the conservation agency ideal point to the history of interagency rivalry and say this is the means of eliminat-
ing it. Another way to look at the problem, though, might be to
point out that much of the wasteful rivalry and delay of the past
originated in resistance to consolidation during some of the earlier

campaigns to combine conservation agencies. Realistically accepting the political impossibility of the ideal consolidation, the answer is coordination at the top, and effective action by cabinet officers to snuff out petty bickering. Secretaries Stewart Udall and Orville Freeman have provided an effective demonstration of how this policy can achieve results. They both started with a good personal grounding in conservationist philosophy, a qualification which Presidents should bear in mind in making appointments to cabinets.

The informal cabinet control system has an inherent weakness in the Department of Defense, critics like to point out, because neither the Defense Secretary nor his Secretary of the Army has the time, and often not the inclination, to ride herd on the Corps of Engineers. The answer to this could be an Assistant Secretary of the Army used for this purpose, who could also be a very useful man for the President in achieving some political value from the management of this major part of his water resource program.

The great deficiency of the informal cabinet accommodations system, even if it were to have enlightened help from the Bureau of the Budget, is the lack of coordinated planning, both for broad long-range goals and for specific day-to-day developments. The answer lies in effective use of the Council on Water Resources, now written into law but still to be tested in actual practice. A broader and better answer, which could be achieved without major controversy or disruption of existing programs, would be a Natural Resources Advisory Council given effective powers by the President's specific direction, with the help of the Bureau of the Budget.

The council might be given a role in the conservation and resource field similar to that of the Council of Economic Advisors on questions of the general economy. It would have no direct executive powers, but its advisory role could bring the proper coordination of long-range planning, and it could become the active agent of the President when agency conflicts developed. This idea was endorsed by the Kennedy-Johnson Natural Resources Advisory Committee in 1961. It is still the best possible answer to the coordination problem today.

The changing face of conservation problems makes it obvious how inadequate most of the old department and agency consolidation schemes would be as solutions to conservation issues. For example, most of the problems have a direct bearing on urban life, which makes little sense of the often-repeated idea of combining the Departments of the Interior and Agriculture into the Department of Rural Affairs. It is not likely that the various committees of the Congress with accepted roles in the conservation field would accept merger or reorganization. Mergers and changes are not essential here in the formal parent committees, but the subcommittees that do most of the work should be drastically overhauled now and from time to time in the future. This is the best way the basic legislation can be written, and the only way for the various committees to retain effective legislative oversight in the field of their responsibilities.

The paths worn by the pork barrel process in both the legislative and executive branches are too deep to be readily erased. To make the most effective attack on the great problems which demand immediate planning and the earliest possible action, conservation forces cannot afford the luxury of leisurely regrouping. The fight has to be made with the tools at hand.

4

During the last weeks of Theodore Roosevelt's Presidency, in February 1909, he was host at the White House to a North American Conservation Conference, once again in response to a Pinchot idea. Canada, Mexico, and the then separate colony of Newfoundland were participants, and there was an agreement on a fine statement of principles including such key sentences as: "Natural resources are not confined by the boundary lines that separate Nations. We agree that no Nations acting alone can adequately conserve them. . . ."

A World Conservation Conference was to be held at the Hague later in the year, but President Taft vetoed the idea and also rejected the continuation of the North American Conference. A continuing conference would have greatly benefited the development of the St. Lawrence Seaway. It would have greatly simplified the problems of the use of international waters and division of water use that have been difficult to negotiate with Canada as well as Mexico. Its most important advantage might have been in providing the instrumentality for migratory bird preserves and breeding grounds.

The United States has been a major exporter of conservation ideas and resource development projects through the various foreign aid programs, the World Bank, and the United Nations. The underdeveloped countries of the world will be fertile markets for resource development ideas throughout the next century. Development of the conservation programs through the United Nations and other international organizations would make possible the best use of these programs in helping to contribute to world stability, and this shift in emphasis and responsibility will likely be a continuing goal of American foreign policy.

But even as the most developed nation of the world, the United States must take the lead in establishing a system for international control, development, and conservation of the marine resources shared by the world community beyond the national rights claimed by the coastal nations. These involve the fisheries of the high seas, the minerals on and under the deep sea floor, and possibly the ocean waters themselves. The potentialities of space go beyond even this ad infinitum potential.

5

The saving grace of the pork barrel conservation system that we have developed is that it has often succeeded in spite of itself, thanks primarily to the American philosophy of public service and our ideal of utilization for the public benefit harnessed to the pulling power of self-interest, sometimes enlightened and sometimes wholly selfish. There have been many defects in the system, but the inexcusable and now irreparable one is the failure of our national government to provide the properly planned leadership which could have avoided the permanent waste and losses that have occurred.

There are no magic solutions for meeting future needs. The solutions will not become cheaper in the future, either. Postponement of action will inevitably mean that it will cost more in the years ahead. Pork barrel politics is an inescapable element of the American political structure. The task of executive leadership is to contain and control these impulses, and to utilize them to achieve the broad conservation goals that are a basic responsibility of our national government. This can and must be done.

Bibliography

« « « » » »

Bibliography

The history of American conservation and development of natural resources has never received adequate attention, either from formal surveys of the nation's history or in the field of specialized monographs. This lack of attention has resulted in a significant gap in the political and economic history of the country; I hope this book will fill a substantial portion of that gap. The bibliography appended here is therefore not a complete one for the subject, but is a full listing of the sources I used in rounding out the background for this book. The book's evaluations and judgments are, of course, based on my own experience in the field.

I am indebted to Mrs. Audrey Warren of the staff of the House Public Works Committee for countless evening hours devoted to technical and editorial help in writing this book. Even though that assistance was personal rather than official, this is perhaps a good place to pay tribute to the fact that the cause of conservation in the United States is presently better served because the House Public Works Committee, which has the broadest responsibilities in natural resource legislation, also has a staff of exceptional ability. The ranking members of the Public Works Committee are the most effective team of legislators in the natural resources field the country has had in many years, and I believe they would be the first to agree that much of what they have accomplished would have been impossible without the quality of back-up work they have had from their committee staff. That work is seldom recognized publicly, and perhaps this notation will fill a portion of that gap as well.

I would like to acknowledge the helpful cooperation of the Library of Congress and the Technical Library of the Tennessee Valley Authority in assembling the bibliographical material. My secretary, Mrs. Mary F. Knurr, provided invaluable assistance in the preparation of the manuscript. My wife Helen has been, as usual, my chief proofreader.

Abbot, Lieut. H. L., and Capt. A. A. Humphreys, *Report upon the Physics and Hydraulics of the Mississippi River; upon the Protection of the Alluvial Region Against Overflow; and upon the Deepening of the Mouths: Based upon Surveys and Investigations*. Philadelphia: J. B. Lippincott Company, 1861.

American Scenic and Historic Preservation Society, *Sixteenth Annual Report, 1911*. Albany, N. Y.: J. B. Lyon Company, 1911.

Baumhoff, Richard G., *The Dammed Missouri Valley*. New York: Alfred A. Knopf, Inc., 1951.

Bennett, Hugh H., *Soil Conservation*. New York: McGraw-Hill Book Company, Inc., 1939.

Biddle, Francis B., *In Brief Authority*. Garden City, N.Y.: Doubleday & Company, Inc., 1962.

Bobbé Mrs. Dorothie, *De Witt Clinton*. Port Washington, N.Y.: Ira J. Friedman, Inc., Publishing Division, 1933.

Brink, Wellington, *Big Hugh: The Father of Soil Conservation*. New York: The Macmillan Company, 1951.

Brown, Leahmae, *The Development of National Policy with respect to Water Resources*. (Unpublished thesis.) Urbana: University of Illinois, 1937.

Carmer, Carl L., *The Hudson*. New York: Holt, Rinehart & Winston, Inc., 1939.

Chalmers, Harvey, II, *The Birth of the Erie Canal.* New York: Bookman Associates, 1960.

Clapp, Gordon R., *The TVA—An Approach to the Development of a Region.* Chicago: University of Chicago Press, 1955.

Clawson, Marion, R. Burnell Held, and Charles H. Stoddard, *Land for the Future.* Baltimore: Johns Hopkins University Press (for Resources for the Future, Inc.), 1960.

Congressional Quarterly Service, *Congress and the Nation—1945-1964.* (A Review of Government and Politics in the Postwar Years.) Washington: Congressional Quarterly Service, 1965.

Coyle, David Cushman, *Conservation: An American Story of Conflict and Accomplishment.* New Brunswick, N.J.: Rutgers University Press, 1957.

Cramton, Louis C., *Early History of Yellowstone National Park and Its Relation to National Park Policies.* Washington: Government Printing Office, 1932.

Darling, Arthur B. (ed.), *The Public Papers of Francis G. Newlands.* Volumes I and II. Boston: Houghton Mifflin Company, 1932.

Davidson, Donald, *The Tennessee.* Volume II: *The New River, Civil War to TVA.* New York: Holt, Rinehart & Winston, Inc., 1948.

Dorsey, Florence L., *Master of the Mississippi: Henry Shreve and the Conquest of the Mississippi.* Boston: Houghton Mifflin Company, 1941.

Douglas, William O., *A Wilderness Bill of Rights.* Boston: Little, Brown and Company, 1965.

Downing, A. J., *A Treatise on the Theory and Practice of Landscape Gardening, Adapted to North America; with a View to the Improvement of Country Residences.* New York: G. P. Putnam's Sons, 1849.

Downing, A. J., *Rural Essays.* (Edited by George William Curtis.) New York: G. P. Putnam's Sons, 1853.

Droze, Wilmon Henry, *High Dams and Slack Waters—TVA Rebuilds a River*. Baton Rouge: Louisiana State University Press, 1965.

Duffus, R. L., *The Valley and Its People—A Portrait of TVA*. New York: Alfred A. Knopf, Inc., 1946.

Elam, W. E., *Speeding Floods to the Sea* (or The Evolution of Flood Control Engineering on the Mississippi River). New York: Hobson Book Press, 1946.

Ellis, Clyde T., *A Giant Step*. New York: Random House, Inc., 1966.

Frank, Arthur DeWitt, *The Development of the Federal Program of Flood Control on the Mississippi River*. New York: Columbia University Press, 1930.

Garrett, Garet, *The Wild Wheel: The World of Henry Ford*. New York: Pantheon Books, 1952.

Gill, Edwin, *DeWitt Clinton—The Man on the Cigarette Stamp*. Raleigh, N.C.: Edwards & Broughton Co., 1953.

Glozé, Alfred R., *Reclamation in the United States*. New York. McGraw-Hill Book Company, Inc., 1952.

Goetzmann, William H., *Army Exploration in the American West—1803-1863*. New Haven, Conn.: Yale University Press, 1959.

Goodrich, Carter (ed.), *Canals and American Economic Development*. New York: Columbia University Press, 1961.

Hansen, Harry, *The Chicago*. New York: Holt, Rinehart & Winston, Inc., 1942

Harrison, Robert W., *Alluvial Empire*. Volume I. Little Rock, Ark.: Pioneer Press, 1961.

Havemeyer, Loomis (ed.), *Conservation of Our Natural Resources*. (Based on Van Hise's "The Conservation of Natural Resources in the United States.") New York: The Macmillan Company, 1931.

Hays, Samuel P., *Conservation and the Gospel of Efficiency—The*

Progressive Conservation Movement, 1890-1920. Cambridge, Mass.: Harvard University Press, 1959.

Hill, Forest G., *Roads, Rails & Waterways—The Army Engineers and Early Transportation.* Norman: University of Oklahoma Press, 1957.

Hislop, Codman, *The Mohawk.* New York: Holt, Rinehart & Winston, Inc., 1948.

Holt, W. Stull, *The Office of the Chief of Engineers of the Army —Its Non-military History, Activities, and Organization.* Baltimore: Johns Hopkins University Press, 1923.

Hornaday, William T., *Thirty Years War for Wild Life; Gains and Losses in the Thankless Task.* New York: Charles Scribner's Sons, 1931.

Hubbard, Preston J., *Origins of the TVA—The Muscle Shoals Controversy, 1920-1932.* Nashville, Tenn.: Vanderbilt University Press, 1961.

Hughes, Emmet John, *The Ordeal of Power—A Political Memoir of the Eisenhower Years.* New York: Atheneum Publishers, 1963.

Hulbert, Archer B., *The Great American Canals.* Cleveland: Arthur H. Clark Company, 1904.

Humphreys, Benjamin G., *Flood and Levees of the Mississippi River.* Washington: 1914.

Ickes, Harold L., *The Autobiography of a Curmudgeon.* New York: Reynal & Company, Inc., 1943.

Ickes, Harold L., *The Secret Diary of Harold L. Ickes:*

Volume I, *The First Thousand Days, 1933-1936.* New York: Simon & Schuster, Inc., 1953.

Volume II, *The Inside Struggle, 1936-1939.* New York: Simon & Schuster, Inc., 1954.

Ise, John, *Our National Park Policy: A Critical History.* Baltimore: Johns Hopkins University Press (for Resources for the Future, Inc.), 1961.

Ise, John, *The United States Forest Policy*. New Haven, Conn.: Yale University Press, 1920.

Kelso, Harold, *Inland Waterways Policy in the U.S.* (Ph.D. thesis.) Madison: University of Wisconsin, 1942.

Kemper, J. P., *Rebellious River*. Boston: Bruce Humphries, Inc., 1949.

Kerr, Senator Robert S., *Land, Wood and Water*. New York: Fleet Publishing Corporation, 1960.

Kerwin, Jerome G., *Federal Water-Power Legislation*. New York: Columbia University Press, 1926.

Kimball, Francis P., *New York—The Canal State*. (The Story of America's Great Water Route from the Lakes to the Sea, Builder of East and West with a Discussion of the St. Lawrence Treaty.) Albany, N.Y.: Argus Press, 1937.

King, Judson, *The Conservation Fight—From Theodore Roosevelt to the Tennessee Valley Authority*. Washington: Public Affairs Press, 1959.

Leopold, Luna B., and Thomas Maddock, Jr., *The Flood Control Controversy; Big Dams, Little Dams, and Land Management*. New York: Ronald Press Co., 1954.

Leuchtenburg, William Edward, *Flood Control Politics—The Connecticut River Valley Problem—1927-1950*. Cambridge, Mass.: Harvard University Press, 1953.

Lewis, Walker, *Without Fear or Favor—A Biography of Chief Justice Roger Brooke Taney*. Boston: Houghton Mifflin Company, 1965.

Lilienthal, David E., *TVA—Democracy on the March*. New York: Harper & Row, Publishers, 1944.

Lilienthal, David E., *The Journals of David E. Lilienthal*. Volume I: *The TVA Years—1939-1945* (including a selection of Journal Entries from the 1917-1939 period). New York: Harper & Row, Publishers, 1964.

Maass, Arthur, *Muddy Waters—The Army Engineers and the*

Nation's Rivers. Cambridge, Mass.: Harvard University Press, 1951.

McGeary, Martin Nelson, *Gifford Pinchot, Forester-Politician*. Princeton, N.J.: Princeton University Press, 1960.

Martin, Roscoe C. (ed.), *TVA—The First Twenty Years—A Staff Report*. University, Ala., and Knoxville, Tenn.: University of Alabama Press and University of Tennessee Press, 1956.

Miller, Nathan, *The Enterprise of a Free People: Aspects of Economic Development in New York State during the Canal Period, 1792-1838*. Ithaca, N.Y.: Cornell University Press (for the American Historical Association), 1962.

Mississippi Valley Committee, *Report of the Mississippi Valley Committee of the Public Works Administration*. Washington: Government Printing Office, 1934.

National Conservation Commission. *Report of the National Conservation Commission*. (60th Congress, 2nd Session, Senate Document 676.) Washington: Government Printing Office, 1909.

Neuberger, Richard L., and Stephen B. Kahn, *Integrity; The Life of George W. Norris*. New York: Vanguard Press, 1937.

Nevins, Allan, *The Evening Post—A Century of Journalism*. New York: Liveright Publishing Corp., 1922.

Nevins, Allan, and Frank E. Hill, *Ford: Expansion and Challenge*. New York: Charles Scribner's Sons, 1957.

Nixon, Edgar B. (ed.), *Franklin D. Roosevelt & Conservation—1911-1945*. Volumes I and II. Hyde Park, N.Y.: General Services Administration, National Archives and Records Service, Franklin D. Roosevelt Library, 1957.

Norris, George W., *Fighting Liberal, the Autobiography of George W. Norris*. New York: The Macmillan Company, 1945.

Olmsted, Frederick Law, Jr., and Theodora Kimball (eds.), *Fred-*

erick Law Olmsted—Landscape Architect, 1822-1903. New York: G. P. Putnam's Sons, 1928.

Owen, Marguerite, *Muscle Shoals and the Public Welfare.* Washington: Committee on Livings Costs, National League of Women Voters, 1929.

Payne, Robert, *The Canal Builders—The Story of Canal Engineers Through the Ages.* New York: The Macmillan Company, 1959.

Pinchot, Gifford, *Breaking New Ground.* New York: Harcourt, Brace & World, Inc., 1947.

Pinchot, Gifford, *The Fight for Conservation.* Garden City, N.Y.: Doubleday & Company, Inc., 1910.

Powell, John Wesley, *Report on the Lands of the Arid Region of the United States.* Washington: Government Printing Office, 1879.

Richards, William C., *The Last Billionaire: Henry Ford.* New York: Charles Scribner's Sons, 1948.

Richardson, Elmo R., *The Politics of Conservation—Crusades and Controveries—1897-1913.* Berkeley: University of California Press, 1962.

Robbins, Roy M., *Our Landed Heritage—The Public Domain, 1776-1936.* Princeton, N.J.: Princeton University Press, 1942.

Roberts, Guy, *Natural Wonders of the White Mountains.* Cambridge, Mass.: Murray Printing Company, 1924.

Roosevelt Theodore, *Theodore Roosevelt, An Autobiography.* New York: The Macmillan Company, 1913.

Russell, Mabelle Geddes, *The Old Man of the Mountain—Past and Present Efforts To Save the Great Stone Face.* State of New Hampshire Recreation Division, 1959.

Savage, Henry, *River of the Carolinas: The Santee.* New York: Holt, Rinehart & Winston, Inc., 1956.

Schlesinger, Arthur M., Jr., The Age of Roosevelt: *The Crisis of the Old Order.* Boston: Houghton Mifflin Company, 1957.

The Coming of the New Deal. Boston: Houghton Mifflin Company, 1959.

The Politics of Upheaval. Boston: Houghton Mifflin Company, 1960.

Scientific American, *Technology and Economic Development.* New York: Alfred A. Knopf, Inc., 1963.

Selznick, Philip, *TVA and the Grass Roots.* Berkeley: University of California Press, 1949.

Shannon, Fred A., *The Farmer's Last Frontier: Agriculture, 1860–1897.* New York: Holt, Rinehart & Winston, Inc., 1945.

Smith, Frank E., *The Yazoo.* New York: Holt, Rinehart & Winston, Inc., 1954.

Stegner, Wallace, *Beyond the Hundredth Meridian.* (John Wesley Powell and the Second Opening of the West.) Boston: Houghton Mifflin Company, 1954.

Sundborg, George, *Hail Columbia—The Thirty-Year Struggle for Grand Coulee Dam.* New York: The Macmillan Company, 1954.

Swain, Donald C., *Federal Conservation Policy—1921-1933.* (University of California Publications in History Vol. 76). Berkeley: University of California Press, 1963.

Tilden, Freeman, *The State Parks—Their Meaning in American Life.* New York: Alfred A. Knopf, Inc., 1962.

Trombley, Kenneth E., *The Life and Times of a Happy Liberal; A Biography of Morris Llewellyn Cooke.* New York: Harper & Row, Publishers, 1954.

Turner, Frederick Jackson, *The Frontier in American History.* New York: Holt, Rinehart & Winston, Inc., 1920.

Udall, Stewart L., *The Quiet Crisis.* New York: Holt, Rinehart & Winston, Inc., 1963.

U.S. Army, *Report of the Federal Civil Works Program as Administered by the Corps of Engineers.* Part 1, Volume 3. Washington: Government Printing Office, 1952.

U.S. Congress. Joint Committee on Atomic Energy, *Hearings*

Before the Senate Section of the Joint Committee on Atomic Energy. Confirmation of Atomic Energy Commission and General Manager. (80th Congress, 1st Session.) Washington: Government Printing Office, 1947.

U.S. Department of Agriculture, Forest Service, *The American Outdoors.* (Management for Beauty and Use.) Washington: Government Printing Office, 1965.

U.S. Engineer Department. *Reports on the Yellowstone:*

Raynolds, Gen. W. F., *1868 Exploration of the Yellowstone River.* Washington: Government Printing Office, 1868.

Hayden, F. V., *Geological Report of the Exploration of the Yellowstone and Missouri Rivers.* Washington: Government Printing Office, 1869.

1871 Report of Yellowstone Expedition of 1870. (Sen. Ex. Doc. 51, 41st Congress, 3rd Session.) Washington: Government Printing Office, 1871.

1872 Engineering Report. (Sen. Ex. Doc. 66, 42nd Congress, 2nd Session.) Washington: Government Printing Office, 1872.

U.S. House of Representatives. Committee on Public Works, *The Civil Functions Program of the Corps of Engineers, United States Army.* (82nd Congress, 2nd Session, House Committee Print No. 21.) Washington: Government Printing Office, 1952.

U.S. House of Representatives. Special Subcommittee of the Committee on Government Operations, *Hearings on Water Resources and Power Report of the Commission on Organization of the Executive Branch of the Government.* (84th Congress, 1st Session.) Washington: Government Printing Office, 1956.

U.S. President's Water Resources Policy Commission, *The Report of the U. S. President's Water Resources Policy Commission:*

A Water Policy for the American People. Washington: Government Printing Office, 1950.

Ten Rivers in America's Future. Washington: Government Printing Office, 1950.

Water Resources Law. Washington: Government Printing Office, 1950.

U.S. Senate. Select Committee on National Water Resources, *Report and 32 Committee Prints*. (87th Congress, 1st Session, Report No. 29.) Washington: Government Printing Office, 1961.

Van Hise, Charles R., *The Conservation of Natural Resources in the United States*. New York: The Macmillan Company, 1910.

Walker, Barbara K. and Warren S. (eds.), *The Erie Canal: Gateway to Empire*. Boston: D. C. Heath & Company, 1963.

Webb, Walter Prescott, *The Great Plains*. Boston: Ginn & Company, 1931.

Wengert, Norman I., *Natural Resources and the Political Struggle*. Garden City, N.Y.: Doubleday & Company, Inc., 1955.

Whitman, Willson, *God's Valley—People and Power Along the Tennessee River*. New York: The Viking Press, Inc., 1939.

Wildavsky, Aaron, *Dixon-Yates: A Study in Power Politics*. New Haven, Conn.: Yale University Press, 1962.

Wildes, Harry E., *The Delaware*. New York: Holt, Rinehart & Winston, Inc., 1940.

Wyer, Samuel S., *Niagara Falls, Its Power Possibilities and Preservation*. Washington: Smithsonian Institution, 1925.

Wyld, Lionel D., *Low Bridge! Folklore and the Erie Canal*. Syracuse, N.Y.: Syracuse University Press, 1962.

ARTICLES

Bates, J. Leonard, "Fulfilling American Democracy: The Conservation Movement, 1907 to 1921." *Mississippi Valley Historical Review*, Volume 44, No. 1, June 1957.

Fesler, James W. (ed.), "Government and Water Resources." *American Political Science Review*, Volume 44, 1950.

Ickes, Harold L., "Not Guilty." *Saturday Evening Post*, May 25, 1940.

Johnson, Emory R., "River and Harbor Bills." *Annals of the American Academy of Political and Social Science*, Volume 2, 1892.

Nelson, E. C., "Presidential Influence on the Policy of Internal Improvements." *Iowa Journal of History and Politics*, Volume 4, 1906.

Noggle, Burl, "The Origins of the Teapot Dome Investigation." *Mississippi Valley Historical Review*, Volume 44, No. 2, September 1957.

Rubin, Julius, "Canal or Railroad?" *Transactions of the American Philosophical Society*, Volume 51, Part 7, 1961.

Shelton, Barrett, "The Decatur Story." *Proceedings of the United Nations Scientific Conference on the Conservation and Utilization of Resources, 1949*, Volume 1, 1950.

Index